MAKE EACH DAY COUNT

*A Christopher thought for
every day of the year*

by JAMES KELLER, M.M.

A Dell Book

NIHIL OBSTAT: JOHN M. A. FEARNS, S.T.D.
             CENSOR LIBRORUM
 IMPRIMATUR: ✠ FRANCIS CARDINAL SPELLMAN
             ARCHBISHOP OF NEW YORK

The nihil obstat and imprimatur are official declarations that a book or pamphlet is free of doctrinal or moral error. No implication is contained therein that those who have granted the nihil obstat and imprimatur agree with the contents, opinions, or statements expressed.

New York, July 16, 1955

Published by
Dell Publishing Co., Inc.
261 Fifth Avenue
New York 16, N. Y.

Designed and produced by
Western Printing & Lithographing Company

Cover design by Jeannette Cissman

First Dell printing—February, 1958

Printed in U.S.A.

"Each day you are preparing for life hereafter as well as for life on earth. Consequently, it is important that you *make each and every day count* for time and for eternity.

"In order to aid you in a small way, at least, this volume has been prepared. These simple daily thoughts are not intended for the advanced in spiritual life, but for beginners. The object of this book is to bring little reminders of God to those who may be starved in soul, but who are not yet ready for more solid spiritual fare. There are millions in our land who are never reached by religion. This is a small attempt to share with them the truth, love and peace of Christ."

—from the *Preface*

PREFACE

During the past 40 years, 63 million people were killed in two World Wars. Countless others were maimed and crippled. The cost in money alone was more than a *thousand billion dollars*.

Within the past few years, 33 thousand Americans were killed and more than 103 thousand wounded in the Korean conflict that cost the American taxpayers another hundred billion dollars.

And still no lasting peace!

Peace to the World Through You

Placing blame is of little value. It is far more important for each individual to do something positive and constructive to restore to the world that precious peace which God wishes us to enjoy here on earth and which He intends should be our happy lot in heaven for all eternity.

Jesus Christ, true Man and true God, came on earth to teach men how to live in peace. At His very birth the angels sang: "Peace on earth to men of good will." (Luke 2:14) Thirty-three years later, when He rose from the dead, His very first words were: "Peace be to you." And then He immediately added: "As the Father hath sent Me, I also send you." (John 20:21)

What a thrilling privilege to be an apostle of peace, a peace-bearer, a Christbearer—yes, a Christopher, in a world that yearns for lasting peace.

And in that extraordinary role you do not work alone.

The full force of heaven is behind you, as far as you wish it.

A Challenge for You

A tremendous challenge faces each of us who lives in the atomic age. The stakes are big. Things are moving fast. Those who are dedicated to good must think and act quickly, honestly and courageously. We may be at the threshold of the greatest peace the world has ever seen—or of the most terrible catastrophe.

What part are you playing in this great drama? What you, personally and individually, do—or fail to do—can have far-reaching effects involving your own destiny and that of millions of your fellow human beings.

God expects you to play a special role, no matter how insignificant it may seem, in shaping the trends of our day and of the critical years ahead.

He has given you talents, few or many, to use not only for yourself, but for the benefit of others as well. He has assigned a special mission to you personally. There is no substitute for you! He has delegated you to apply in person at least a small bit of His love and truth and justice to the vital spheres of influence, especially in government, education, literature, entertainment and labor relations. He wants you to be a Christopher.

Inner Power Essential

To be truly effective as a Christbearer, however, it is essential that you develop and sustain your inner power by daily prayer and reflection. The more God-centered your interior life, the more influence for good you are bound to exert externally.

This cannot be done overnight. It is by availing ourselves day by day of all the helps God has provided for us, especially by prayerful consideration of the sublime eternal truths that give meaning to life: why do I exist? from whence do I come? where am I going? The answers can only be found in God's unchangeable truths.

One day you will appear before Him to render an account of every thought, word and deed of your life. Each day, therefore, you are preparing for life hereafter as well as for life on earth. Consequently, it is important that you *make each and every day count* for time and for eternity.

The Purpose of This Book

In order to aid you in a small way, at least, this volume has been prepared. These simple daily thoughts are not intended for the advanced in the spiritual life, but for beginners. Its object is to bring little reminders of God to those who may be starved in soul, but who are not yet ready for the more solid spiritual fare. There are millions in our land who are never reached by religion. This is a small attempt to share with them the truth, love and peace of Christ.

As our model in this respect, we endeavor to follow the inspiring standard set by the great Apostle, St. Paul. When he wrote to the first Christians of Greece, he must have burned with a desire to make these people of Corinth perfect followers of Christ in as short a time as possible. But he was wise and considerate enough to know that this was not possible. He realized it was important to make haste slowly—to pursue a patient, long-range approach.

One of the best evidences of St. Paul's tender understanding is to be found in his first epistle to the Corinthians (3:1-2), where he wrote: "And I, brethren, could not speak to you as unto spiritual, but as unto carnal. As unto little ones in Christ. I gave you milk to drink, not meat; for you were not able as yet. But neither, indeed are you now able; for you are yet carnal."

The Role You Can Play

The more you realize how much you count from the point of view of God, how important you yourself are in applying His divine law and order to a world that always drifts towards disaster when it forsakes Him, the more enthusiastically and thoroughly you will go about the task of strengthening and deepening your spiritual roots.

Everything you think, say and do will take on a new and richer meaning. You will find refreshing and invigorating satisfaction in the realization that you, whoever you are, can be a co-worker with Almighty God in renewing the face of the earth.

Once you have brought a divine sense of purpose and direction into your life, you will bring into play that "bit of missionary" that God has implanted in you and which He wishes you to use in changing the world for the better.

You will grow in the love of God and man. You will look for opportunities to serve. Yes, you will gradually find it easy to "make each day count."

James Keller

THE CHRISTOPHER MOVEMENT

1. The word *Christopher* is derived from the Greek word, *Christophoros*, meaning *Christbearer*.

Back in the third century, the story is told, a giant son of a heathen ruler longed to serve someone greater than himself. First he enlisted in the ranks of a great king, and then of the devil. But he was disillusioned in both.

Hearing finally that Christ was the King of kings, he desired to serve Him above all others. He discovered he could do this by helping those in need. One way to do this, he thought, would be to carry travelers across a dangerous stream nearby.

One day, while this powerful man was bearing a small child across the river, he found his burden so backbreaking that he could scarcely reach the other bank. On looking up, he was surprised to find that he was actually bearing the Christ Child, holding the world in His hands. At the same time, he understood that those who would carry Christ to all people must be willing to work hard and even to suffer.

Without realizing it, this stalwart man had become a Christbearer—a Christopher. Since that time he has been known far and wide as St. Christopher.

2. *Aim of the Christophers.* (a) To stir up a sense of personal responsibility and individual initiative among millions. (b) To encourage each one to do something practical and constructive in restoring the spiritual truths upon which this nation is founded to all phases of private and public life. (Among these is the "*Self-evident truth*" that each human being derives his rights from God, not

9

government; that the chief purpose of government is to secure and protect these God-given rights.) (c) To help in a particular way to raise the standards of government, education, literature, entertainment and labor relations.

Most of the turmoil of our day is due to the fact that those against God, a handful at most, have swarmed into the above fields that have such a powerful influence on the lives of all people the world over. These fields will never be any better than the people in them. Little is accomplished by complaining or criticizing: "It is better to light one candle than to curse the darkness." If another handful go as Christbearers into these same fields, a trend for the better is bound to come!

3. *No Organization*. In order to emphasize the importance of each individual in playing a personal role in shaping the future, the Christopher movement has no organization (beyond its headquarters at 18 East 48th Street, N. Y. C.), no memberships, no chapters, no meetings and no dues.

4. *Limitations*. The Christopher movement confines itself to one phase of a big problem. It is merely an attempt to supplement, not replace, basic and essential organizations. It restricts itself to emphasis on primary truths, while recognizing the importance of all the truths that flow from them.

5. *The Distinguishing Mark*. Love of *all* people for the love of God should be the distinguishing characteristic of anyone who would play the role of a Christopher. In no case should there be a return of hate for hatred. Those who would be bearers of Christ must be ready for all the ingratitude, suffering, rebuffs, and countless disappointments which the Master encountered. Each must strive to be kind while still remaining firm, to be able to disagree without becoming disagreeable. "*Love your enemies, do good to them that hate you and pray for them that persecute and calumniate you.*" (Matthew 5:44)

With this motivation, the most difficult task can become a labor of love.

6. *Emphasis on the Individual.* Because God has implanted in every human being a desire to be creative, to make a certain contribution to the peace of the world that no one else can make, the Christopher approach stresses individual initiative. Our policy is to point out elementary principles and then leave it to each person to work out his own method of blending, integrating, or incarnating the divine into the human. This allows for greater freedom, within reasonable limits, and encourages that element of originality, imagination, and enterprise which is possible only when the individual feels a personal responsibility in changing the world for the better.

7. *No Placement Bureau.* We have purposely refrained from setting up any placement bureau. We feel that it is better for each to go into a job of his own choosing, when and where he likes. Furthermore, we are convinced that it is an important experience in the missionary approach of the Christopher movement for such a person to go through the difficult, and often discouraging, ordeal of finding an opening in a career that counts. God blesses the very effort of trying.

8. *Dependence on God.* By the very nature of our work, a deep conviction of dependence on God, of being merely an instrument, however unworthy, in the hands of God, is absolutely essential. The closer one is to Christ, the more one is bound to accomplish. Competence is needed, to be sure. But ability without godliness can be a great danger even for those who have dedicated themselves to a good cause.

9. *Our Channels.* At present several millions over America are at least acquainted with the Christopher idea. Our aim is merely to suggest and encourage. We leave it to each individual to find for herself or himself

whatever special information or training is needed. Our contacts with all of them are through Christopher talks, literature, movies, radio and television.

   a. Christopher News Notes are sent each month without charge to about one million persons. A Christopher column "Three Minutes a Day" appears in 61 daily newspapers.

   b. Nine Christopher books have been published: 1) *You Can Change the World,* 2) *Three Minutes a Day,* 3) *Careers That Change Your World,* 4) *One Moment, Please!,* 5) *Government Is Your Business,* 6) *Just For Today,* 7) *All God's Children,* 8) *Stop, Look and Live,* and 9) *Make Each Day Count.*

   c. Christopher radio and television programs are now presented each week on more than 1300 stations in the United States, Canada, Alaska, Hawaii, Puerto Rico and Mexico.

10. *No Christopher Clubs.* Because we restrict ourselves to developing individual initiative and personal responsibility, *we do not authorize Christopher clubs or groups of any kind,* or the use of the Christopher name in connection with any project that has resulted from the Christopher idea. We leave it to each to decide whether he will work alone or join any one of hundreds of excellent organizations. Each individual speaks and acts for himself, not for the Christopher movement.

11. *Financial Support.* In keeping with our policy of no memberships, no subscriptions, no dues, we merely announce our needs and depend entirely on God to provide, through voluntary contributions, the nearly one million dollars a year now needed for the support of all Christopher projects (staff, literature, television films, radio transcriptions, etc.).

To make sure that all contributions come from conviction rather than from pressure of any kind, no one is solicited for assistance, and there are no collections, benefits or fund-raising drives. (All donations to the Christophers are deductible from one's taxable income . . . The Christophers are incorporated under the legal title: "The Christophers, Inc.")

12. *The Christopher Position.* The Christopher movement was started in 1945. The purpose of the Christophers is to restore the love and truth of Christ to the marketplace. Begun and carried on under Catholic auspices, the Christopher movement has the voluntary support of countless Americans of all faiths and in all walks of life. Inasmuch as the movement has no memberships and no meetings, each person participates in the work of the Christophers as far as he can and will.

You, too, can be a Christopher. You—whoever you are—can do something to carry the love and truth of Christ into the very heart of modern twentieth century life.

God has put a bit of the missionary in you. If you take the time and trouble to play the role of an apostle or Christbearer, whether by prayer, word or deed, you may do much to bring lasting peace to the world.

Prayer of the Christophers

Lord, make me an instrument of your peace.
Where there is hatred, let me sow love;
Where there is injury, pardon;
Where there is doubt, faith;
Where there is despair, hope;
Where there is darkness, light;
And where there is sadness, joy.
O, Divine Master, grant that I may not so much seek to
    be consoled, as to console;
To be understood as to understand;
To be loved as to love;
For it is in giving that we receive;
It is in pardoning that we are pardoned;
It is in dying that we are born to eternal life.

ST. FRANCIS OF ASSISI

The Christophers
18 E. 48th St., New York 17, N. Y.
Father James Keller, M.M., Director

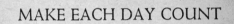

MAKE EACH DAY COUNT

SHE WALKED 5000 MILES

On New Year's Day, 1953, a woman started on foot from Los Angeles to New York. Her purpose was to present a peace petition to the United Nations.

She travelled for a year, averaging about 25 miles a day. She detoured on her trek to touch the Mexican and Canadian borders. Finally, after a 5000 mile transcontinental walk, she arrived in New York. She said, "I intend to be a wanderer on the face of the earth until mankind has learned the way of peace."

You don't have to walk from one end of the country to the other to be a missionary of peace. More than 1900 years ago, Jesus Christ gave a formula for "peace on earth" that can be put to work anywhere. When enough people can be found who are of such good will that they bring these divine principles into their own thoughts, words and deeds, and apply it to the world as far as they can reach, then will mankind experience that precious peace for which all men yearn.

There is something that you can do today in your home, classroom or office, in your shop, on your farm or anywhere else that will clearly show you are determined to be a zealous apostle of peace.

"On earth peace to men of good will." (Luke 2:14)

꯫ Let me be an instrument of Thy peace, O Jesus.

YOUR BIT OF RESPONSIBILITY

In one election district in Long Island, New York, that numbers 869 registered voters, the turnout at primary elections averages only 14 individuals.

In short, 855 persons who enjoy the God-given privilege of participating in self-government fail to go to the polls at a most important time.

If those who live off the benefits of free government fail to make their influence felt in the election of candidates and other important electoral officials they are in effect sabotaging the very process which provides them with liberty.

God has put a bit of responsibility for the administration of human affairs in the hands of everybody.

Down through the ages the chief reason why men have fallen into slavery was because the majority of citizens have failed to shoulder that bit of responsibility.

They adopted a "Let George do it" attitude. And the "Georges," sure enough, were there to do it, but they were the corrupt, self seeking or disloyal.

This tendency to "Let George do it" can be changed at any time. You can do something to remind others of their responsibility to vote to make government their business. Don't underestimate your role—you will be fulfilling the will of God himself.

"Bear ye one another's burdens and you shall fulfill the law of Christ." (Galatians 6:2)

Raise up more among us, O Lord, who will shoulder their responsibility toward all.

SAFECRACKERS GET LOOT—ON OWNER

If Albert Altmark, Brooklyn construction company president, hadn't interrupted thieves trying to open a safe in his office, he might be $7800 richer today.

The safe was empty but Altmark wasn't. He returned from a nearby bank and found two young men working on the safe in his garage-office. So they concentrated on Altmark and robbed him of the $7800 he had just withdrawn from the bank and was about to tuck away in his safe.

On all sides today relentless efforts are being made to wrest from individuals their most precious possessions—their faith, their ideals, their virtue. All of these are gifts of God and therefore the most valuable things we have.

But those who would hurt mankind, or who would wish to destroy God, are ever on the alert, and concentrate on these higher values first. Once they have these, they know, it is easy to get the rest.

We must protect these treasures of heart and soul both in ourselves and in our institutions, particularly in our youth and in our schools.

Our best protection is for us to get enough good people into vital spheres of influence—government, education, labor relations and communications—and there will be less chance of the evil-doers multiplying about us.

"The devil, as a roaring lion, goes about seeking whom he may devour." (1 Peter 5:8)

❧ Let the good flourish and prosper among us, O Lord, and keep us from evil.

A WOMAN'S DARING

A 39-year-old London housewife, who was awarded a medal for bravery in fighting incendiary bomb fires during the blitz, recently died trying to scale Britain's highest mountain.

Mrs. Elizabeth Emery, a veteran climber and courageous woman, lost her footing on the ice-caked slopes of 4406-foot Ben Nevis and plunged into a chasm. For 20 hours she swayed in the freezing blasts suspended by a 120-foot safety rope.

Rescue teams tried to reach her before nightfall but failed. When they did the following noon, she was dead.

It is difficult to place limits on what a brave woman can do. And a housewife is no exception. Tales of their valor are constantly coming to our notice.

Imagine what a change would take place throughout the world if they applied their God-given power for good to influencing public affairs.

We are convinced that if a few million members of the 42 million families in America will individually take it upon themselves to show as much initiative and daring in fighting for truth, goodness and beauty in literature and entertainment, as the advocates of crime, violence and immorality display in pushing their wares, they can easily outplay and outsmart them.

"Who shall find a valiant woman? far and from the uttermost coasts is the price of her." (Proverbs 31:10)

◄§ Inspire the women of our nation, O Lord, to make their influence felt.

NO ONE ASKED HER

A New Jersey woman employed as a clerk in the school system, was hired in September 1950 and had collected $12,000 in salary until someone recently asked her a pertinent question. The school board demanded to know why the woman hadn't worked a single day since she was put on the payroll.

"I would have come to work if anyone had asked me to," she frankly admitted.

There is such a thing as cutting corners, and there is lack of initiative because of human nature being what it is. There is, nevertheless, a certain point where it is a question of dishonesty in taking wages for service not performed. To accept wages for work not done is in reality taking money out of other people's pockets. For this reason it must be treated as any other theft.

Dishonesty in any job is condemnable. It is all the more when it is in a job of vital importance, as government, education and the like. The theft is then against the common good. The loss is not only one of money but of public service as well.

"But about the eleventh hour he went out and found others standing, and he saith to them: Why stand you here all the day idle? They say to him: Because no man hath hired us. He saith to them: Go ye also into my vineyard." (Matthew 20:6-7)

᪥ Give me a true zeal for Thy Cause, O Lord.

HOMEMAKING COMES FIRST

More than nine million women now hold jobs outside the home, according to the Life Insurance Institute.

Many thought that the number of working wives during World War II was approaching the point where it would interfere with normal home life. At that time it hit an all-time high of seven million married women employed in a large variety of jobs.

In some cases, it is an economic necessity for a wife or mother to be the breadwinner. With a sick husband unable to support his family, or when a widow is left alone to shoulder that burden, there is little other choice.

But statistics show that four million of these working wives take paying jobs to boost the family income to the $5000-$10,000 a year income bracket and thus provide more material conveniences and comforts.

It is understandable that people should try to improve their lot provided they do not undermine and eventually break up the home for the sake of a few more advantages. Some realize too late that their divorce or their delinquent child is the penalty they pay for a few conveniences.

The wife and mother is the soul of the home. Once she departs from it, except for serious reasons, it begins to fall apart. Our nation's true greatness depends on homes that are founded on and operated according to God's unchangeable law.

"He that hath found a good wife hath found a good thing and shall receive a pleasure from the Lord."

(Proverbs 18:22)

≈§ Keep all homemakers in Thy protection, O Lord.

ONE BY ONE

An ant crawled into a radio transformer in a clover field near Philadelphia and immediately burned to a crisp.

Another ant followed and was electrocuted by the high voltage. More and more ants piled into the transformer. Finally, the mechanism stopped and radio service was disrupted in the entire area.

These thousands of ants' charred bodies became carbonized and clogged the tubes and delicate wiring of the instrument. Technicians had to replace the encrusted machinery with an emergency unit until the original parts could be reconditioned.

How a few thousand ants could turn off radio reception in an area would be hard to conceive, were it not for a story like this. It is an effective reminder of the power of the individual.

Much like these ants, if a sufficient number of persons intent on doing evil infiltrate into our government, educational system, our mass media of communication, they can poison them at their source or break them down completely. By the same token, if good and loyal citizens take it upon themselves one by one to get into these vital spheres, we can expect the peace and stability that the Lord intended should be our lot.

Do what you can to arouse as many as possible to a realization of the tremendous possibilities given them by God to change our country and world for the better.

"The Lord will raise thee up to be a holy people."
(Deuteronomy 28:9)

ა§ Convince us, O Lord, of the power we can wield for Thy sake.

THIEF LEAVES HIS ADDRESS

When detectives arrested a 33-year-old Kansas City man for a $200 tavern robbery, he wasn't the least bit surprised. In fact, he was expecting their visit.

The man was in such a hurry to make his getaway that his billfold dropped from his pocket. It contained his driver's license, social security card and telephone number. All the police had to do was call at the man's home.

Wrongdoers are not always so easily caught as this one. But one way or another they eventually are the victims of their own mistakes.

God has planned His universe in favor of the good and against the wicked. In the long run, the man who lives a life of virtue and service of others is happy not only in the next life but in this one too.

Don't remain satisfied, however, merely to avoid evil, but do all the good you can. Do it where it counts the most—in the fields that influence for better or worse the lives of everyone.

If we truly love God and our fellowman, we will, for instance, make every effort within our power to see that all schools are staffed with the best possible teachers, who are given the respect and support they deserve.

"And we know that to them that love God, all things work together unto good, to such as, according to his purpose, are called to be saints." (Romans 8:28)

◄§ Give me a love of what is right and good, O Lord.

FORECASTING HIS OWN DEATH

In August, 1954, Raymond M. Eastman of Des Moines, while driving in his new sports car, clipped another car and smashed into a bridge. He was killed.

Three years before the same Mr. Eastman, an advertising writer, described in one of his articles the thoughts of a motorist about to be killed in an accident.

Here are excerpts from Eastman's article:

"Ten seconds to live. He massaged his eyes with thumb and middle finger, trying to rub out some of the sand ... Nine seconds to live. He'd driven almost eight hours since lunch, and was beginning to feel it ... Eight seconds to live. Lousy driving in the rain ... Four seconds to live. Something looked wrong through the blurry windshield. He made out an old unlighted slow-moving truck ahead ... One second to live. He was floating right into the rear corner of the truck bed. He opened his mouth to scream ... No seconds to live."

It is difficult for most of us to visualize our own death. And yet we easily associate death with others. Without getting morbid about it, it is a holy and wholesome thought for one and all to recall frequently that one day, sooner or later, each of us must appear before the Judgment Seat of God to render an account of our stewardship.

By so doing we will be preparing ourselves for our entrance into eternity.

"In all thy works remember thy last end, and thou shall never sin." (Ecclesiasticus 7:40)

&ŝ Convince me of the brevity of this life, O Lord.

GOOD IN THE WORST

Al Newman, owner of a Bronx restaurant, was surprised to receive a letter containing a money order for $1.70. It read:

"Enclosed is a check for $1.70 which my brother and I owe you for two dinners we had in your place eight years ago. We were both broke at the time and we slipped out of the restaurant without paying the check. I'd like to pay off now and apologize for trying to beat you out of the check."

Impressed by the man's honesty, Newman invited him and his brother for an identical dinner at the restaurant's expense and said the money would be given to charity.

"This restores my faith in human nature," Newman said. He added that recently a patron had cashed a $75 rubber check and his faith in people had dropped very low.

We should not wait for experiences like these to believe the goodness that God has placed in human nature. By believing in it, despite all, we bring it out in ourselves and in others.

Make it a point to look for the good in everyone.

Rather than waste valuable time and effort bemoaning the mistakes of others, try to imitate Jesus Christ Who spent Himself even unto death in order to rehabilitate weakened human nature and redeem those who had fallen.

"Then came Peter unto Him and said: Lord, how often shall my brother offend against me, and I forgive him? Till seven times? Jesus saith to him: I say not to thee, till seven times; but till seventy times seven times."

(Matthew 18:21, 22)

SET YOUR HEART HIGH

When a 58-year-old New Haven, Connecticut, man was hungry for steaks nothing stopped him from having his fill. Not even the lack of money.

The man recently walked into a New Haven restaurant and ate two steaks. Everything went along fine until he was presented with the check. He didn't have the money to pay for the hearty meal. Police asked him why he didn't have the money.

"I haven't had a steak since the last time I got arrested for the same thing," replied the man with the penchant for steaks.

The old adage, "where there's a will there's a way," can work for good or evil. We've seen it proved both ways time and time again. Even when a man sets his mind on eating steaks there is little to stop him.

One of the most effective ways to prevent juvenile delinquency is to implant in young people at an early age a determination to lead a life with a purpose. It will get them off to a good start channeling for good the talent, little or much, that God has entrusted to them. When not put to good use at an early age, it can easily be used for harm.

"Where thy treasure is, there is thy heart also."
(Matthew 6:21)

CAUGHT IN HIS OWN TRAP

Sometimes we set our own booby traps.

A Colorado man trying to protect his summer cabin during the winter months rigged up a .22-caliber rifle so that when the door was opened the gun would fire at the intruder. Returning the following June he found the windows had been smashed. Suspecting that the cabin had been entered, he rushed through the door and was shot in the chest by his own device.

He crawled to the highway where he was picked up by a motorist who took him to a hospital in serious condition.

Human nature being what it is, it is only proper to care for oneself and one's possessions. The use of locks, safe-deposit boxes, and the like, is essential.

We can overdo it, however. Becoming too preoccupied with personal safety and security, we fall into a lack of balance. We do so, for example, when we are too violent in punishing others for their encroachment on our domain or possessions.

We often become the victims of our own excessive zeal to catch others doing wrong. The best cure is to aim on every occasion to try to rehabilitate others, especially those who do great harm.

"Which of these three, in thy opinion, was neighbor to him that fell among robbers? But he said: He that showed mercy to him. And Jesus said to him: Go and do thou in like manner." (Luke 10:36-37)

⊷ Never permit me, O Lord, to be hard on others for my own advantage.

BE YOURSELF

A girl from the Midwest wrote a glamor columnist that she felt inferior because she didn't dress or talk like other girls do in New York City.

The advice she received was invaluable, especially for young people. The columnist said that there were so many look-alikes in New York that a change would be refreshing.

She told the girl to be herself, to be natural at all times, become an individual rather than a carbon copy.

She added:

"Do smile and speak in a friendly tone. Do increase your vocabulary. Don't imitate anyone. Don't 'put-on' a voice for an interview or in conversation."

Too many young people think being different means being out of step with society. They forget that only by developing their own personalities can they ever hope to rise above what is known as the "average person."

God has placed something in each individual which He entrusted to no one else. This "individuality" is not to be suppressed, but put to work for the good of all.

Don't be a "carbon copy," but the original that God made you. There is some task which, if you do not do it in life, will never be done without you.

"For even as a man going into a far country, called his servants, and delivered to them his goods. And to one he gave five talents, and to another two, and to another one, to every one according to his proper ability . . ."
(Matthew 25:14-15)

❧ Help me, O Lord, to discover and use the distinctive energy You gave to me for helping others.

LOVE ACROSS THE SEA

Possibly it was the name that attracted nine-year-old Anita Rae Teague of Barnsley, England, to send her year's savings to four-year-old Anita Rae Bartlett of Dallas, Texas.

The little English girl read that Anita Rae was dying of an incurable disease. She rushed to her piggy bank which contained 12 shillings, or $1.68, which she earned by doing errands. In her own handwriting she wrote this letter to the mother of the Texas tot.

"I am Anita Rae, too, and I am sending you my new 3-penny pieces, 6-penny pieces and a shilling I have saved in my piggy money-box to buy a little present for my namesake.

"Does Anita want anything special? If she does, mummy and I will try to get it for her. Please do not be sad. We will pray every night for Anita—Love from Anita Rae Teague."

Love is the strongest force in the world. It is above time and space and reaches out to all. God has entrusted a bit of it to all of us.

Love should be practical, however, and not remain a feeling or a thing to talk about. Reach out today to try to touch the lives of those about you with God's love.

Use in whatever way you can the modern means we have of affecting all with the love of God—government, education, radio, television, books, the press.

"My little children, let us not love in word, nor in tongue, but in deed, and in truth." (1 John 3:18)

⮿ Teach us to love, O Lord.

EVIL NEVER TRIUMPHS

Crime has a way of catching up with those who think they can escape paying the penalty.

A 23-year-old Connecticut man thought he could evade the law, but it found him where he least expected it would—in a movie.

The young man stole a rowboat and felt confident that no one had detected the theft. Several weeks later, he was watching a movie in a neighborhood theatre. By this time he had almost forgotten about his "perfect job."

Then he heard an usher paging him and not suspecting a ruse he walked to the lobby. There he was met by policemen who had been working on the case every day and decided on this trap. The thief planned everything but this was one of his blind spots.

Men frequently succeed in evading the law. As a result, they often jump to the conclusion that they fooled everybody. They make one big mistake. They forget that God never allows evil to triumph over good for very long. Even if they deceive others for the few fleeting years of a lifetime, they soon face the tribunal of God.

But this does not mean that we should be content to spend our life on earth only avoiding evil. If we spend our time doing good, it is impossible to make many mistakes.

God sees our good actions as well as our bad.

"But I say to you, that every idle word that men shall speak, they shall render an account for it in the day of judgment." (Matthew 12:36)

∾ Make me conscious of Thy ever watchful eye, O Lord.

COSTLY COUNTERFEITING

A 34-year-old Fort Worth, Texas, lithographer was struck by an idea recently which he felt would make him a rich man.

The skilled craftsman thought it would be easy to make plates for counterfeit money. His first attempt was so successful that he was encouraged to continue. He turned out $9000 worth of bogus $20 bills before Secret Service agents caught up with him.

A father of three children, he had two friends pass the bills in 11 states from California to Alabama. They managed to circulate $4000 worth before the scheme was detected.

The temptation to look for the short cut or the line of least resistance is a strong one. There is doubtless a "lazy streak" in most of us. On the other hand, we were made to work for our living and work out our salvation in patience.

For this God gives us sufficient grace. A life of work can be a full and happy one. A life of service to others is invariably a most satisfying one.

Rather than spend valuable time and effort trying to dodge your obligations and responsibilities, why not deliberately and cheerfully seek them as your share in providing peace in the world. God expects you to carry your share of the load. Everyone else does too!

"In the sweat of thy face shalt thou eat bread till thou return to the earth, out of which thou wast taken . . ."

(Genesis 3:19)

EVERYONE CAN DO SOMETHING

A young lady in Carbondale, Ill., was impressed by the constant emphasis the Christophers place on the power of each and every individual for good. She cited as living proof the example of her aunt, who has been on crutches for 35 years as a result of an attack of polio at the age of 2. She wrote that "she does more than a dozen women with 2 good feet would do."

To prepare for a career, this crippled woman entered college and took radio and speech courses and then started a children's show on the local radio station. She takes a carload of children to church every Sunday, teaches a class and organized a choral group that entertains at hospitals, veterans' and old people's homes, etc. She is always on the go, working with children and their parents, groups and individuals.

Her niece said she is a lively example of "what one person can do."

There is not one individual in the world who is not capable of doing some good that will lighten the burden of others.

No matter how handicapped, busy or lacking in talent you may think you are, there is much that you personally can do—if you really want to get out of yourself and start working for the glory of God and the good of souls.

Countless persons need the care and affection that only you and others like you can give. Once you start looking for the opportunities that God is offering you, you will see how great the need is, and experience the joy of working for Him.

"The harvest indeed is great, but the laborers are few."
(Matthew 9:37)

WHEN WOMAN TAKES A STAND

A 49-year-old London woman clerk displayed unusual courage when two robbers pointed pistols at her and tried to snatch the payroll. Far from being frightened by the guns or their demand she struck them across the face. Apparently she put a lot into her punch because she dislocated her right arm.

The shocked gunmen fled without the payroll.

A 60-year-old Indianapolis grandmother also showed a vigorous approach in dealing with a thief. She got her dander up when a man pointed a pistol at her and dipped his other hand into the cash register of her shop.

The brave lady quickly slammed the drawer on the robber's knuckles and slapped him in the face with her right fist. That was enough to make the bandit jump over a three-foot counter and flee down the street.

We certainly don't recommend that all women follow such a daring pattern. But we do heartily encourage them to take a stand where there are no such risks involved. God has blessed women in particular with a sense of truth, reverence, and decency. What a refreshing change for the better if each good woman in America took at least one positive step to bring these important values into all levels of government and education, and into providing better literature and entertainment.

Those who would foul up these vital spheres of influence are cowards at heart. Most of them run away in fright when good women take a stand.

"The Lord is my helper: I will not fear what man shall do to me." (Hebrews 13:6)

STEPS TO BETTER GOVERNMENT

Here are a few steps, proposed by the Christophers, that you may find practical in encouraging the personal participation on the part of each citizen that is essential for the proper functioning of American government:

1. Inquire about the management of public affairs from authoritative sources. Keep informed by reading newspapers, magazines, etc. Listen to speeches, discussions, and debates and then form your own opinion about candidates and issues.

2. Pray for those in public office that they may render conscientious service worthy of the responsibility entrusted to them by the people.

3. Encourage those with character and competence to dedicate themselves to careers in public service. Government can never be any better than the people in it. Pay tribute to those in government, regardless of party, who are doing a good, honest job. Branding all government employees as "no good" often results in driving good workers out.

4. Study the candidates. Look up their past records, what they stand for, whether they have a reputation for living up to their promises.

Think up additional practical steps of your own that may help others to play an effective part in protecting the blessing of freedom that God has entrusted to us. What you, personally and individually do, may have far-reaching effects.

"Thy will be done on earth as it is in heaven."

(Matthew 6:10)

MORE STEPS TO BETTER GOVERNMENT

You have a God-given right to participate in the administration of good government. But with that right goes an obligation if you are to play the role that the Judge of nations expects of you. These few suggestions may help you to apply your ideals in a practical way.

1. Participate in political meetings. Make your voice heard in the selection of candidates and workers as well as in the formation of policy.

2. Check on the voting record of your present representatives. Ask your local newspapers to print their record.

3. Stimulate others to vote (within the limits prescribed by your State laws). Explain where and when to register and vote.

4. Offer your services for essential chores and "leg work" in some pre-election job of your own choosing. Help to arrange for transportation and baby sitters for those who might not otherwise be able to exercise their privilege of voting.

5. Consider legitimate political activity as a moral obligation to God and country. (Failure to fulfill this responsibility may be a serious sin of omission.)

6. Vote for those, regardless of party, who stand for the preservation of free constitutional government which we, under God's Providence, enjoy.

It is up to you to do your part as a good citizen. You must decide how, where and when you will play your role. It is between you and your conscience—between you and God.

"Render to Caesar the things that are Caesar's."

(Matthew 22:21)

ACCENT THE GOOD

Appearing before a Senate Committee in Washington D.C. which was investigating the causes of juvenile delinquency, two public officials recently gave two practical suggestions:

1. Probate Judge George Edwards of Detroit said that one of the best ways to eliminate juvenile delinquency is to reawaken interest in home life. Instead of glorifying glamor girls, he said, praise the mother who stays home and cares for her children.

2. Leroy E. Wike, executive of the International Association of Chiefs of Police, claimed that juvenile delinquency will continue so long as parents place their own interests and desires above the welfare of their children. Then he added:

"If parents in all walks of life can be sold, by our modern advertising methods, on the merits of chlorophyl, toothpaste, lipstick and shaving creams, then it would not be perversion to 'commercialize' the values of rectitude, integrity and industriousness.

"Our cinema, television and radio have a terrific impact on the actions, mannerisms and ideas of adults and juveniles alike. Why cannot these media diverge from the present level of distorted values to portrayal of the eternal values of righteousness and honor?"

You personally can do something to see that the normal rather than the abnormal side of life is accentuated. A prayer, a word, or some positive effort on your part may accomplish much.

"Be not overcome by evil, but overcome evil by good."
(Romans 12:21)

37

A $300 TEMPTATION

Three-year-old Rose Wetjas happily tripped alongside her mother one day on a shopping expedition in Pittsburgh. Curious to explore whatever caught her eye as most children are, Rose spotted a package on the street and picked it up.

Her mother, Mrs. Dorothy Wetjas, asked her daughter to throw the dirty package away. But the girl was fascinated by it and slipped it into her mother's shopping bag. Mrs. Wetjas opened the bundle at home. In it was $300.

Taken by surprise, the first thought that entered her mind was her husband's unpaid $2000 hospital bill. This money would help pay part of it. The temptation was a strong one but Mrs. Wetjas resisted it. Immediately she turned the money over to the police.

"My conscience wouldn't permit me to keep the money," she explained.

Those who develop a good strong conscience early in life seldom get into serious trouble. They are ever conscious of their obligations to God and to others. They usually have a healthy sense of self-control and know that God will supply His grace when they make an honest attempt to cooperate with His Divine Law.

In return God gives them a reward that neither money nor position can buy. It is that peace of mind, heart and soul that only those enjoy who recognize and live up to their responsibilities.

Do all in your power to restore a sense of conscience to modern life.

"I can do all things in Him Who strengtheneth me."
(Philippians 4:13)

LABOR RELATIONS BECOME
HUMAN RELATIONS

The personnel director of a large factory in Pennsylvania claims that seeing a Christopher TV program helped him to shift from "negative to positive." The gentleman started off his letter by saying that he belonged to no church and concluded with this remark: "P.S.—I didn't ask my secretary to type this letter because I have been regarded around this office as a little hard-boiled." He pointed out that he had gotten into the habit of "terminating interviews rather abruptly, visualizing the applicant just as a routine contact."

Because of the Christopher idea however, he wrote that "my reception of applicants has undergone complete revision . . . Now I receive each applicant as though he is the most important person in the world because, as you say, he is a child of God. It is consoling to know that even when I can't give these people a job, I can help them to regain self-confidence, hope and the ability to go on. I have received satisfaction in my work, never before achieved . . . I feel that by this more friendly approach, in my own small way, I am lighting a candle."

It took only a word of encouragement to bring out this man's great potential. Imagine the refreshing change for the better if even a few hundred thousand would integrate their belief in Christ into their dealings with workers and thus transform "labor relations" into "human relations."

"Thou shalt love thy neighbor as thyself."
(Matthew 22:39)

TAKING THE BUMPS

Two-year-old Kevin O'Connor, a chicken bone caught in his throat, was being rushed to a Philadelphia Hospital by an ambulance. The slightest delay might mean the difference between life and death. So the driver didn't mind the bumps in the road. Suddenly the ambulance hit a small hole. It made Kevin cough. Up came the bone that had lodged in his throat and the nurse quickly snatched it. The boy was examined at the hospital where doctors found him well enough to return home.

Many people spend a lifetime dodging trouble, little realizing that, if they had deliberately braved some of the bumps along the way, they might have solved many troubles for themselves and countless others.

By striving to avoid anything of inconvenience or discomfort, many people actually bring upon themselves more than a few heartaches and headaches.

To do almost anything worthwhile in life today means to take up a cross—to invite trouble and hardship. But there is a hidden blessing for everyone who "takes the bumps" cheerfully and voluntarily. The sense of purpose that sparks, for instance, a devoted parent or teacher, helps everything to take on a new and refreshing meaning.

When you regard yourself as an instrument in God's hands the very difficulties you encounter often go unnoticed. Everything you do can become a labor of love.

Christ Himself expected everyone interested in working with Him to welcome the cross, not run away from it. He put it very plainly:

"If any man will come after Me, let him deny himself, and take up his cross daily, and follow Me." (Luke 9:23)

YOU ARE NEVER TOO OLD

A 78-year-old man in Pittsburgh, a former public official, recently showed he could continue to be a force for good. Impressed by the Christopher slogan of "better to light one candle than curse the darkness," he decided that age is no obstacle to being a Christopher.

After his retirement, he personally initiated an investigation that exposed graft in government. Still more, he encouraged one of his sons to become a school official. He persuaded his second son to become active in union affairs at the mill where he worked.

This young man, now vice-president of the union, has in turn stimulated three of his friends to run for public office in order to promote more honest and efficient government.

It is safe to say that no one is ever too old to do some good—by prayer, word or deed. God has given each of us a mission in life to perform. It may be that our greatest good will be accomplished in the twilight of our lives.

Then again a strong, vital purpose that absorbs one's interest and talent, especially when one has extra time, adds new meaning and zest to what might otherwise be very humdrum living.

You would do a Christlike service to some elderly persons by showing them that they still count—that they can still be an influence for good.

"Neglect not the grace that is in thee." (1 Timothy 4:14)

THEY HIT FOR THE WORLD

Jesus Christ set a big goal for every one of His followers. His Twelve Apostles took him very literally. They made a desperate try to reach the "whole world" of their time with His message of love and truth. During their short lifetime they succeeded in a phenomenal way.

Whenever Christ's followers have felt a deep and personal responsibility to bring His truth and love to the world itself, they have acted daringly and have been blessed with results that have left their mark on history.

On the other hand, whenever those who call themselves Christians have lowered their sights, becoming merely local-minded, and forgotten their world objective, they have in effect betrayed their cause and left the door open to the misery that inevitably follows.

Only when more take it upon themselves to fulfill this sublime commission will the dream of lasting peace become a reality.

Those who spread hatred of God and their fellowman from one end of the earth to the other can never be accused of being small-minded, or lacking in vision, imagination and enterprise. Their chief strength is our weakness. The best way to remedy this is to do what Christ said:

"All power is given to me in heaven and earth. Going, therefore, teach ye all nations, baptising them in the name of the Father, and of the Son, and of the Holy Ghost, teaching them to observe all things that I have commanded you and behold I am with you all days even to the consummation of the world."

(Matthew 28:18-20)

A SIXTY PER CENT BURN

A two-year-old Long Island girl was critically burned while playing with matches and given a slight chance to live. Doctors said the girl, Barbara Jackson, was doomed because she had lost 60% of her own skin and there were not enough skin donors.

Newspapers took up the plea and immediately offers began to flood the hospital. Three people—Barbara's 15-year-old brother, a 39-year-old fireman and a 29-year-old telephone lineman—were chosen for the grafting operation. Richard Beecher, the fireman, and father of three children, said his son had recently survived a severe case of pneumonia and vowed he'd try to help other children if God saved his son. James Allen, the lineman, said that the night before the appeal for Barbara was made, he punished his three children for playing with matches. The skin grafting operation was not dangerous, but it meant that each donor had to remain in the hospital for two or three weeks.

In times of emergency, more than a few gallant souls usually show extraordinary generosity. They are willing to go to great lengths of self-sacrifice in order to help others in need.

If the same sense of courage and devotion could be stirred up in such a way that it would go to work on a day to day basis in preventing trouble in education, government, and other vital fields, rather than after disaster takes place, many catastrophes could be averted. Working from emergency to emergency is not enough. God expects us to protect our blessings.

"Watch ye, therefore, praying at all times."

(Luke 21:36)

ONE MAN CHANGES A UNION

In New Jersey, a union man deliberately stayed away from labor meetings because his local was dominated by a radical minority. His sister, a teacher, who is interested in the Christopher movement, pointed out to him that one of the reasons subversives gain control is because honest, well-intentioned people are not on the job.

She explained that he had no right to complain about conditions if he didn't even bother to attend meetings. She well knew the meaning of the expression "the absent are always wrong." She told her brother it was his obligation to get into the thick of things and fight for the truth, even if it meant hardship and failure.

This made sense to him. Not only did he begin to attend meetings, but he persuaded other members to take part in union activities. As a result of his positive action, they were able to inject new life into the union.

Eventually this man, who had previously refused even to attend the meetings, ended up as president of his local!

Wherever those bent on evil obtain a footing in government, education, communications or labor unions, it is usually due to the fact that they have been very much on the job while those who should know better are "among the missing." The solution is within the grasp of almost everyone. God blesses those who live up to their obligations.

"Why are you fearful, O ye of little faith."

(Matthew 8:26)

⚜ O Lord, teach me never to shirk responsibilities that involve the well-being of others as well as my own.

SHE OVERLOOKED THE BRAKE

A 32-year-old San Francisco woman was driving through a web of traffic when the car suddenly stalled near an intersection. To compound the confusion the auto rolled back and crashed into the car behind it.

By this time a crowd had gathered to listen to what an approaching policeman would say to the frightened woman. Speaking in a pleasant yet firm voice, the officer asked: "What do you think that's for?" and pointed to the brake pedal.

"I haven't the least idea. What is it for?" the woman blandly blurted out.

An eight-day jail sentence gave her an opportunity to think about a lot of things, especially about her obligation to know how to stop her car as well as how to start it.

There is much talk these days on the "right to know" and the "right to be informed." But that God-given right should not be over-simplified or distorted.

With every right goes a responsibility, first of all to know the full truth, the whole truth, not merely some selected or slanted portions of it. Do your part to see that all men are given at least their right to know what our Founding Fathers aptly termed the "self evident truth" that all men are created by God.

"I am the way, the truth and the life." (John 14:6)

❧ Grant me the grace, O Lord, to fulfill the responsibilities that are an essential part of all my rights.

AT ANY COST

Some years ago, the sympathy of the country went out to Mr. and Mrs. Georgescu, the parents of two boys who were held captive by the Communists.

The parents were promised the release of the boys if they would consent to engage in espionage for the Reds. If they refused they were threatened with the death of the boys. It was a terrible decision to make for a couple who sincerely loved their children. Yet these were people who knew that there is never really any compromise when the decision is a definite choice between right and wrong.

Bravely, they put the case before the U.S. government and prayerfully awaited the outcome. For seven years they waited, never really being sure that their sons were alive. But the Communists had overplayed their hand, reckoning without the integrity of the couple and the vehement denunciations their shameful action would bring upon their heads. Pressure was brought to bear from many sources and finally the Georgescu boys were returned home safe and sound.

Stories like this are bringing home to us forcefully that fact that there are certainly values in life which are superior to any human consideration. They come from God. This is something we must not forget. Truth, honor, integrity, freedom,—all these and more are dearer than life itself.

"If any man come to me, and hate not his father, and mother, and wife, and children, and brethren, and sisters, yea and his own life also, he cannot be my disciple."

(Luke 14:26)

46

THE PEAK OF GREATNESS

Dr. John McCall, a famous University of Alaska glacier-ologist, once climbed the dangerous Mt. McKinley and found it such a hazardous experience that he vowed never to do it again. He kept his vow—until just recently when a small party of men headed by Pfc. George Argus, 25-year-old Brooklyn GI, decided to make the trip up.

Dr. McCall warned them that snowslides and avalanches are such a constant danger on Mt. McKinley that it is foolhardy for even practiced mountaineers to attempt it, much less amateurs. But heedless to his warnings they went ahead.

When George Argus became marooned 11,000 feet up with a broken hip and another climber was killed, it was Dr. McCall who headed the rescue party—breaking his vow in order to save another man's life.

In his heart every man is inspired by the example of heroism especially when it takes the form of great love of our fellowmen. These examples keep us going through the humdrum of every-day life.

Our every-day existence can also be daring. Though less spectacular, the devotion to duty, to our country, to our family, to a friend, can be nothing short of heroic. It is in the eyes of God, Who will judge us.

"Greater love than this no man hath, that a man lay down his life for his friends." (John 15:13)

FAITH IN REVERSE

If you happen to be one of these people who "knock on wood" to avert some disaster—and smile at yourself for doing it, you may be interested in learning what Dr. Judd Marmor, a University of California psychiatrist, has to say about this old superstition.

He stated that knocking on wood is one of the most common of 80,000 superstitions, and apparently stems from a primitive belief that protective gods dwell within trees. While some people make this gesture in all seriousness, most persons do it jokingly. Yet it is usually indicative of a deep-lying fear of antagonizing some vengeful "authority," who may disapprove of our doing too well at anything.

Dr. Marmor said that this "call on magic" to protect one against possible evil, is a sign that the person who knocks on wood is usually very immature.

A person who indulges in superstitious practices is usually one who lives in fear. And worse still he lives without any effective faith in God.

A person like this must learn to love—to get out of himself and turn toward others. This love will dispel his fears and increase his faith, because, as St. John said: "God is Love."

"I am the Lord thy God . . . Thou shalt not have strange gods before me." (Exodus 20:2-3)

❧ Lord, increase our faith.

THE REAL THING

"Ersatz" is a useful German word meaning "substitute"; something put in place of the real thing.

Hitler and his Nazi followers knew that man needs to believe in something greater than himself. They perverted this instinct away from God, and channeled it towards a substitute concept: "Das Volk," the mystical German People. His book, *Mein Kampf* ("My Struggle"), became the Bible of the new belief.

Young people were taught that they were the children of the state rather than children of God. In school, they were taught to end their childish letters with "Heil Hitler!" instead of the traditional "Grüss Gott."

In our own lives, we may try to substitute a person or thing as our goal and steadfastly ignore the Real Thing, only to discover eventually, as the Germans, that our substitute is just that—a substitute. We must remember that God is the only Real Thing in all of life. By realizing this we will never need to fear being fooled by the "substitutes."

We should show the same zeal as Hitler's followers in promoting a recognition of God in our institutions, especially government and education.

"Go ye into the whole world, and preach the gospel to every creature." (Mark 16:15)

Increase my zeal to have Thy name known, O Lord.

OUR COMMON DEBT

Nineteen-year-old airman Anton Tople of Yugoslavia recently took his oath of allegiance as a citizen of this country. He is one citizen of whom this country may be justly proud.

He escaped from Trieste more than five years ago and later enlisted in the U. S. Air Force. When the time came for him to name a beneficiary for his $10,000 life insurance policy, he named the United States Government.

Asked why he did this, he explained, "There is no price tag on my obligation to America or the value I place on living in America. My insurance is all I have. This I give with humble gratitude."

We all have the natural tendency to take for granted that which is close to us. One of the great blessings given us is a free government. Our appreciation of it, however, is limited to "patriotic" gestures and words. Seldom does it take the form of deeds.

The example of this immigrant should bring to mind our indebtedness. Let us work in whatever way we can to make our nation strong under God.

"Unless the Lord build the house, they labour in vain that build it." (Psalms 126:1)

◢ Accept our thanks, O God, for the land thou hast given us.

THE RULE OF LAW

A 16-year-old boy in Buffalo, N.Y., applied for a job with a company which makes plastic shipping seals. The company has a rule that all employees must be over eighteen. But the boy didn't let this stop him. He merely gave his age as eighteen.

The employer did not investigate to see whether or not the boy spoke the truth. He hired him. Eight days after the boy started work, he stuck his hand into a scrap cutting and grinding machine, injuring it so badly that it had to be amputated.

The upshot of the matter was that the boy lost a hand, and the employer lost $8,000—the amount he was ordered to pay the boy as compensation for the injury.

Sometimes with the best of intentions we "interpret" the law in our own favor, or take the law in our own hands. We believe the law did not have us in mind. The results are usually bad, and sometimes disastrous.

If everyone did this, the consequences would be chaos. For the good of all we should obey legitimate authority, for all authority is from God.

Keep the law in little things and you will have no difficulty in the greater things.

"Let every soul be subject to higher powers; for there is no power but from God." (Romans 13:1)

⇜ Inspire us, O Lord, with a respect for authority.

A BLIND MAN TO THE RESCUE

Charles Vines, a blind Korean veteran, heard the shouts of two teen-age girls and a man who were drowning. He plunged into the treacherous Pascagoula River near Lucedale, Miss. and began swimming in the direction of the screams.

The terrific current made Vines exert every ounce of energy to reach one of the girls. He made shore with one girl, when the other one whom he had pushed near the bank was again carried away by the swirling water. The brave man struck out again and returned the girl to safety, and set out for the man who had jumped in to rescue the girls but who had himself been sucked down by the rushing waters.

Near exhaustion, Vines summoned up what strength he had left and hurled himself back into the river and brought the other man to shore.

Few realize the power for good that is hidden within them regardless of their handicaps. Rather than wait for an emergency to bring it out, why not look for ways and means of serving God and one's fellow men in the countless little challenges that confront each of us in our daily lives?

No matter how handicapped we may think we are, God has put in our trust a bit of the peace of the world. He expects us to decide for ourselves how, when and where we shall deliver it.

"He who soweth in blessings shall also reap blessings."
(II Corinthians 9:6)

⇜ Help me, O Lord, to bring out the power thou hast given me.

A MORE DEADLY DISEASE

Not long ago, the Philippine Congress appropriated $1,000,000 for a most unusual but very pressing purpose. The money is being spent to rid Mindanao Island of rats!

Within the past ten years, the whole island has been overrun with field rats, which have multiplied at such an alarming rate that they have defied all control. Millions of these rodents have devoured the rice and corn crops of the fertile land, forcing the starving people to migrate away from the area.

The President has offered a $100,000 reward to any scientist who can provide a formula that will kill the rats, and at the same time not harm other animals.

Difficult as it is to fight against a plague of rats, it is a far greater problem to meet the subtle, hidden attack on the minds and souls of men that is being deliberately propagated over the earth today.

Merely being against this deadly disease is not enough. Do your part to spread far and wide the Truth that overcomes error, the Health that banishes disease, the Light that eliminates darkness.

"Fear ye not them that kill the body and are not able to kill the soul, but rather fear him that can destroy both body and soul in hell." (Matthew 10:28)

ᏋᏋ Let me be for light, O God, not merely against error.

MISPLACED ZEAL

Two men in Paris planned to the minutest detail the theft of expensive copper piping from a municipal warehouse. They stole a truck, painted it the same color as the city-owned vehicles, drove to the warehouse and began loading.

It looked like a perfect crime. Nobody noticed the difference so they speeded up operations. This was their undoing.

A shrewd foreman paid little attention to the two workers at first. But when they began to show unusual hurry at their task, it aroused his suspicion. He knew that municipal employees seldom showed such zest for their jobs. Could these two be having a change in heart? He decided to look into the matter.

He soon discovered they were nothing but thieves pretending to be conscientious public servants. They had overplayed their part and were soon in the hands of the police.

There is a temptation for all of us to take it easy, to look for the line of least resistance, to do as little as we can. We often become so preoccupied with material security that we overlook our obligations to the very work that provides our security.

You would accomplish much by encouraging those who are half-hearted at a job to give it the same devotion and whole-hearted interest that the corrupt and subversive display.

"For the children of this world are wiser in their generation than the children of light." (Luke 16:8)

IT BEGINS IN THE HOME

In Paterson, New Jersey, a count was taken and it was discovered that 5,700 school windows had been broken since July 1st, 1953. This amounts to an enormous extra expense for school authorities.

The situation was so serious that the Mayor of Paterson made a public appeal calling for a curb on vandalism of public school buildings.

The mayor said that this could not be effected without the aid of the parents—for even though the law enforcement authorities and school custodians may bend every effort to restrain the children from their costly pranks, it could only be stopped altogether by correct disciplining by the parents.

The parent obviously can never be fully replaced in a young person's life. God meant it that way. Teachers in our schools will tell you this often from sad experience.

That is why it is of first importance that we maintain our family life in our country. Anything you can do to bolster the home, by combating divorce, marital infidelity, deliquency and promoting general Christian morality in public life, is an inestimable contribution to our nation's future.

"Wherefore a man shall leave father and mother, and shall cleave to his wife: and they shall be two in one flesh." (Genesis 2:24)

MORE THAN ONE KIND

An insect exterminator in Houston, Texas, nearly sacrificed the lives of his two little daughters to his business.

Rat poison is part of an exterminator's stock in trade so it wasn't unusual that there was quite a large supply in his home. It was kept high on a shelf out of the children's way, and it probably never occurred to him or his wife that the two girls might find that an additional reason to investigate.

One morning, when their mother wasn't looking, the little girls, aged 5 and 3, climbed up on a stool and helped themselves to what appeared to them to be a new kind of jam. They scooped large portions out of the jars and spread it thickly on slices of bread and ate it with gusto.

Their mother discovered what they had done in time to rush them to the hospital and save their lives.

There are more than physical poisons around us in life. Many things appear harmless to us, but they are moral or spiritual "booby traps." Unlike children, we have no excuse for not investigating all things before using them. This applies more to spiritual things than to what we eat, for our souls are our greatest possession.

"Watch ye, and pray that ye enter not into temptation. The spirit indeed is willing, but the flesh is weak."

(Matthew 26:41)

Grant me the grace to see clearly what is harmful to my salvation, O Lord.

TO BUILD OR TO DESTROY

Recently police officials in New Haven, Conn., have been greatly worried by a widespread outbreak of vandalism all over the city. Monuments have been defaced by pranksters, and buildings have been set afire. The senseless destruction has caused the city an enormous amount of expense and concern.

The newest prank seems to indicate that the vandals are adults. Recently, several trees, each about 25 feet high, were cut down during the night, falling across the streets and blocking traffic until they could be removed.

Each tree was cut about four feet from the ground, apparently by means of an axe—a height too great for youngsters.

Everyone at times feels the urge to be destructive; it is a natural instinct which must be curbed. The best way of curbing it is to channel this energy into constructive channels by devoting oneself to building instead of destroying.

It is a depressing thing to see, as in this story, grown adults behaving as children and tearing down, at a moment in history when we need the positive energies of all to build a better world and further the cause of peace.

"When I was a child I spoke as a child, I understood as a child. But, when I became a man, I put away the things of a child." (1 Corinthians 13:11)

&§ Grant me the grace, O Lord, of growing into a mature and Christlike personality.

STUMBLING UPON A TREASURE

When Dr. Hans R. Teichert, a Chicago art dealer, bought a painting in a New York antique shop for $450 little did he dream that the 25 by 20½ inch work of art was actually worth $1,000,000.

Dr. Teichert asked art critic Dr. Maurice H. Goldblatt to appraise it because he had been honored by the French Government and the Louvre in Paris for earlier studies of Leonardo da Vinci's paintings. Dr. Goldblatt concluded the painting was a da Vinci valued at $1,000,000.

The critic said an amateur had tinkered with it and overpainted several parts. When the touched up parts were removed he recognized the work which is done on wood as da Vinci's original "Madonna and Child." Checking back it was found the restored work had been exhibited in London in 1882. The painting also hung unrecognized in a home in Broseley, England, at the turn of the century.

The laws of God and nature have been disregarded and glossed over for a long time. You can do something no matter how small to bring them back into the mainstream of life—to restore to all people the priceless treasure of truth which is their sacred heritage.

"In this is my Father glorified; that you bring forth very much fruit, and become my disciples." (John 15:8)

◦§ Let me be an instrument, O Lord, helping the world rediscover Thy truth.

LINCOLN'S RESPECT FOR GOD

Abraham Lincoln was a great President because he was first and foremost a man of deep respect for Almighty God. His greatness stemmed from the fact that he held fast to those spiritual truths which served as the basis for all his concepts and deeds.

When Lincoln was only 19, he made this statement: "I never behold the stars that I do not feel that I am looking in the face of God. I can see how it might be possible for a man to look down upon the earth and be an atheist, but I cannot conceive how he could look up into the heavens and say there is no God."

Whenever young people are given a thorough grounding in religious truths, they usually lead lives that are free from crime, even if they are not altogether perfect.

If through neglect in their home-training or education they do not gain a familiarity and reverence for eternal values, they seldom get them later in life. That is why so many without spiritual roots, lead negative, superficial lives if they do not succumb to the corrupt influence that deprives them of the true joy of life that God intended to be their lot.

Do all in your power to bring to the youth of America the divine truths that must be the foundation of any lasting peace.

"Unless the Lord build the house, they labor in vain that build it." (Psalms 126:1)

Help me, O Lord, to make Thy truth known to young and old.

SHE TOOK A STAND

In Newark, New Jersey, a 14-year-old boy entered a hardware store with an automatic pistol and finding it empty except for the proprietor, a 64-year-old woman, he demanded that she turn over the contents of her cash register.

The woman looked at him for a long moment and suddenly, with no thought of fear, shouted at him, "Now get out and stay out!" And with those words she flew around the counter at him and hit him with her closed fist right in the mid-section.

The boy was so surprised and terrified at the woman's fury that he pocketed his pistol and ran out as fast as he could.

Many times we hesitate to perform a worthy action because of a doubt about our abilities. Still, as a rule, the man who musters up the courage to decide gets all the ability necessary.

If we take a stand, we will surprise ourselves by our own initiative and daring. Furthermore, God helps most those who try to give most.

"For he that hath, to him shall be given: and he that hath not, that also which he hath shall be taken away from him." (Mark 4:25)

◄§ Give me the fortitude to take a stand on all matters that count, O Lord.

AN OUNCE OF PREVENTION

A nine-year-old youngster in Glendale, N. Y., gave his mother a delightful surprise on Valentine's Day. After he had sent greetings to some of his classmates, he worked especially long on one more valentine.

Finally, after finishing it, he took a ladder and pinned it in the center of the archway between the living and dining rooms. "I was surprised and proud," his mother wrote us, "that it was a valentine to God. It stated simply 'I love God!' Everyone who saw it was impressed and felt a little ashamed at never having thought of sending such a message of love to God."

If more could be done to channel the God-given enthusiasm and energies of young people into noble and inspiring outlets, we would not be faced with the alarming fact that the million children who were apprehended as juvenile delinquents last year will increase by another half million in the next few years, according to official estimates.

Much harm could be avoided by appealing to the idealism of the average young person and pointing out the full, fruitful and fascinating life that can be his if he starts out at an early age to prepare for a useful and constructive career.

"He that doth the will of God, abideth forever."
(1 John 2:17)

⋙ Allow me, O Lord, to do my bit in bringing out the good in every young person.

EASY DOES IT

In Los Angeles, Calif., a little 3-year-old girl went to the drugstore with her mother. While the mother was busy making purchases, the child became intrigued by the chewing gum machine. She stuck her finger into the slot to investigate.

But when she tried to draw the finger out, she found that it was stuck fast in the machine.

Everyone in the drugstore tried to help her release the finger—her mother, the pharmacists, bystanders, but to no avail. Finally the police ambulance crew was called, but they too were unable to get the finger out.

There was only one thing to do. The ambulance men sawed off the part of the gum machine which held the finger, and took the child with the attached piece of machine to the hospital. But it was not necessary to make the whole trip. On the way the bumpy ride jiggled the child's finger free.

It is not frenzied efforts that get the job done, but rather quiet thoughtful action.

Both God and Nature, His handmaid, cooperate with the one who maintains his calm and his faith.

All our efforts for peace in the world could be greatly improved if we relied more on God and prayer. Pray that the councils of nations will learn the way of God to obtain peace.

"Blessed is the man that trusteth in the Lord, and the Lord shall be his confidence." (Jeremias 17:7)

Give us trust and confidence in Thee, O Lord.

NATURE'S WAY

An amusing note entered the last formal report of the American Bankers Association concerning burglar alarm systems used by banks as protection against robberies.

It seems that of all the fine systems man has designed to scare away criminals, the most effective is still a woman's scream. The records show that the majority of instances when a would-be-burglar has fled in fright from the scene of his crime, has been due to the piercing shrieks of a frightened, and sometimes indignant woman.

The Association makes a subtle reminder to those who might possibly be considering robbing a bank, that there are nearly twice as many women as there are men bank employees.

We take a legitimate pride in the advances and achievements of our modern science. But every now and then we are humbled when we discover that nature's ways are far superior to our finest inventions.

The Divine Intelligence invented nature; the human mind invented modern science. We should never hope nor dream of the second equaling the first.

Whenever you can, instill a sense of the greatness and mystery of God and His nature. Make your voice heard in the fields or careers that count.

"The heavens show forth the glory of God, and the firmament declareth the work of His hand."

(Psalms 18:2)

ᴥ Teach me always to be humble before Thy works, O Lord.

BEGIN IN SCHOOL

A young lady studying in California noticed that a trend away from God and country was being fostered on her college campus by a small group in the Student Council. Like most of us, her first inclination was to "mind her own business" and stay aloof.

As she thought about it, however, her conscience would not rest. She came to realize that she would be "minding her own business" in a truer sense if she acted to correct the abuse. She told classmates that they all had an obligation to keep student activities on a high level, free of domination by a minority that was obviously working to destroy the truths on which our country was founded. Instead of remaining quiet, our student friend induced a leading student with high ideals to run for the Student Council. Her friend was elected easily.

The tendency to "sit back" begins early in life, and at school. The chances are, however, that those who do so for the first part of their life will do so the rest of their life.

Our student days are valuable opportunities to learn the "missionary approach" as well as academic matters.

Encourage young people to take a part in school activities, and guide them in the right direction. Point out how students, your friends or your children can make their influence felt among their classmates.

"Remember thy Creator in the days of thy youth."
(Ecclesiastes 12:1)

◅§ Inspire our youth, O Lord, with the zeal of Thy word.

MISGUIDED DARING

In Baton Rouge, La., two teen-age University students, 18 and 19, decided to go off on a spree one night.

In a reckless mood, they stole a state ambulance for transportation. With sirens screaming they made their way from one night club to another, stopping at each to fortify their enthusiasm with liquor.

At first they were enjoying themselves hugely. But as the evening wore on this amusement began to pall. They looked about for new and more adventurous entertainment. They touched the zenith in bright ideas when they drove the "borrowed" ambulance out to the airport, and "borrowed" a plane for a midnight flight.

They took off with the unsuspecting operations specialist giving instructions. But the flight came to a sudden end, when the untrained pilot lost control of the plane and it crashed into a house, killing him, injuring his partner seriously and two of the occupants of the house.

The spectacle of misguided energy and daring is always a painful one. One cannot but think of the good that could be accomplished if it were harnessed and channeled in the direction that God intended it should be.

These two University students had it in them to do great things; they could have been leaders in the world when the world needs leaders more than ever. What they could do will probably ever go undone.

"I must work the works of him that sent me, whilst it is day: the night cometh, when no man can work."

(John 9:4)

⤳ Inspire us, O Lord, to devote all our energies to Thy Cause.

THE HARSH REALITIES

A large amusement gallery in Stockholm, Sweden, recently received and duly set up for operation a new amusement "gimmick" manufactured in New York.

The new game is a sort of "try your skill" slot machine which is played by one's aiming a bomb on a moving target—in this instance a city shown on a film strip. Of course, one scores by making the highest amount of direct hits. It is called "The Atomic Bomber."

But somehow or other, the youngsters did not find this idea so amusing. In fact 100 of them made a demonstration protesting the management's installation of this game as quite objectionable. The management was forced to get rid of the machine.

No one can complain about the protests of these young people. There are plenty of other subjects for amusement purposes than those dealing with death and destruction.

On the other hand, is it not equally true that often we turn away from subjects like war and atomic bombs, no matter where they appear, in an attempt not to face the reality of these horrors.

If more would use their God-given power to restrain and control them, they could help shape the future for peace. Young people with high ideals could accomplish much by taking up careers in the atomic energy field and helping to direct it so that it will serve man instead of destroying him.

"Peace, peace, and there is no peace." (Jeremias 6:14)

IN HIS NAME

A teacher in a secondary school tells us about a young man who was, in her estimation, the most difficult case she had ever handled.

He was a boy with definite criminal tendencies. He had been caught stealing cars, molesting small girls, and committing many acts of violence. All the usual techniques had been applied, but to no avail. All the teachers were sure that he would eventually land in prison—all but this one teacher.

She refused to believe that nothing could be done to put this boy on the right path. Having tried everything else, she decided to use what she knew to be her greatest asset—her faith in God and her reliance on Christian charity.

Her persuasive kindness got a hearing with the boy, and little by little she helped him to see himself as a child of the Living God,—the Loving Father Who rewards our good actions and punishes our evil ones. In a comparatively short time the boy changed his whole outlook and became a model pupil.

The greatest help we can give anyone is a faith in God. It is the one cure of all ills if correctly applied.

Too often we, who believe in God, are party to the great silence about Him in public life and in our institutions. Our forefathers were not so silent about Him. We should strive to imitate them in proclaiming the love of God.

"Going therefore, teach ye all nations."

(Matthew 28:19)

THE PRICE OF PEACE

President Eisenhower recently illustrated the cost of war to society. He asserted that every weapon made was a "theft" from those "who are hungry and are not fed, those who are cold and are not clothed." He said, "The cost of one modern heavy bomber is equivalent to the cost of:

A modern brick school in more than thirty cities.

Two electric power plants, each serving a town of 60,000 population.

Two fine, fully equipped hospitals.

Fifty miles of concrete highway.

We pay for a single fighter plane with a half million bushels of wheat.

We pay for a single destroyer with new homes that could have housed more than eight thousand people."

When we realize the fabulous cost of modern war, we better appreciate the value of peace. The thought of the billions of dollars that could be devoted to feeding and clothing people all over the world should urge us to increase our efforts for bringing peace to all.

First, we should pray for peace. Then we should urge those devoted to the cause of peace to get into government, atomic research, education, writing, labor relations and every other vital field that affects the destiny of most men.

"Peace I leave with you, my peace I give unto you."

(John 14:27)

❧ Give us peace in our time, O Lord.

GEORGE WASHINGTON CHANGED HIS MIND

In the life of George Washington, we see outstanding examples of his sense of responsibility to God and country that carried him through many black moments of discouragement when all seemed lost.

In his volume, *The Soul of Washington*, Joseph Buffington tells us that one day at Valley Forge, when the more than half-naked men had eaten no meat for many days, and when Congress had failed once more to provide or even to suggest any way for getting food and clothes the ebb was reached and Washington wrote out his resignation as commander-in-chief of the Army.

Among the generals sitting in council, Henry Knox spoke out, reminding him of the pen-knife his mother had given him as a child. Upon the knife was the inscription, "Always obey your superiors." When General Knox spoke out, referring to the knife, Washington asked what that had to do with his resignation?

"You were always to obey your superiors," replied Knox. "You were commanded to lead the Army. No one has commanded you to cease leading it."

Washington paused, and then answered, "There is something in that. I will think it over."

Half an hour later he tore his resignation to pieces.

Encourage a sense of responsibility to God and one's fellowman in young and old alike. It is a powerful asset in bringing out the best in all.

"Let every soul be subject to higher powers: for there is no power but from God." (Romans 13:1)

⚜ Keep me ever reminded, O Lord, of my responsibilities. Pp. 34-35, Buffington.

THE EVIL ARE SELDOM CARELESS

In Ossining, N. Y., a hotel proprietor was collecting the price of a room, when he was struck by the strange appearance of one of the dollar bills which was handed to him.

The serial numbers were upside down on either side of George Washington's portrait. The blue seal was on the left side of the portrait instead of the right. And the signatures of the Secretary of the Treasury and the Treasurer of the United States were near the top instead of the bottom.

The proprietor examined it carefully, and then accepted it. He took it because he knew that no counterfeiter would try to get away with so clumsy a job. It was one of the rare freak dollars which occasionally get misprinted in Washington. The proprietor has it framed on the wall of the hotel restaurant.

Evil-doers take the time and trouble to be clever. Those who follow Christ should be even more intelligent, alert and painstaking.

What a refreshing change will take place over the world once this picture is reversed. When more of the good, ordinary people become convinced that their God-given talents should be used for the best causes in life— for peace, for morality and spiritual living—the change will come.

"For the children of this world are wiser in their generation than the children of light." (Luke 16:8)

⎉ Help me to dedicate my talents to Thy cause, O Lord.

LIGHTS IN DARKNESS

Mayor Morrison of New Orleans recently received two very unusual letters from a German who had spent some time in the Crescent City.

In one letter, the man explained to the Mayor that he had failed to pay his fare on a streetcar one day, since all he had was a $10 bill. Enclosed was a dime to pay the belated fare.

And the other envelope enclosed a letter to the streetcar company praising the conductor for his courtesy and understanding, and the company for having such polite and considerate workers.

Stories like these are very cheering in a time when many believe that no one can be trusted, and that all are "out for themselves."

It is simply a question of refusing to go with the crowd, to drift with the current. Most people have decent instincts and fine ideals. God has given them these qualities and expects them to apply them to modern life. But often they are either ashamed to be singular, or to appear better than others.

Just a little more courage is needed. Hold your ground and show the way to others rather than be led into evil by them. Do this in the sphere of vital influence, in government, education, radio, TV, writing and the like.

"So let your light shine before men, that they may see your good works . . ." (Matthew 5:16)

 § Give me the courage to lead the way to my brethren, O Lord.

THE ROLE OF WOMAN

Julia Ward Howe was visiting in Washington, D. C., in December, 1861. Signs of war were everywhere. The railroads were guarded by soldiers, and the streets were crowded with men in uniform singing war songs, among them the stirring tune, "John Brown's Body."

After hearing the song, Mrs. Howe found herself mentally composing new words for the tune—words that would lift the minds and hearts of the soldiers to God, words that would remind them that "God's truth is ever marching on."

Her song turned out to be the great "Battle Hymn of the Republic."

The words were published a short time later in the *Atlantic Monthly*, and soon all the North was singing the song. It is said that the first time President Lincoln heard it he was so moved that he cried out, with a tear in his eyes, "Sing it again!"

Because Julia Ward Howe showed the imagination and initiative to bring a spiritual note into the troubled times in which she lived, she provided a splendid example of what one person can do.

If you are truly interested in leaving the world a bit the better for your being in it, you too can do something that may have far-reaching effects. What you attempt may be known only to God, but He will bless your slightest effort.

"According to your faith, be it done unto you."
(Matthew 9:29)

&§ Grant, O my Savior, that I may constantly seek an opportunity to bring Thy love and truth to all men.

SENT FROM GOD

You probably read how Lieutenant Genevieve de Galard Terraube was captured by the Reds at Dien Bien Phu and later released by the Vietminh. This young woman's heroism in time of great stress has brought her two of her country's highest awards, the Legion of Honor and the Croix de Guerre. Moreover, she has been recommended to receive the top Red Cross honor, the Florence Nightingale Medal.

During the terrible time before the fall of the fortress, Lieutenant de Galard Terraube wrote a cheering letter to her mother in which she said, "God is here to protect me."

This is not the first time the power and mercy of God were manifested in a woman. More and more today the real power of woman is becoming clear.

Christianity emancipated woman and we are beginning to reap the benefits. In a sense, the masculine world of the past has led to wars and disorder. The feminine influence is needed.

More women of high ideals are required in our government, schools, in communications, radio, TV, and writing, as well as in the home.

"Who shall find a valiant woman? Far and from the uttermost coast is the price of her." (Proverbs 31:10)

  Raise up great women among us, O Lord.

WISDOM VERSUS LEARNING

On page 11 of Ernest R. Hull's book, *Formation of Character*, there is presented one of the best comments on the role of education we have seen. He points out that most citizens expect youth will be intellectually well-informed, clever, conscientious, morally upright, sanely religious, strong and healthy.

But then he warns, "Our boy may become a very Hercules of physical health and strength, and yet a perfect dolt. He may be clever as the devil—and yet as wicked. He may be as good as gold and pious as a saint, and yet a flabby helpless creature. He may be the pink of aesthetic refinement and yet a sensual libertine. He may be a perfect genius and yet as fantastic as a goblin. The best qualities in one line may be discounted or even cancelled by some glaring disability in another—the head of gold and the trunk of brass and the legs of iron and the feet of clay—a bundle of disparities rather than a man."

Education is highly regarded in our land. This is something to be proud of. Still we should guard against seeking education for its own sake, failing to pay attention to the quality of our education. Thank God, our educational system is a good one. We must try nevertheless to improve it, and keep it on a high level.

This can best be done by encouraging the cream of our youth to get into this exalted profession.

"From thy youth up receive instructions and even to thy grey hairs thou shalt find wisdom."

(Ecclesiasticus 6:18)

MAKE THE GOOD BETTER

A 65-year-old nurse in San Jose, Calif., recently lost a purse containing $19,000. She reported to the police that she had dropped the purse somewhere, but they were impressed by the fact she seemed so calm about the loss. When they questioned her about this, she replied, "I never worry. I believe in the goodness of people."

Her faith in the goodness of human beings was quite justified, for a gas station operator found and returned the purse with all contents intact.

A belief in the goodness of man is a wholesome point of view and the basis for a healthy optimism. But we should not push it too far. Man has his shadowy side; we are a fallen race.

Besides, if we believe in the absolute goodness of mankind, there is little incentive for us to make things better. It is only when we see the weak and defective side of human nature honestly, especially in ourselves, that we are inclined to change and improve things.

Believe that mankind is basically good, but work all the harder to make it better by making your influence felt in the careers that count.

"And God saw all the things that he had made, and they were very good." (Genesis 1:31)

GOD AND MAN

Ernst Bergmann wrote a book entitled *The German National Church*, in which his views on religion give a comprehensive insight into Nazi thinking. Here is an excerpt from page 72:

"This kind of Christianity was sheer brain disease of the human race, a mental affliction, which lasted thousands of years. Hopelessly we struggle with the problems. All that Man can do now that he is freed of 'dementia Christianity' is—to become a beast again. As an animal, Man has today to begin again."

Whenever God goes out, man goes out too. It is an obvious lesson from history that every regime that has departed from belief in God or from His ways has brought about a degradation of mankind.

Man's inherent dignity is a tenet of Christianity, and when he loses one he loses the other.

None are needed to sow this idea anew in all the vital spheres of influence. Make your voice heard wherever you can to remind men that they are children of God and are of infinite value.

"For you are bought with a great price."

(1 Corinthians 6:20)

🖎 Keep us in mind of our great worth, O Lord.

WHY ARE YOU SOLICITOUS?

An 84-year-old man in Philadelphia, Pa., was recently taken to a hospital after collapsing in the street.

It was discovered that he was suffering from acute starvation, although in his vest was sewn the sum of $1153.

Social workers were called in, and it was found that this man was alone in the world, without relatives or friends. For fifty years he had been a railroad worker, but now he was too old to work. He had a great fear of living on charity, and so he was trying desperately to live as meagrely as possible on his remaining savings so that they would last him the rest of his days.

The social workers took over the case and are helping him use his money wisely so that he may live without starving.

A fear of insecurity is a basic human impulse. It is a legitimate and useful fear as long as it does not distort our values or turn things upside down.

If we keep first things first, we need not fear. Christ has assured us that if we trust God for the morrow, we shall have all we need.

"If then ye be not able to do so much as the least thing, why are you solicitous for the rest?" (Luke 12:26)

◈ Teach us to trust Thee, O God, in all things.

LIVE BY THE DAY

About a month or so ago, Italy was the victim of a rumor which somehow got started and spread like wildfire through the nation. The rumor was to the effect that on a certain Monday in May the world was scheduled to come to an end.

Large numbers of people were reported to have attended church and prayed at length.

One near tragedy occurred when a panic-stricken 69-year-old tramp told his friends "If the world is going to end, I might as well get it over quickly," and jumped over a railroad bridge, plunging to his death.

The strange thing is that no one seems to know how the false rumor started. Many Italians were convinced that it was false only when Tuesday morning dawned bright and fair.

Prophets of doom show up in every age and in every field. We even find them in religion. But we were warned to "Beware of false prophets." Those who predict the end of the world do as much harm as those who promise a heavenly utopia on earth in the future.

"You know not the day nor the hour."

(Matthew 25:13)

◄§ Help me, O Lord, to keep my mind on the work at hand.

THE FORTITUDE OF WOMAN

A 28-year-old woman in Paris, France, recently made an attempt to climb up the outside girders of the 984-foot Eiffel Tower.

She started up bravely. But this was no easy undertaking. The vertical height and the sharp iron girders require more than ordinary endurance to conquer. When she had climbed 345 feet she was forced to give up, for she had reached the point of exhaustion and her hands were bleeding from many cuts.

When asked why she had attempted such a fantastic feat, she explained that her grandfather had once tried to scale the Eiffel Tower and failed, and that she had made the attempt because she wanted to "save the family honor."

There is a great role for women to play in our modern world. They can make a contribution men cannot make. True, many women have gone into the mainstream and sought careers. But not enough have tried to inject the feminine note in public affairs. Too often, as the lady in the Eiffel Tower did, they have fallen short of their true vocation—which is to imbue our society with moral feeling and a spiritual sense. More women who will do this are needed in the careers that count if we are to achieve peace.

"Who shall find a valiant woman? far and from the uttermost coasts is the price of her." (Proverbs 31:10)

᪥ Raise up, O Lord, women who will do Thy will among us.

79

IN HIS IMAGE

A mother in Trenton, N.J., left her month-old baby in its carriage in her yard while she went to answer the phone.

There was no reason to be afraid for the child's safety, the mother felt, as she would only be gone a few minutes. But when she returned she was horrified to find two small boys each about five years old, using her infant for a football. They were tossing the child into the air and kicking it about.

The mother screamed and rescued her child which was by now in a critical condition. It was taken to the hospital with multiple skull fractures and abrasions of the body.

The boys when questioned by the police seemed very bewildered by the whole affair. They said that they had thought that the child was a doll.

It is almost inconceivable that two children might mistake a child for a doll. And yet, on another level, is not the great error of our times a false conception of man? Man is regarded as an animal by those who deny God and in totalitarian countries He has been treated like an automaton or a pawn.

There is great need for those who believe that man is made to the image of God to make their voices heard in government, education, communications, and labor-management relations. Only when human dignity, based on divine worth, is recognized everywhere will there be peace.

"And to the image of His own likeness He made him."
(Wisdom 2:23)

≈§ O God, allow me to see Thy image in all men.

VIRTUE IS ITS OWN REWARD

Justice Lee L. Ottaway gave significant advice to some young offenders who had come before him in the Supreme Court. The gist of his grave, but kindly, talk was that the worst thing about being a criminal is that criminals are always unhappy.

He said, "As a lawyer I defended those charged with crimes, and as an assistant district attorney, I prosecuted criminals. Since I have been on the bench I have had contact with many more, and I can say that they are never happy people.

"A man who starts out in the criminal field seals himself to live among unhappy people for the rest of his life."

Many learn too late that virtue and real happiness are inseparable companions. Vice can bring temporary pleasure or the illusion of happiness but not lasting satisfaction.

Thus it is that the criminal will necessarily and always be unhappy, while he who works for others and gives of himself for the common good of all will gain a happiness and place that is forever closed to the selfish man.

Make an experiment. Begin to work or increase your efforts in Christ's name for others for a certain period of time, say 3 months, and see if your happiness and peace of soul are not increased.

"He that shall lose his life for my sake, shall find it."
(Matthew 16:25)

&§ Teach me to seek happiness only in Thee, O Lord.

MIRACLE UPON MIRACLE

It always makes our hearts glad to hear about the miracles of modern surgery.

Recently, a most unusual operation was performed on a new-born baby girl, who 20 years ago would certainly have died. The child was born with a blind esophagus—a condition in which a section of the tube which joins the throat to stomach is missing and which, uncorrected, causes the victim to strangle because of being unable to swallow.

Immediately on discovering the condition, the doctor operated, separating the esophagus from the windpipe and stitching the two ends together. Twice during the operation the child's heart stopped beating, but the doctor massaged the tiny heart—fighting desperately for her life—and now the child is alive and well.

Saving a life is like cooperating with the Almighty, Who keeps us all in existence.

Our great studies in science, however, should never become a source of prideful boasting. It should rather be an incentive to further humility.

Modern science, especially modern medicine, may well be a "miracle"; life itself is a greater miracle.

"O Lord our Lord, how admirable is Thy name in the whole earth!" (Psalms 8:2)

৵৻ Imbue in us an awe in face of Thy gifts, O Lord.

WHEREON TO STAND

A little girl, 6 years old, was missing one day from her home in Los Angeles. The frantic parents notified the police. An alarm was sent out, and for 16 hours they searched for the youngster.

Finally, a policeman came across a little girl who answered the description of the lost child. He spoke gently so as not to frighten her: "Little girl, aren't you lost?"

The child drew herself up to her full height. She spoke with dignity, "I'm not lost. It's my house that's lost."

Anyone, young or old, who has been trained in the home, church and school in true values is never really lost. No matter what changes or mishaps may take place, such a person is guided by an inner strength that is rooted in God's unchangeable and eternal truth.

If you would play the role of a Christopher, or Christ-bearer, you would do well to develop and deepen your inner life by study, meditation and prayer.

Any external activity that you engage in will be effective almost in direct proportion to the interior strength of mind, heart and soul that you develop within you.

There is great need today for people like you to apply the changeless truths of God to our changing times. Nurture your inner power and you are bound to do much good.

"Neglect not the grace that is in thee." (1 Timothy 4:14)

☞ Let me be rooted in Thy love and truth, O Lord, so that I shall never be lost.

A WOMAN'S STRENGTH

In Capetown, South Africa, not long ago, a crazed lioness left the jungle and made her way into the city. She prowled about the streets roaring her defiance at civilization while citizens fled before her.

The lioness was not long in finding a prey. She threw herself through an open door where a small family lived and attacked the father and his two small children who were playing together. But she had not reckoned on the mother.

The mother, attracted by the screams of her family, came running into the room, and without any hesitation threw herself on the back of the beast and tugged at its ears until her husband was able to get his gun and shoot the animal.

Few women are aware of the great power for good that God has entrusted to each of them individually. Time and again emergencies prove their heroism. And it is invariably bravery with a purpose—a willingness to sacrifice even life itself in order to protect others.

If women would apply that power on a day-to-day basis to regenerating modern life, a refreshing change for the better would quickly take place.

It would be well for all of us to ponder over this warning of the Apostle Peter:

"Be sober and watch, because your adversary the devil, as a roaring lion, goeth about seeking whom he may devour; whom resist ye, strong in faith." (1 Peter 5:8)

❧ Enable me, O Lord, to tackle each day's problems as an effective way to anticipate emergencies.

OUR FIRST CONCERN

In Edgewater, N.J., a great fire started at a warehouse, razing it to the ground and causing injury to 100 firemen and property damage amounting to $1,000,000.

Investigation proved that the fire had started when six boys and a girl, all aged 14 to 17 years, slipped into the rear of the building to do some cigarette smoking. They were careless with the matches and soon a small blaze had started. They tried to put out the fire themselves but it spread too quickly for them to control. Panic-stricken, they fled from the scene.

Later, all the teen-agers were arrested and then paroled in the custody of their parents. But in remarking about the case, the Police Chief said, "What disturbs me is that they don't seem in the least contrite about it."

If you show a little interest in young people, you may do much to stem the tide toward juvenile delinquency. It will require time and patience to restore a sense of conscientious responsibility to teen-agers who have been neglected by their parents or who have been taught that there is "no difference between right and wrong."

In the worst of the teen-age offenders there is a latent goodness that can be stirred up to such an extent that it will overcome the destructive tendencies that they display. By trying to reclaim even one young offender you will be playing a truly Christlike role.

"Suffer the little children to come unto me and forbid them not, for of such is the kingdom of God."

(Mark 10:14)

Have mercy, O Lord, on all teen-agers who make mistakes.

THE CLAIMS OF TRUTH

A high school teacher was taking graduate work in a large Eastern University. One day the professor declared: "There is no power in democracy—bar none—greater than the majority."

Our teacher-student, a social studies major, challenged this statement with the question: "Does not even the majority have to comply with a law higher than itself?"

"No," the professor said flatly.

"Then how," the student pursued, "do you account for such evils as the murder of six million Jews by the Nazis? If the majority decrees it is all right to be anti-Semitic to that extent, does that make it all right?"

"Of course not," the professor replied. "But that would not happen here. It's against the democratic process." "Precisely," said the student. "Then it proves the point that majority rule is not the essence of the democratic process. Unless the majority is governed by a Higher Power, mob rule will take over. It is obvious then that God is the basis for the democratic process."

Many well-meaning persons in our day are confused and led astray by half-truths or distortions of the truth. You can do a real service by speaking up on such occasions. To do this requires a bit of daring and courage, but you will never regret taking a stand for the law and order of God.

"Everyone therefore that shall confess me before men, I will also confess him before my Father who is in heaven." (Matthew 10:32)

⊷ Strengthen me, O Jesus, to show courage where Thy truth is concerned.

THE HEART OF THE NATION

In 1953, 31,980 marriage licenses were issued in Los Angeles County, while 15,668 divorces became final. This means that for every two marriages there was one divorce in that area. This is a ratio more appalling than that of the notorious divorce mills of Reno and Las Vegas where the ratio is only one divorce to every five marriages.

In revealing the figures, Supervisor Kenneth Hahn said, "America became great largely because of the unity of the home. We must stem the rising tide of divorce."

In nearly all parts of the United States the trend is toward more divorces rather than fewer. Slowly but surely the consequences of this widespread rebellion against the marriage vows is undermining the country. If you do a little investigation on your own, you will probably be amazed to discover the disturbances that follow in the wake of 100 divorce cases: breakup of the home, children deprived of proper environment and training with many drifting into crime and corruption.

There is something you can do to prevent at least one divorce. First of all, pray for those who are tempted to break up their marriage. Then, in a friendly, sympathetic way, do what you can to seek a solution, despite the fact that most others are encouraging divorce. You will be happily surprised to see how God will bless your efforts if you strive sincerely and tactfully to be a peacemaker.

"What therefore God has joined together, let no man put asunder." (Matthew 19:6)

&֍ Bless, O Lord, the families of our land and keep them together.

A BIG DIFFERENCE

A housewife in Ridgewood, N. J., had just finished her weekly marketing. The grocery boy carried her packages out to her car, and following her instructions, put them on the back seat.

Just before the woman got behind the wheel, she thought about the carton of eggs that she had bought. A sudden lurch of the car could easily break the eggs on the back seat. So she put the carton on the seat beside her where she could keep her eye on them as she drove.

Starting off, all went well, until she made a left turn. The eggs started to slide off the seat. As she grabbed frantically for the package, the car swerved off the road and hit a tree. The housewife suffered a badly cut knee, and $500 damage to her car.

It is difficult for most in the hurried pace of modern life to make a distinction between what is of first and secondary importance. Some become so preoccupied with the incidentals of living that they gradually lose sight of what life is all about—why they are here, where they came from, and where they are going.

You can perform an important service as a Christopher by keeping first things first and by encouraging others to do the same.

"Seek ye therefore first the kingdom of God and his justice, and all these things shall be added unto you."

(Matthew 6:33)

&§ Help me, O Lord, to see the difference between essentials and incidentals.

THE HIDDEN ENEMY

Not long ago, scientists in Florence, Italy, had to wage an intense chemical warfare to save some of Italy's most treasured art works from termites.

It was discovered that millions of African white termites were undermining the foundations of the 15th century Palazzo Pitti, in which are housed some of the world's finest paintings.

An amusing note to the whole proceedings, was the fact that when the war against the termites was well underway, the scientists discovered that the pests had made their way to the Palazzo Pitti from their own headquarters in the adjoining Institute of Entomology.

Much of the catastrophe of our day is due to the fact that we discover too late the harm done by human termites who labor intensively, quietly and secretly to undermine government, education and the other vital spheres of influence.

As happened in Florence where the termites started their disastrous work under the very noses of scientists, so does evil spring up in the very midst of the followers of Christ who have been negligent in playing the apostolic role assigned to them by God. The more you strive to be a Christopher, or Christbearer, the more you will note and correct defects around you.

"*And what I say to you, I say to all: 'Watch.'*"

(Mark 13:37)

Inspire me to be so alert in doing good, O Lord, that I will be quick to detect what is false and evil.

THE DAY OF RECKONING

A short while ago, the FBI arrested the vice-president of a suburban bank in Philadelphia. The 57-year-old man was charged with having stolen funds from the bank and having made false entries in the records to cover the amount of $146,000.

The amazing thing about this robbery is that the thefts had been made in small sums over a period of 35 years! The trusted bank official had begun defrauding his company from the age of 22, and having gotten away with it for so long, he was quite certain that he would never be caught.

The discovery of his thefts was made simply enough during a routine inspection by federal bank examiners. When faced with the evidence, he confessed and told the examiners that he had taken the money *"for general daily living expenses."*

Many a person foolishly tries to convince himself that because he is "getting away" with a violation of God's law, he is therefore deceiving everyone. He may go to great pains to fool others—but he never completely fools himself. And, much as he would like to dodge it, he knows deep in his heart that he cannot fool his Maker. The day of reckoning must eventually come, when he will hear the Supreme Judge say to him:

"Render an account of the stewardship: for now Thou canst be steward no longer." (Luke 16:2)

✍ Help me, O Lord, to live honestly all the days of my life.

USE YOUR TALENTS FOR GOOD

Sacks of potatoes were being thrown on an outbound truck in the state prison in Joliet, Ill., when a guard noticed that one of them seemed unusually heavy.

He called another guard and they investigated. Inside they found a 30-year-old prisoner who wasn't due out of prison until 1975.

The prisoner weighed only 135 pounds, so he thought he could get away with it. He told the warden that he really wasn't planning to run away, he only wanted to see the 500-mile speedway at Indianapolis. The warden replied kindly that he was sorry but he would have to be a little late and would probably get to see it in 1976.

It is always a source of surprise to observe the extraordinary imagination and resourcefulness that an individual can show when he is trying to get out of trouble.

If people in general would show the same enterprise and daring in keeping freedom as they do in trying to regain it after their liberty has been taken away from them, the world would be much nearer peace than it is today.

It is in the nature of weak men to take the lazy, negligent way until it is too late. But it is also within the power of man to rise above his weakness, fortified by God's grace, and prevent the trouble that often plagues him.

"Children of this world are wiser in their generation than the children of light." (Luke 16:8)

Let me anticipate trouble, O Lord, rather than struggle to get myself out of it.

THE MORAL UNIVERSE

The South Side neighborhood in Chicago, Ill., recently experienced quite a little upset because a 21-year-old man undertook to teach his 16-year-old sister how to drive.

The girl had no permit to learn to drive. But her brother permitted her to take the wheel while he sat beside her and told her what to do.

She evidently didn't follow his instructions well, because she found herself in danger of running down a dog. She swerved to avoid it and rammed into a parked station wagon. The station wagon rolled into a row of garbage cans. The garbage cans smashed into the back stairway of a house causing the whole stairway to collapse.

The owner of the house, hearing the commotion, went to investigate and fell 20 feet to the ground from the second floor, down the missing stairway.

The brother and the girl were both fined.

When men are taught God's laws and then fail to follow them, the harm that they do seldom stops with them. It often spreads with chain reaction effect, involving many innocent persons.

By the same token, those who learn His truth and then not only apply it to their own lives but take effective steps to make it known and respected by as many others as they can reach, accomplish good that can scarcely be measured.

"Can the blind lead the blind? Do they not both fall into the ditch?" (Luke 6:39)

‿ Let me be a doer of Thy law, O my God, not a hearer only.

ON THE BEAM

A man set out in a 23-foot ketch from the shores of Seattle, Wash., to make a leisurely sail along the coastline of the United States.

It proved to be a fine trip. He sailed all the way down to Panama and then turned through the Canal and headed towards Miami. But after some days he became very tired, having sailed some 7000 miles, and fell asleep at the tiller.

He was greatly surprised when a sudden jerk brought him to consciousness, and he found that he had run aground on Miami Beach.

A Coast Guard patrol boat came to his rescue and pulled the ketch off the sand.

Some people who have led exemplary lives over a long period of years make the same mistake that this enterprising sailor of the seas did. After successfully braving and overcoming innumerable obstacles, they fall asleep at the wrong time and then run aground in one way or another.

In these critical times when so much is at stake, it is important that you keep alert. Take care not to succumb to the countless temptations that would lead you off your course and possibly "beach" you. Your continued determination will be a test of your faith in God and your fellowman.

"He that shall persevere unto the end shall be saved."
(Matthew 10:22)

⋘ Help me to push on, O Lord, despite all odds against me.

TRUSTEES OF ETERNITY

A runner in a brokerage is what a delivery boy is to a grocery. But the packages which are the charge of the runner are practically always of far greater value than a delivery boy's.

A 65-year-old runner for a brokerage on Wall Street was making some deliveries in the course of the day when he opened his brief-case to check his packages and discovered that they weren't there.

He immediately called the police, who searched the area which had been covered by the runner. But they didn't find the missing bonds.

The total value of the bonds was $100,500.

The more you realize that your mission in life is similar to that of a messenger, the more conscientious you will be about protecting and delivering the trust that God has placed in your hands.

Try to reflect and pray frequently over the fact that the Father of all has put a tiny bit of the peace of the world in your hands. He did this because He wants you to play a part in seeing to it that His will is "done on earth as it is in heaven."

Take great care that you do not underestimate the confidence that Christ places in you. There will be little chance of you failing in any way if you realize the privilege that is yours.

"As the father hath sent me, I also send you."

(John 20:21)

🔊 Thank Thee, O my Jesus, for allowing me to be Thy messenger.

DEEDS OF GREATNESS

Two little boys, 5 and 8, were playing in a park in Milwaukee, Wisc., while a little girl was skipping rope near by.

The 8-year-old suddenly had the desire to show off. Talking very loudly so that the little girl could hear, he volunteered to show his friend how people hanged themselves the way they do in movies.

He borrowed the rope from the little girl and while she and the smaller boy stared open-mouthed, he climbed a nearby tree and tied one end of the rope to a limb. The other end he tied about his neck. The 5-year-old boy gave a gasp of admiration as his friend jumped—a gasp which quickly turned to one of fear, for the rope wasn't long enough to permit his friend to land on the ground as he had expected. He was slowly being strangled, with his feet a mere inch from the ground.

The younger boy didn't hesitate a moment. He grabbed his friend's pocket knife and climbed the tree, cutting the boy down, and then cut the rope from his neck thereby saving his life.

In every youngster there is a bit of greatness, put there by God Himself. But He expects us to work long and hard to nourish and develop it in them. Rarely do they realize they possess it themselves. If you do your best to bring out the good that is in every young person, you will be blessed for all eternity.

"As long as you did it to one of these my least brethren, you did it unto me." (Matthew 25:40)

Let me find my happiness, O Lord, in helping young people.

MAKE IT YOUR BUSINESS

In 1951 Kansas City was the victim of a severe flood, causing extensive and costly damage.

Although this was regrettable, the United States Circuit Court of Appeals was somewhat surprised when suit was brought against Government agencies, including the Weather Bureau, for more than $1,000,000 in damages from the flood.

The suit was filed by six Kansas City firms. They charged the Weather Bureau with giving out misinformation about the flood crest and failing to give sufficient warning that the area was in danger of being flooded.

But the court ruled that the governmental service provided by the weather forecasts in no way relieves the individual citizen of his responsibility to exercise his own judgment in such matters.

Most tend to blame others for not giving them proper warning when they are overtaken by trouble. Too frequently people say: "Why didn't someone do something about this?" Too seldom does anyone turn the light of inquiry upon himself and honestly ask: "Why haven't I done something about it?"

"Better to light a candle than to curse the darkness" is an expression we use frequently in the Christopher movement. Make it your business to "light a candle" rather than to use valuable time complaining about defects in government, education, labor relations, and in the literary and entertainment fields.

"Be not overcome by evil, but overcome evil by good."
(Romans 12:21)

❧ Inspire me, O Lord, to be a doer, not a complainer.

DON'T FORGET THE MAIN ISSUE

In Omaha, Nebr., two middle aged men who were life-long friends, went to a local tavern and sat reminiscing over old events, and rehashing old jokes. But before the night was over one of them had landed in the hospital and the other was in jail.

At the very end of their visit they became involved in a heated argument which developed into a fight. Later when questioned as to the cause of the trouble, they explained that it had started with an argument because each had insisted on paying for the other's supper.

One of the chief obstacles to the average person in trying to accomplish a bit of good is the tendency to forget the main issue. It is the Devil's way of sidetracking those who could play an important role in changing the world for the better.

If you would play the role of a Christopher or Christ-bearer, do your part to bring into the marketplace the great truths of God that are the indispensable foundation stones of peace. Make sure at all times that you are not deflected from your main objective. Keep first things first.

"Blind guides, who strain out a gnat, and swallow a camel." (Matthew 23:24)

꧁ Give me the wisdom, O Holy Spirit, to keep my mind on the goal.

TINY NUT CRIPPLES PLANE

A giant plane, carrying 43 passengers and crew members, was recently forced to crash-land on the outskirts of Chicago when its landing gear stuck.

Only the skill of the crew prevented a major tragedy. The plane's right main landing gear would not come down as it prepared to land at Chicago's crowded Midway airport. It was ordered to the Glenview Naval Air Station where it came to earth like a wounded bird.

Expert mechanics labored over the plane for three hours before they found what caused the mechanical failure. And what they found was almost unbelievable.

A nut about as small as a pencil eraser and costing approximately one cent, had dropped into a channel, or had been picked up on the runway, and had prevented a pin from being withdrawn. This in turn kept the landing gear from falling.

Little things, whether good or bad, often determine the well-being—or lack of it—for countless persons. One individual in a vital spot in government or education who is either disloyal or careless can jeopardize the safety of a large number of persons.

But by the same token, one person in a position of influence who takes great care to be loyal to God and country and to work for the best interests of all can often prevent disaster. Never underestimate your own personal power for good.

"Do not you say . . . they are white already to harvest."
(John 4:35)

YOU CAN BE A CHRISTBEARER

Back in the third century, the giant son of a heathen ruler longed to serve someone greater than himself. First he enlisted in the ranks of a great king and then of the devil. But he was disillusioned in both.

Hearing finally that Christ was the King of kings, he desired to serve Him above all others. He discovered he could do this by helping those in need. One way to do this, he thought, would be to carry travelers across a dangerous stream nearby.

One day, while this powerful man was bearing a small Child across the river, he found his burden so backbreaking that he could scarcely reach the other bank. On looking up, he was surprised to find that he was actually bearing the Christ Child, holding the world in His hands. At the same time, he understood that those who would carry Christ to all people must be willing to work hard and even to suffer.

Without realizing it, this stalwart man had become a Christbearer—a Christopher. Since that time he has been known far and wide as St. Christopher.

You, too, can be a Christopher. You—whoever you are —can do something to carry the love and truth of Christ into the very heart of modern twentieth century life.

God has put a bit of the missionary in you. If you take the time and trouble to play the role of an apostle or Christbearer, whether by prayer, word or deed, you may do much to bring lasting peace to the world.

"As the Father hath sent me, I also send you."
(John 20:21)

TEEN-AGER SPEAKS UP

Here is a letter from an 18-year-old girl, a freshman at a Colorado university, which recounts how she made her voice heard for good!

"My university is a pretty nice place," she tells us. "The social activities are swell, the kids super, and the professors about as fair as they can be. All in all, the university is tops. There's just one thing that's missing— God. Try as you might, you can't find Him anywhere."

An Episcopalian, this young lady reported that no one seemed to be doing anything about the absence of God on the campus. So she wrote a letter to her university newspaper pointing out that the university had been founded on a religious basis, yet was promoting "downright atheism."

"Our Lord should be more evident on the campus and in people's hearts. Where is religion at this university?" she demanded. After that things began to pop, she said. Her letter made a definite impression on the faculty and students.

The vast majority of teen-agers in America are basically good and well meaning. Unfortunately they are heard from too little, and some people therefore get the impression that most teen-agers are questionable if not bad.

If more young people with high ideals would speak up for the love and truth of Christ, as this freshman in Colorado did, they could do much to shape the peace of the world in which they will live.

"Thou shalt love the Lord thy God and Him only shalt thou serve." (Luke 4:8)

WORDS, WORDS, WORDS

A lawyer in Brussels, Belgium, recently set out to discover for himself whether or not a court really listens to a lawyer's courtroom speech. For a long time he had been suspicious that such speeches are a waste of time.

One day, right in the middle of presenting his case, he switched suddenly to a law book, and read through 20 paragraphs, before anyone even mentioned it.

It appears that the prosecutor had noticed the switch, but he was at a loss as to what to do about it, for the judge had quietly fallen asleep some time before, and to awaken him would cause embarrassment to everyone. But since the lengthy reading from the law book grew longer, and the judge slept on peacefully, the prosecutor was forced finally to awaken him.

Rather than talk about trouble, make it your business to do something about it. Those who are out to wreck the world are usually men of few words. They devote their time and energy to translating words into action.

On the other hand, the very ones who have in their custody the Truth that can make the world free, are too frequently long on words and short on action. The Devil doesn't mind a bit if we merely pass resolutions and never get down to the serious business of actually blending God's truth into modern life.

"Be ye doers of the word and not hearers only, deceiving yourselves." (James 1:22)

SO RICH AND YET SO POOR

Recently in Paris, the police arrested a man who looked as rundown and bedraggled as the hotel where they found him. Yet, when he was searched they found $1,000,000 worth of diamonds hidden in his clothes.

The police were satisfied that this was the man who had perpetrated the daring jewel robbery of a few weeks before. But they were puzzled why, with so much wealth on him, the robber appeared so poor.

To their great surprise, the burglar confessed that he hadn't eaten for some time, and that he was very hungry. Although he had a million dollars in jewels, he didn't have enough money to buy a meal. It seems that no one would buy the jewels from him.

In a desperate attempt to find satisfaction in material things, large sections of humanity are today suffering from spiritual malnutrition. While seeking every possible physical advantage and bodily pleasure, they have neglected their souls. As a result they have developed lopsided, incomplete personalities.

Rather than condemn such persons, make it your business to bring to them in every possible way the spiritual nourishment for which they are starving. With gentleness and kindness make up for what they lack.

"As long as you did it for one of these, my least brethren, you did it to me." (Matthew 25:40)

⋞ Permit me, O Lord, to serve those who are starving in soul or body.

FIFTY PERSONS GAVE THEIR SKIN

A 7-year-old girl in Long Island, New York, reached across the kitchen stove to get her lunch box. Her dress caught fire, and she was burned from head to foot.

The child was rushed to the hospital in critical condition. For some time it was doubtful whether or not she would live. But when she had survived the danger line, the widowed mother was faced with a grave consideration. Her little girl would be disfigured for life unless the doctors could obtain enough skin to graft on in place of that which had been destroyed.

For such a widely burned area a great deal of skin was required. The frantic mother sent out a public appeal, hoping against hope that someone would be sympathetic enough to help. She immediately received not just one, but offers from fifty persons to give her child their skin.

Emergencies bring out the deep-seated generosity in many a person. It is proof of the good that is in every man. True, he usually reacts best when emergencies occur—on a crisis-to-crisis basis. But with a little encouragement, some will dedicate themselves to the apparently difficult but deeply satisfying task of serving others in Christ's Name. Taking a temporary loss for love of God is a guarantee of great gain for eternity. As Christ said:

"He that humbleth himself shall be exalted."

(Matthew 23:12)

Teach me, O Lord, the wisdom of winning by losing.

THEY ADOPTED TWO BLIND CHILDREN

A young New York couple, Mr. and Mrs. Francis Lynch, not long ago adopted their second blind child from the Boston Nursery for Blind Babies.

Mr. and Mrs. Lynch have no children of their own, and when they adopted a child they decided it should be a blind baby, named Susan. Little Susan is now four years old, and perfectly healthy in all other respects.

The couple hadn't planned to adopt another child right away. But one day when they had to make a trip to the Nursery, they met two-year-old Elizabeth Ann, and immediately wanted her for their own. Nursery officials said that it was the first time in their experience that a couple had wanted to adopt two blind children.

You may not be able to imitate this unusual generosity in taking on the responsibility of giving a home to two such handicapped little ones, but there is something that you can do along these same lines.

You might, for instance, take some job (or continue in it if you have one) that is for the benefit of others but that, at the same time, is a thankless and difficult one. God blesses those in a particular way who deliberately choose the unpopular and often unpleasant tasks out of love of Him and others.

"The Son of man is not come to be ministered unto, but to minister and give his life for many." (Matthew 20:28)

TREASON AT THE LAST SUPPER

The Last Supper should have been one event at which every possible trace of evil and human frailty should have been absent.

It was one of the most sacred occasions of the Saviour's life. It marked the institution of the Holy Sacrifice. Taking bread, Christ said, "This is My Body which is given for you." And in like manner with wine, He solemnly added: "This is the chalice, the new testament in My Blood, which will be shed for you."

Scarcely had He uttered these sublime words than He had to continue sorrowfully: "But yet behold, the hand of him that betrayeth Me is with Me on the table."

What a terrible disappointment it must have been for the gentle Christ to know that even then Judas was traitorously plotting against His very life. One of the twelve He Himself had selected as one of His close associates was profaning this holy occasion by preparing the way for Christ's ignominious death on the following day.

As a further disturbing note, the other Apostles began to quibble about their own personal prestige. St. Luke notes it very specifically: "And there was also strife among them, which of them should seem to be the greater."

If Christ Himself was confronted with such a display of human weakness on this sublime occasion, you should not be surprised nor scandalized at the smallness or even treachery that may stalk your path if you strive perseveringly to be a Christopher or Christbearer.

"I am the living bread which came down from heaven."
(John 6:41)

105

WINNING BY LOSING

Good Friday teaches a powerful lesson to all who would learn the lesson of winning by losing.

Jesus Christ, hanging on the cross, uttered nothing but words of love and compassion even when he was being crucified. To the world it seemed that He had lost as no other person had. His disgrace was complete, but in His divine heart He knew He had won.

He loved unto death even those who were His worst enemies. One of the most sublime prayers He ever uttered was: "Father, forgive them, for they know not what they do."

If each of us would say these words from our heart and mean them in their fullest sense, we would be making the first big step toward the peace of the world.

"Father forgive them." Brutality, sordidness, corruption, bitterness, immorality, are being merchandised on a scale never before witnessed. One wonders if those who make it their business to foul up the hearts, minds and souls of countless others really realize the terrible damage they are doing.

Men despair of changing these very ones in any way except by force. Stern measures are often needed but if they come from a loving understanding that is more interested in correcting evil than merely finding fault, the worst of men can be transformed.

"Father, forgive them, for they know not what they do."
                                                    (Luke 23:34)

~§ Let me learn to put love where there is no love, O Lord, so that I may find love.

THE FATHER OF ONE AND ALL

The first and last expression of Jesus before He died on the cross began with the word "Father." As he looked down on His crucifiers from the gibbet, with exquisite tenderness toward them, He cried: "Father, forgive them, for they know not what they do." His last words were "Father into Thy hands I commend My spirit."

If Jesus Christ, our Redeemer, could open and close His three-hour agony on the cross with the simple but sublime appeal to His Father and our Father, surely the thought of Almighty God being the Father of all mankind should permeate every thought, word and action of our lives.

Every human being in the world has been made in His image, has come from His divine image. To each He has given the priceless privilege of free will and therefore has allowed them one and all to choose good or evil, to be loyal to Him or to deny Him.

But regardless of how much men may stray away from God, rebel against Christ, refuse His invitation to become adopted sons, and vent their hatred on their fellow human beings, they still remain God's children by creation.

If you see this precious worth of each individual, as Christ did, then you will strive without let-up to redeem and rehabilitate even the worst.

"Love your enemies, do good to them that hate you."
(Matthew 5:44)

&⸱ O Heavenly Father, let me see Thy image in every creature.

THE WOMEN AT THE TOMB

Mary Magdalen and the other holy women were the first to return to the tomb after the burial of the Crucified Christ.

The Apostles and disciples of Jesus were not as alert and bold as these women. Still stunned by the terrible ordeal of Calvary, they were apparently not ready for the fulfillment of Christ's promise to rise from the dead.

One can see these daring, loyal women hurrying along the road to the tomb just after the break of dawn on that first Easter morn. And it was Mary Magdalen, out of whom Christ cast seven devils, who led the way. Sparked by the faith, hope and charity that a loving Saviour had generously shown her, she seemed to sense that this was the one great occasion on which she could prove her complete confidence in Him.

An extraordinary reward was to be hers. The first person to whom Jesus Christ appeared after His resurrection from the dead was Mary Magdalen. In addition, she was given the first commission to "go" in Christ's name. He bade her to tell the glad tidings to His disciples.

How filled with joy must have been her heart and those of the other women as they went swiftly to tell the great news to the disciples. But how shocked they must have been at the cool reception they received from the Apostles as St. Luke records it: "And these words seemed to them as idle tales; and they did not believe them."

In doing the work of Christ, expect skepticism from those who should give you the most encouragement.

"As the Father hath sent me, I also send you."

(John 20:21)

HE ATE TOO MUCH

Police in New York couldn't help but smile when they entered the small east side restaurant very early one morning and found their suspect, obligingly, fast asleep at a table.

The owner of the restaurant had reported that every night for a week, a burglar had entered and helped himself to a free meal, cigarettes and chewing gum. He never seemed to touch anything else, however, and the police guessed that the thief was someone who was destitute and driven to steal food because of hunger. But when they found their man they were surprised. They hadn't expected the arrest to be so easy.

The man explained, sleepily, that he always left as soon as he had eaten. But that night he had eaten too much and had become so drowsy that he had fallen asleep.

Those who spend their time living off others hurt themselves in more ways than one. Above all, they cannot have much peace of heart, for conscience reminds them they are cheats, both in failing to carry their share of the load, and in taking from others what does not belong to them. Sooner or later they pay the penalty for side-stepping their responsibilities.

"Depart from me, you cursed, into everlasting fire that was prepared for the devil and his angels, for I was hungry and you gave me not to eat."

(Matthew 25:41-42)

SO NEAR AND YET SO FAR

A cattle raiser and his son who had a thriving ranch in Clear Lake, South Dakota, wanted to buy a fine bull. In fact, they wanted to buy the finest bull they could find.

So they decided to attend the Western Stock Show in Denver, Colorado. For there, surely, they would have a wide selection from the finest animals in that section.

It was a long trip, many miles away. But they made it with no mishaps, and after a day's scouting around, finally made the choice of the finest Angus bull at the sale.

They bought the bull for $5050 and started for home. But the father and son had little to say to each other on the way back. They were both feeling a little sheepish. The bull they had bought had been raised on their neighbor's farm up in South Dakota, less than a mile from their own.

In our day, countless persons are searching for the Way, the Truth and the Life. Little do they realize how close they are to it at all times.

A rare opportunity presents itself in our day to bring the love and truth of Christ to the countless millions who are looking in vain for someone to make it known to them. Those who are dedicated to falsehood go to endless trouble to reach everybody with their errors. Can you in conscience do any less with the truth?

"Go ye into the whole world and preach the gospel to every creature." (Mark 16:15)

&§ Help me, Almighty God, to play the role of missioner as far as I can.

IT'S EASY TO BLAME OTHERS

In Palermo, Sicily, not long ago, a sixteen-year-old boy found himself in serious trouble with the law.

The youngster was not a very good student, but he possessed an unreasonable pride and an ungovernable temper. Although he was never willing to work very hard at his studies, he nonetheless was always very put out when he failed to receive good grades.

On one occasion he became particularly furious with his instructor because he failed one of his courses. Nothing could convince him that it was his own fault that he had failed. He was so angry that he secured a pistol, and fired four shots at the unfortunate teacher, wounding him in the arm.

It is a human tendency to blame others for our own shortcomings. Parents who neglect to give their children the proper home training too frequently take it out on teachers for what they themselves have allowed to develop. Those who fail to vote or take any interest in better government are usually the first to complain when things go wrong in the administration of public affairs.

You will never make a mistake by first looking into yourself when trouble arises to find if, and where, you yourself have failed. If you examine your own conscience in this way, it will be a strong inducement for you to improve rather than merely disapprove.

"Before thou inquire, blame no man: and when thou hast inquired, reprove justly." (Ecclesiasticus 11:7)

⇜ Help me, O Lord, to search my own heart before blaming others.

111

SHE THREW AWAY $5000

A judge in San Francisco listened patiently while the couple before him listed their grievances. It was clear that these two had never learned to "*bear and forbear.*" Small hurts had been stored away in their memories, rankling and growing, till their life together seemed to be no more than an occasion of new and better methods of revenge.

The case was brought to a climax when the husband's attorney demanded that the wife tell the court what she had done with $5000 cash which she had had in her possession, but which belonged to both.

"*Oh, I threw it over the bridge into the Bay,*" the woman said calmly. "*You see, my husband throws away all his money gambling. So I figure I can throw mine away, too.*"

Rather than make a bad situation worse by becoming impatient with the faults and mistakes of others, you can do much to correct the trouble by showing greater love and forbearance than usual and thus make up for what is lacking on the part of another person.

One of the simplest ways to start to be a Christopher or Christbearer is to show kindness to those around you, especially to your own household. From there you can carry the habit, cultivated at home, into the office, classroom, shop, farm or wherever else you may be.

"*By this shall all men know that you are my disciples if you have love one for another.*" (John 13:35)

✍ Give me the good sense, O Lord, to lessen frictions rather than to aggravate them.

MUSIC WITH A PURPOSE

The jail in Dyersburg, Tennessee, is noted for its reasonable and humane treatment of prisoners. Often in the evenings, passersby may hear the sound of singing voices or of a guitar playing a merry tune.

The sheriff is of the opinion that even criminals should be allowed a little fun now and then.

But on one occasion he was not too pleased with this apparently innocent amusement. There was one prisoner who had a guitar, and who whanged away at it every night for long hours at a time.

He played very loudly, and what was worse, he played very badly. The sheriff stood it as long as he could. Then one night his nerves could suffer no more. He went to speak to the prisoner. But he found more than a noisy guitar player. Three other prisoners were keeping time to the music by sawing away on the bars with hacksaws.

Men use various ways to cover up evil. It is proof that men know the difference between right and wrong when they strive to appear as "*good*" when they are actually perpetrating "*evil.*"

The most dishonest persons want honest people to handle their affairs. Those who lead immoral lives wish to appear decent and respectable. The very ones who resort to falsehood and deceit go to great lengths to make others regard them as upright.

"*Deceitful souls go astray in sins.*" (Proverbs 13:13)

❧ Impress on me, O Lord, the importance of living honestly.

FAITH IN THE WRONG WAY

A man wanted to buy a badly needed new suit. He asked a friend to go with him to the corner store and help him to choose one.

But the friend objected. "No," he said, *"I'll be glad to go with you, but you mustn't buy it at the corner store. I know where we can get the same values for half the price."*

So, of course, the man let his friend take him to this far away spot, where, believing that he was buying wholesale, he chose a suit for $50.

He was delighted with his purchase until he ran into the neighborhood butcher wearing an identical suit to church that Sunday.

"Hey!" he said grinning. *"Where did you buy that suit?"* The butcher grinned back. *"Oh, I suppose the same place you bought yours . . . At the corner store. A real buy for $30, wasn't it?"*

It is a remarkable thing that so many people put great confidence in mere hearsay and yet are so slow to show as much faith in the ageless truths of God.

But one thing is certain. However misplaced faith may be—even to the extent of being bilked, it is still an expression of trust. Channel that confidence towards supernatural truth and you will bring about a great gain for everybody.

"I do believe, Lord: help my unbelief." (Mark 9:23)

⋙ Inspire me with apostolic zeal, O Lord, in helping others to believe in Thee.

ONE YOUNGSTER AND A BUCKET OF GREEN PAINT

A three-year-old youngster thought he would surprise his father by painting the family automobile.

He found a bucket of green paint and a brush and set to work. The boy put plenty of energy into the task and covered every bit of the car except the roof—which he couldn't reach. When it was finished, he toddled into the house and proudly informed his parents of his deed.

When his father investigated his son's handiwork he found he was telling the truth. Headlights, tail lights, windows, doors, door handles—everything he could reach was a glittering green. The roof was still brown.

The desire to act creatively is an innate one, and shows itself at an early age. But it does not express itself very intelligently before the age of reason is reached. This is no reason to suppress it. God put it there, and He expects that it be used.

Our part as adults and teachers of the young is to guide and channel their energies so that they will attain their full power later on. For this we cannot start too early.

The best way to attack this important task is not to wait for little Johnny to display his genius in the strangest ways but to give him little tasks which are useful and interesting.

"It is a proverb: A young man according to his way, even when he is old he will not depart from it."

(Proverbs 22:6)

🔊 Inspire, O Lord, all who train the young to be wise, kind and patient.

HE NEVER CAME BACK

A Pittsburgh man, planning a trip to Florida in his car last winter, was anxious to find someone to help with the driving.

Having put an advertisement in the newspaper, he waited for the phone calls. They came—15 of them. The trusting man picked the one he thought best filled his qualifications.

Several days later with his car loaded with clothing, luggage, typewriter and a radio-phonograph, the Pittsburgher was ready to hit the highway. But before he started he thought it would be best to let his driver get the "feel" of the car. He told his new-found 26-year-old friend to drive the auto around the block.

The helper apparently was willing to do more than share the driving, for he never returned. Next day, police arrested him in Wheeling, W. Va.

How many there are who are scrupulously careful about the minutest details, but who disregard the main issues!

For example, how many of us pay so much attention to the multitude of details of daily living, but show not the slightest regard for what happens to our government, our educational system, what comes into the home in the form of entertainment on TV, radio, books, newspapers, magazines, and the like.

We shall always pay the penalty for neglect in these important matters. Resolve today to try harder to keep your eye on the main issues.

"What does it profit a man, if he gain the whole world, and suffer the loss of his own soul?" (Matthew 16:26)

ONE WAY TO A HAPPY MARRIAGE

A pastor in England says that he has saved many marriages simply by showing the married couple motion pictures of their happy wedding day, whenever a serious misunderstanding develops that could split the union.

The clergyman takes movies of the newlyweds as they leave his church then suggests that they see him if they quarrel.

"By the time the film is half over most couples are holding hands," the 51-year-old pastor explained. "And by the time it's over they're as happy as they were when they walked out of my church on their wedding day."

It is good for all to get back to fundamentals from time to time. But we ought not to wait until trouble or emergencies force us to do so. These can be averted if we do it with regular frequency.

Not only the marriage ceremony, but the Ten Commandments and the many revealed truths of God should be kept at our finger tips. Keep familiar with the basic principles of your religious and moral life.

In your own way, use every opportunity to remind others of these essentials. Strive also to apply them in a practical way to education, government and other vital spheres of influence. Like those who are helped to recall their marriage vows, people live much better lives when they are conscious of what God expects of them.

"But seek ye first the kingdom of God and his justice, and all these things shall be added unto you."

(Luke 12:31)

24 HOURS UNDERWATER

His skin blue and wrinkled like a prune, a "skin diver" stayed underwater for more than 24 hours to set a world endurance record.

The diver, Ed Fisher, camped on the ocean floor off Miami, Fla., for 24 hours and 2 minutes. His head ached from the water's pressure, but he was very happy over his accomplishment with his associates who kept a vigil over him in two boats.

Fisher had no direct contact with the surface and made the dive to test a new breathing device. For nourishment, he drank soup, ate candy and speared fish which he ate raw. He consumed his food by removing a mouthpiece which fed him air.

The 26-year-old swimmer was exhausted, but apparently escaped without injury.

Endurance record-breakers serve the very good purpose of pointing out the enormous potentialities we have within us, but which we never use—or even discover.

They are strong reminders to those who would retire into their own little worlds to "launch out" and make their influence felt in the world. We play up our limitations too often and overlook the powers of endurance entrusted to us by God.

If one man can sit on the ocean floor for 24 hours, imagine what we can do to change the surface of the earth, if we would be willing to submit to a like hardship in raising the standards of government.

"That which you hear in the ear, preach upon the housetops." (Matthew 10:27)

A BLIND BOY BASEBALL PITCHER

A nine-year-old blind boy can throw a baseball straighter than some boys with full sight can because a kind county fair concessionaire took the time to teach him.

The boy, Jack Farnham of Springville, N. Y., and a student at the State School for the Blind at Batavia, didn't think he had a chance in the world of knocking down the bottles in a baseball throw concession. But the operator urged him on and offered to give the youth a few practice throws.

The man told Jack just where to throw the baseball. He gave him the direction, height and angle which lined up the pitch with the bottles. Jack caught on immediately and when the bottles stopped falling he had a stuffed teddy bear tucked under his arm.

"It was honest," the man told doubtful observers. "The boy is really remarkable. Believe me I don't give anything away."

Every now and then we are surprised by a demonstration of what a handicapped person can do. God in His goodness and wisdom has placed in us a law of compensation by which we gain something which more than makes up for what we lose.

There is a great potential in handicapped people. We should try to help them to find it by encouraging them and finding outlets for their hidden talents.

What a great satisfaction to have assisted in turning a broken and crippled life into a useful and happy one!

"Lend to your neighbor in the time of his need."
(Ecclesiasticus 29:2)

237 HOURS ON A FLAGPOLE

His ankles throbbing with pain, a 51-year-old professional flagpole sitter from Detroit descended his lofty perch after almost 10 days in which he broke his world's record.

When the man reached the bottom of the pole on which he stood for 237 hours and 35 minutes, his ankles were swollen twice their normal size. He looked haggard and in need of nourishing food.

The man proudly announced that he had broken his old record of 192 hours set in Milwaukee in 1952. He was paid $1000 for his exhausting and painful feat and immediately left for the hospital to have his ankles treated.

What some will do for glory or fame never ceases to amaze us. It seems to be a great waste of time and energy. But, on the other hand, we can see in these remarkable feats a proof of what man can do against the greatest odds if he has the will and the perseverance.

Everyone has some of this great power of accomplishment. And, fortunately, it can be turned into constructive and useful channels. Set yourself a goal and strive toward it with all your might. You can expect hardships and suffering, but in the end you will be amazed at your own powers.

These God-given powers lie within you waiting to be tapped and harnessed for use in the service of mankind. God will see that you conquer every obstacle.

"Every one strives that they may receive a corruptible crown, but we an incorruptible one."

(1 Corinthians 9:25)

THE PROBLEM OF BEING SUCCESSFUL

To gamble away $28,000 in seven years and go into debt for more than $4000 is the price a 45-year-old Liverpool, England, man said he paid for being "too successful."

Seven years ago, William Garrett won $28,000 in a soccer sweepstake. Before this he had won $4600. If money was this easy to make, Garrett reasoned, then why work for it. So he let his business interests wane and concentrated on gambling.

Each week for the past seven years he bet an average of $420. He told the Bankruptcy Court that he finally lost all his cash and also two homes, property, a coal business and his car. He had but $52 in his pocket and owed $4700.

When the official receiver told Garrett he couldn't be trusted with money, the disillusioned man said that all this happened because he had become "too successful."

Most are convinced that they can handle "success." But many are unable to do so. Wealth and possessions are means to other higher ends, yet some people make them into ends themselves. How often does a man become financially successful only to find that he has lost all his other values and has become self-centered and unhappy. It is simply a case of the "tail wagging the dog."

The best way to avoid letting success or your possessions dominate your life is to consider them as a trust and to use them for the good of others.

"To what purpose is this waste?" (Matthew 26:8)

HIS LIFE FOR $2

Cesare Pizzoccheri was breathless as he slowly read the results of the week's soccer games in Lodi, Italy.

As he neared the end of the list he began to realize that he had picked every game correctly to that point. Now his heart began to pound faster as his eyes raced over the remaining scores. When he came to the final score, the 49-year-old man dropped dead.

Thinking he had won what sometimes amounts to a million lire, Pizzoccheri was so overcome with emotion that he suffered a heart attack. Perhaps he would probably still be living if he had known that 137,690 other persons also picked every game perfectly.

Pizzoccheri's share of the pool was 1285 lire—about $2.

There is constant danger of putting too much stress and strain on the wrong things. There is hardly any doubt that if we put the proper amount of emphasis on the right things our lives will be far happier.

There is a balancing force in the law God has given us to love Him above all things and our neighbor as ourselves. If we follow this command, automatically our lives will straighten out and become as full and satisfying as is possible this side of heaven.

When the stress is on self we invite trouble. When it is on God and others, we can look for—and get—peace of heart, soul and mind because there is a proper balance in our lives.

"Seek ye first the kingdom of God and his justice."
                                            (Luke 12:31)

MAKING A BAD SITUATION WORSE

"He should have seen my son," was all a 38-year-old Harlan, Kentucky, man could say after he shot and critically injured the driver of a truck which struck his son.

The father witnessed the accident and became so incensed that he ran into his home and returned with a shotgun. As the driver stepped from the truck to investigate he was hit in the chest and side by a blast from the gun.

Seriously injured, the 13-year-old boy received fractures and a brain concussion.

The youth's father said his son was standing beside the road when the truck hit him. The father was charged with intent to kill.

One can understand the terrific emotional pressure a father undergoes under such circumstances. But, all the same, we must understand still more how important it is for us to keep ourselves under control in a crisis. Taking the law in one's own hands in this fashion cannot be condoned. If it were, life in society would become impossible.

There are, fortunately, other ways of dealing with such cases. It is possible to be firm and just in correcting abuses and neglect. Losing one's temper only makes a bad situation worse.

Also, there are times when we must leave to others or to the law courts the needed correction. Sometimes we have to leave it to God. He in the end will make all things right.

"Thy Father who seeth in secret will repay thee."
                                                            (Matthew 6:4)

LIVING TO EAT

After eating what ten men would normally consume at one sitting, a French coal miner bowed to his rival in an eating contest when he could not find room for a 12-egg omelet.

The loser, Gustave Porion, and the winner, Andre Pollaert, a butcher, actually ate a dinner of soup, hors d'oeuvres, chicken pies, a chicken with peas, a duck garnished with cauliflowers, a steak with green beans, ham and salad, cheese, tarts and petit-fours. They followed each dish with appropriate wines.

Since nothing was left on either of their plates, the judge declared the contest a draw. So both men started over again on the same menu! An hour later—and pounds heavier—they were still deadlocked.

Then the 12-egg omelet was put before them and the coal miner decided to call it quits. The award went to the butcher.

Although such an example is extreme, a tendency to excess in food and drink is common to many. While gluttony is a sin to which few will admit, we all show in one way or another whether we eat to live or live to eat.

An easy way to develop a sensible balance in this respect is to show a concern for those who suffer for lack of food here in our own country and over the world. If you helped only a few of the two-thirds of humanity that goes to bed hungry every night, you would be taking a big step in the right direction.

"For I was hungry and you gave me to eat."

(Matthew 25:35)

A TEEN-AGER TAKES A SKI LIFT

It may sound impossible or at least improbable but an 18-year-old Italian youth stole a Swiss ski lift piece by piece and transported it to Luino, Italy, his home.

Police said this clever thief made several trips to nearby Switzerland and each time pilfered a part of the lift. This included the motor and 400 yards of steel cable.

So well did the thief carry out his long-range plan that it took police six months to unravel the mystery of the disappearing ski lift.

One cannot avoid admiring the imagination, the determination and the patience of this teen-ager. The pity is that all these excellent qualities which he had in abundance were dedicated to the wrong goals. If he had only harnessed these constructive forces for a worthy and noble goal he would then go far in improving the condition of the tired old world in which he himself must live.

Every teen-ager has these same qualities to some degree. It is one of the most important tasks of our time that we help our youth to realize these energies and to harness them to the great project of restoring the peace of Christ to the world.

If we can encourage the most inspired and talented of our young people to develop their resourcefulness and prepare to take up careers in government, education, labor relations or the creative end of literature and entertainment, the future of our world would be much brighter than it is today.

"Lift up your eyes and see the countries, for they are white already to harvest." (John 4:35)

CAUGHT AFTER TWENTY YEARS

A 44-year-old man who escaped from the Ohio State Reformatory 20 years ago was recently apprehended although he had long been leading the life of a respectable citizen.

In 1932 he had been sentenced to one to twenty years for forging a $40 check. In 1934 he walked away from the prison while working in an honor section.

First he worked as a coal miner, then as a welder and tool maker. In 1943, he enlisted in the U. S. Navy and received the Purple Heart and Silver Star for heroism in the Battle of the Bulge. After he was discharged, he returned to his Ohio home town and bought a hotel and restaurant.

He claimed that he forged the check when his employer would not pay him, but that later he made restitution.

A chief purpose of punishment is to stimulate an individual to turn over a new leaf and lead a better life. There is a danger in being so unforgiving and merciless that more harm than good is done in being relentless after a change for the better has taken place.

Extremes must be avoided. Those who break the law must be punished. But they must also be rehabilitated in a Christlike way.

"Neither will I condemn thee. Go, and now sin no more." (John 8:11)

᪦ Help me, O Lord, to recognize justice but to temper all I do with mercy.

WRECKING HIS HOME TO SAVE A CAT

A Lexington, N. Y., man practically tore down his home to free a kitten who was trapped in the walls and wailing to get out.

This man's wife tried to find a way to free the animal but all efforts failed. She called the fire chief, but he ran up against the same concrete wall which encased the kitten.

When her husband arrived home he immediately began opening holes in the outside wall wherever he heard a "meow." Nine holes later, he made contact with the frightened pussy and pulled it to safety.

"I certainly was glad we could rescue the kitten," he said. "It was such a friendly little fellow we would have hated to see anything happen to it."

To work with determination to execute what we have set before us without counting the cost is the mark of a mature and Christ-like character. We must be constantly on our guard against the opposite tendency in us which is faint-heartedness. We should decide upon our goal and pursue it vigorously.

If we really wanted to bring about better government, better education, better labor relations, and better literature and entertainment, we would find a way to do it. It is only when we half want to improve these vital spheres of influence that we sit on the sidelines and complain. Start today to find a way to change them for the better.

"Be not faint-hearted in thy mind." (Ecclesiasticus 7:9)

Grant me the determination to do great things for Thy sake, O Lord.

CONSCIENCE AND $100

One person in New York State wasn't bothered too much by his conscience when he failed to pay his state tax.

He figured it was something to be proud of since the State Tax Department hadn't detected it. But just when he was forgetting about his "perfect bit of manipulation" the voice of his conscience started to occupy his thoughts.

Then one day he sent a letter to the tax department in Albany. When it was opened, officials found a $100 bill attached to a sheet of paper marked with this one word: "Conscience."

We never cease to be amazed at the power of conscience. It has at times proved itself superior in power to money, prestige, pain, even torture and death. Here it is just a tax collector, but the only collector which could get the money from this man.

We should value our conscience highly, since it is a priceless gift of God to each of us. The difficulty is, however, that its voice can grow weak or strong as we treat it well or badly.

The consciences of the young should be our special concern. What an injustice to a child to have his conscience undeveloped or warped when starting life because of the carelessness of parents and teachers. God will hold us accountable for the conscience of others as well as our own.

"The kingdom of God is within you." (Luke 17:21)

Make me attentive to the voice of my conscience always, Lord.

THE POWER OF SHERIFF JOHN

Policemen in Pasadena, Calif., pleaded with a seven-year-old girl to tell them of the accident which could have taken her life or inflicted serious injury. But she stubbornly refused.

The youngster, police said, rode her bicycle into the side of a car and escaped unhurt. But when police asked her for information about the near-tragedy she kept mum because television's "Sheriff John" had warned her never to talk to strangers.

Police continued to question the tot using every means at their disposal to get her to "talk." But regarding the police as strangers she held her ground and remained silent to the end when she was told to go on her way.

A little incident like this one is eloquent in reminding us of the enormous potential for good in television. Too often we are tempted to sit back and complain that some programs are mediocre or worse, and write TV off as a mere thing of amusement and diversion.

Until more awaken to the great opportunities inherent in television for influencing its listeners for the better, not much is likely to be done in improving it. What a vast change in TV would take place if just a few hundred of our youth with love of God and the needed ability were to aim at taking a job in this important field as a life work to improve the tone of that medium or of realizing more of the fine possibilities in it.

"That which you hear in the ear, preach ye upon the housetops." (Matthew 10:27)

✎ Bless all who are providing and will provide our TV programs, O Lord.

A PISTOL STOPPED TRAFFIC

Traffic screeched to a halt when a 45-year-old Lynn, Mass., man waved a pistol in the air and stumbled across a traffic-laden square in a determined bid to reach the other side.

The man had made countless attempts to cross the street but would get just so far each time when traffic stopped him. Exasperated, he decided to take forceful steps. He went home and got his .32-caliber pistol.

When he started across the square the next time with the gun in full view, motorists graciously and obligingly stopped. He made it to the other side but only to be met by policemen who arrested him for drunkenness and carrying a pistol without a permit.

We all start life as children, but it is our job as the years pass by to mature and become adults. Often this seems to take many years. How often do we find elderly people who have definite traits of childhood.

This man gave a display of a childish tantrum. Insisting on having his own way, he fell into a murderous rage when he was crossed. If many acted like this, life in society would be impossible.

The sign of maturity and adulthood is to show the respect for others that God expects of us. If we are busy enough paying attention to our duties, we won't have time to forget the rights of others.

"When I was a child, I spoke as a child, I understood as a child, I thought as a child. But when I became a man, I put away the things of a child." (1 Corinthians 13:11)

⊸§ Help me to grow in wisdom and strength, O Lord.

THERE'S GOOD IN THE WORST

The weather was cold and crisp in Detroit on the day that a large hard snowball went crashing through a candy store window, accompanied by shouts of boyish laughter.

The annoyed proprietor walked to the door and looked out, but the culprit had fled. With a sigh of resignation, he went about his business. That was the third broken window for the month!

It was late in the evening when one of his clerks brought him an envelope. *"Some kid left this for you,"* he told him. Inside the envelope the surprised storekeeper found a dollar and a note which read: *"Sir, I am sorry I broke your window. I hope this will cover the costs."*

The note was unsigned. The storekeeper told reporters that he would like to find the boy to return his dollar and give him a box of candy. He said, *"In days like these when you hear so much about the destructiveness of kids, it's refreshing to get a note like that."*

One of the great consolations of anyone striving in Christ's name to bring out the best in his fellow man is to find goodness, where it is not expected, and to try to encourage it.

"I came not to call the just, but sinners to penance."
(Luke 5:32)

↝ Inspire me, O Lord, to do my part in bringing out the good that is to be found in the worst of men.

131

THAT ONE BLOT

A short time ago, a petition was filed at the State Pardon Board in Harrisburg, Pa., by 57-year-old Bert Levy, asking that the Board remove the record of his conviction of a holdup 27 years before.

Levy is famous for his introduction of guerrilla tactics to the United States and British Armies during World War II. A book he wrote is still considered one of the best on the subject. Now ill and penniless, he has stated that his reason for requesting this complete pardon is that it was the only blot on his record.

God has implanted a deep yearning in every human being to complete his life with a *"clean slate."* In His boundless mercy, He makes allowance for the weakness of man by offering him complete forgiveness for any sins he may commit. His only requirement is that the sinner should confess his mistakes with sorrow, be willing to do penance and resolve to the best of his ability not to fall again.

"Whose sins you shall forgive, they are forgiven them."
(John 20:23)

➤§ Teach me, O Lord, to forgive others as generously as Thou dost forgive my mistakes.

A TIME TO SIT TIGHT

A 12-year-old girl and her 9-year-old sister recently were stranded all night on a 1000-foot high canyon ledge in Yuma, Arizona.

The girls had been to a picnic and had wandered off and become lost. The couple in whose care the children had been, sought help from the sheriff, who immediately sent out a posse to look for them. Everybody was deeply concerned, because one misstep in the darkness could send the children plunging to their death.

But the two young girls acted with calm and courage when they saw they were lost. Knowing the danger they were in, they sat down right where they were, and calmly waited to be found.

Many persons are just as *"lost"* spiritually, intellectually and emotionally today as were these two children. Living in spiritual darkness they are ever in danger of making a false move that could be catastrophic.

You can play the role of a Christopher or Christbearer by bringing the truth of the Prince of Peace to those who are confused, befuddled or completely lost.

"I am the light of the world: he that followeth, walketh not in darkness, and shall have the light of life."
(John 8:12)

−§ Inspire me, O Holy Spirit, with an ardent desire to share the truth with those who have strayed far from Thee.

A REAL TEST

We seldom think of driving carefully as one way in which to translate into action the precept of Christ: *"Thou shalt love thy neighbor as thyself."* And yet it offers a valuable opportunity to spiritualize one more part of modern life.

The National Safety Council recommends a seven point program to show motorists how, in a very practical way, they could show to other drivers the same courtesy they expect for themselves.

You may be interested in their seven recommendations:

1. Share the road by driving in the proper lane.
2. Allow ample clearance when passing.
3. Yield the right of way to other drivers and pedestrians.
4. Giver proper turn and stop signals.
5. Dim headlights when meeting or following vehicles.
6. Adjust driving to road, traffic and weather conditions.
7. Respect traffic laws, signs, signals and road markings.

It is easy to *"talk"* about being considerate of others. How we apply that principle of love of our fellow man to everyday life, however, is the real test of our sincerity.

The way you drive a car, behave at home or in a crowd, do your shopping or treat your employees or boss is a fairly good yardstick of how much you are trying to bring the peace of Christ into the world.

"By this shall all men know that you are my disciples, if you have love one for another." (John 13:35)

⚜ Help me, O Prince of Peace, to recognize that the peace of the world begins at my doorstep.

DISPUTES THAT HURT OTHERS

The morning traffic rush was at its height in Oklahoma City when two stubborn drivers held lines of cars backed up for blocks.

A young woman was trying to make a left turn at an intersection. A man coming in the opposite direction was trying to get through the intersection at the same time. They met in the middle, and there they stayed. Each was determined to get through first, and neither would yield.

With front bumpers locked, they screamed at each other. They paid no attention to the angry honking of horns behind them. Eventually, the police arrived to settle the argument. They impartially booked both offenders on charges of obstructing the traffic.

Many a good cause suffers because of the needless bickering of a few members. If principles were involved, it would be a different matter. But most arguments are over matters of little consequence.

In the family circle or in your club, school, or place of business take care not to be drawn into such disputes lest important issues be forgotten or sidetracked. Remember that the good of many persons is often held up because two people insist on arguing about "*who comes first*."

"*Whosoever will force thee one mile, go with him other two.*" (Matthew 5:41)

&§ O Lord, grant me the wisdom to be able to disagree without becoming disagreeable.

THE HIDDEN POWER IN EVERYONE

In Oklahoma City, a grandmother was left in charge of her 3-year-old grandson. The child had gone to the bathroom when suddenly a fire broke out in the house. It soon became a roaring blaze.

Realizing the great danger, the woman hurried to get the child to safety. But he had become terrified by the flames licking around the window and the acrid smell of smoke, and refused to open the door. She pounded at the bathroom door with the flames searing her face and hands—pleading with the child. Finally, he opened the door and let her in. It was just in the nick of time. A few moments later the whole house was ablaze. The grandmother was burned severely.

It is always inspiring to observe what a high price individuals are willing to pay to help those unable to help themselves. On the spur of the moment they become heroes. They will lay down their own lives in a desperate attempt to save the lives of others.

Such generous daring is proof of the great power for good that God Himself has implanted in each individual. Would that each could learn to bring it into play on a day-to-day basis instead of waiting for an emergency to bring the best out of them.

"Greater love than this no man hath, that a man lay down his life for his friends." (John 15:13)

&3 Help me to discover, O my God, the power Thou hast entrusted to me to be used for the good of others.

A DECEPTIVE DEATH

A rather odd tragedy occurred in Richmond, Va. Four people, two men and two women, were speeding along on a highway one foggy night when the driver lost control of the car. It went off the highway, through a field, and finally became stuck in a mud hole. Fortunately, no one was hurt and the car was not wrecked.

In the excitement, the only thought of the occupants was to remove the car from the mud hole. They sat in the car planning what to do. No one guessed that the exhaust pipe under the car had been pulled loose where it entered the muffler and would bring death to them all.

Detectives who found the bodies said that the amount of carbon monoxide seeping into the car must have taken less than twenty minutes to overcome the four.

Although we have survived three tragic, costly wars, in which the loss of life and property reached astronomical proportions few are aware that we are in the midst of a far more deadly war that threatens our very survival.

Like the poison gas that is imperceptible a godless philosophy of life can bring fatal results.

Do all in your power to reach the multitude with the only truth that can make it free. Remember Christ's warning:

"Fear not they that kill the body, and are not able to kill the soul." (Matthew 10:28)

◆§ Protect me, O Lord, from evil and let me in turn be a guide and comfort to others who are deceived.

137

THE DEVOTION THAT ALL NEED

Joseph Tagg had been a shepherd in the hill country of England for many years. At 86, though his sight had begun to fail, and his steps were less sure and steady, he still took his sheep faithfully out to pasture, guiding them where the best grass lay.

His dog Tip was old too. For twelve years this faithful collie had helped his master herd the sheep. But now he began to hover closer to old Joseph, more concerned for his welfare than for the sheep.

At the beginning of last winter it was suddenly noticed that old Tagg had disappeared. Searching parties went looking for him, only to return sadly without having found him. After fifteen weeks of severe winter weather, two shepherds accidentally found him lying dead in the snow. Beside him was his faithful dog, weak and hungry, but alive.

The devotion of animals to those who have loved and cared for them is often a lesson to man. Each and every human being has been specially endowed by God with an immortal soul and with great attributes of mind, heart and body to assist him in fulfilling the one great purpose of his life—to serve God and his fellow man. The two go hand in hand, as the Apostle John reminds us:

"He that loveth not his brother whom he seeth, how can he love God whom he seeth not?" (1 John 4:20)

&s O Lord, let me show my love for Thee in my devotion to those less fortunate than myself.

AT THE EXPENSE OF OTHERS

New York detectives recently rounded up a man they suspected of burglary. Unless such suspects are caught in the act, it usually takes long hours of questioning to get some semblance of the truth. So they had prepared themselves for a long session and began with the routine questions.

They were wholly unprepared for the answer they received when they asked him what he did for a living. He told them with a sigh, "I steal. I don't get much, but it's a living."

It has always been a temptation for man, with his weak nature, to seek the line of least resistance in providing for his wants. Invariably, he favors himself and can easily rationalize himself into the attitude that he has a right to something for nothing, that he can avoid work and live off others.

You will gain much peace of heart and soul as well as prepare for your appearance before the Judgment Seat of God if you make it a policy to be honest in all things. You have countless opportunities to be honest—in business dealing, in paying just debts, in putting in an honest day's work for every day's wages, and in numerous other ways.

"Nothing is covered that shall not be revealed: nor hid that shall not be known." (Matthew 10:26)

Let me keep ever in mind, O Lord, that one day I must answer to Thee for all my thoughts, words and deeds.

BETTER LATE THAN NEVER

There's a 61-year-old man in London, England, who calls himself "the world's most rejected painter." For 40 years, Arthur Perry has tried to make a success at being an artist. During these four decades he has submitted 251 paintings to Britain's Royal Academy, and only one has ever been accepted.

Recently, he stated that he has finally decided that "perhaps, after all, art is not my line." So now, although he plans to retire from painting, he is not by any means retiring from effort. He is merely changing his occupation.

Now, at 61, he plans to spend as much time as he can in trying to improve government and thus help everybody.

It is "better late than never" to take a conscientious interest in public affairs. God entrusts to many the power to play a part in bringing His law and order into the mainstream of life.

But if true peace is to become a reality in our time more persons with great faith in God and man will have to devote their time and talent to bettering the administration of government—on a local and state, as well as national, level.

"Neglect not the grace that is in thee."

(1 Timothy 4:14)

ċ Inspire me, O my God, to work for the well-being of others.

A POWER FOR GOOD OR EVIL

At a recent convention of the Radio-Television Broadcasters Association, its president, Mr. Harold E. Fellows, delivered a timely and powerful address.

Calling on newsmen in radio and TV to do all they could to weed out the undesirable influences from their ranks, he said: "A few among our own profession have as little sense of responsibility and integrity and as little direct respect for the truth as an habitual murderer has for human life.

"One of the purposes to which such a professional society as ours should be devoted is that of digging out of the profession, the malcontents and ne'er-do-wells, the liars and libelers, the irresponsible and the unjust."

If you belong to an organization of any kind, do your part to see that it lives up to its high ideals and responsibilities. By helping it to keep its own house in order, you not only protect it but strengthen it to serve as an instrument of God, in promoting the welfare of both its members and the world at large.

By taking an active interest yourself and stimulating others to do likewise, you can accomplish much for the good of all. God will give you all the help you need!

"I can do all things in Him who strengtheneth me."
(Philippians 4:13)

Keep me ever reminded, O Lord, that I have responsibilities as well as rights.

FOR THE PROTECTION OF ALL

In Ephrata, Pa., a State Policeman stopped a 60-year-old farmer, and asked to see his driver's license.

The man explained ruefully that it was some time since he had bothered to get one. On further investigation the policeman discovered that "some time" was all of 23 years!

The man was taken before a justice of the peace, where he explained that his first license had been issued thirty years before, but that after the first seven years he just "hadn't bothered" to get another. In all those years he said that this was the first time he had ever been stopped by the police.

It is to the advantage of all motorists as well as pedestrians that some reasonable practice be followed to make sure that all who would like to drive an auto are competent to do so. Men make laws to protect themselves and their fellowmen.

The revealed laws of God as well as the laws He put in nature are given us for the benefit of all. Imagine what bedlam would follow if everybody decided to throw out, for instance, the Ten Commandments.

Make yourself a "committee of one" to promote a normal healthy respect for that true law and order which takes its origin from God.

"If you love me, you will keep my commandments."
(John 14:15)

✑ Deepen in me, O my God, a reverence for Thy law.

HELP THE TEEN-AGERS

A 14-year-old St. Louis youngster was walking along a Mississippi River bluff 125 feet high, when he missed his footing and fell, plunging to almost certain death.

But he did not die. His fall was cushioned by a pile of weeds and leaves. He suffered a broken arm, but that was all.

Police said that this boy was especially fortunate because right beside this pile of leaves was another pile of broken bottles.

Teen-agers today are confronted with many problems. In countless different ways they are being constantly bombarded with the idea that bodily pleasures provide the height of happiness, for one example.

In succumbing to what is obviously attractive, young people often take one step too many and plunge into an abyss of immorality, brutality and other forms of crime.

You can do something to prevent this tragedy for at least a few by spreading far and wide the saving doctrine of Jesus Christ. He teaches that the body is sacred and should be treated with respect and reverence because it actually houses the immortal soul.

"Know you not that you are the temple of God, and the Spirit of God dwelleth in you?" (1 Corinthians 3:16)

❧ Grant me the grace, O Lord, to do my part in encouraging young people to know their true worth.

FEW TEACHERS GET RICH

Recently, a man died in Los Angeles, whose only employment in all his adult life had been that of a teacher in high school. His salary had never been more that $294 a month.

After many years he had retired on a small pension. When he died it was a great surprise to those who knew him to discover that he had left an estate of almost a million dollars.

It was disclosed, upon investigation, that the teacher had amassed the money over a period of many years, by making regular investments—small but sound—in oil stocks, government bonds and real estate holdings.

Few teachers will ever amass a fortune like that. As a matter of fact, most of them will go through life barely making ends meet. Those who dedicate themselves in a Christlike way to teaching the children of all do not demand special consideration. But to do their job well, they must be assured of the normal security that you would expect if you were in their position.

You can render an important service not only by encouraging those with character, as well as competence, to take up a career in the teaching field and fill one of the nearly 100,000 vacancies, but also in taking whatever steps you can to see that all teachers receive the moral and material support they both need and deserve.

"In this is my Father glorified: that you bring forth very much fruit." (John 15:8)

&§ Inspire many more, O Lord, to become devoted teachers.

PREPARE FOR THE FUTURE

A man in Eau Claire, Wisc., had lived for many years on a busy thoroughfare. He decided that when the time came when he could afford it, he would find a home away from the honking of automobile horns and the screech of tires.

After much looking around, the man was sure that he had found the ideal site—in the city and yet secure from the noise of the traffic. His new house was located at the far end of a dead-end street.

But the man wasn't there long before he discovered that he had merely jumped from the frying pan into the fire. Recently, he reported the ninth incident of an automobile mistaking the dead-end for a through street, plowing through his front yard and smashing the front of his house.

Many think that by running away from the great problems that vex mankind they will find peace and quiet for themselves. They rarely do. They soon discover that trouble has a way of pursuing them wherever they go.

Those who are usually happiest in this life are the ones realistic enough to take their sojourn on earth as God intended it should be: a brief work-out in preparation for the rest and joy that will endure for all eternity.

"He that hateth his life in this world keepeth it unto life eternal." (John 12:25)

 Let me help myself, O Lord, by helping others.

THE PATIENCE OF EVIL-DOERS

There are two thieves somewhere in New York City, who recently set something of a record in proving that patience is rewarding.

It was two hours before closing time in a small uptown tavern when the two men came in and sat down. To the onlooker they would have appeared to be no more than two friends enjoying an evening. In fact they seemed to be having so pleasant a time that the bartender was reluctant to break it up when it was time to close.

So he was completely taken by surprise when after politely reminding them that he was about to lock up for the night, the two men suddenly approached him with pistols pointed at his heart. They quickly emptied the cash register of $200 and made their escape.

Those who have an evil purpose show extraordinary patience in pursuing their objective. No amount of trouble or inconvenience seems too much for them.

Christ Himself gave a pointed reminder to those who claim to be His followers. They should certainly be far more shrewd, alert and painstaking than those who seek lawfully or unlawfully, the fleeting pleasure and rewards of this world.

"The children of this world are wiser in their generation than the children of light." (Luke 16:8)

⁀§ Grant, O Lord, that I may show as much initiative and daring for Thy truth and justice as others show against it.

SHE DIED THAT THEY MIGHT LIVE

In Javojoa, Mexico, a teacher had just dismissed her first-graders. She warned them to be careful not to walk too close to the Mayo river. It had rained heavily recently, and the river was swollen.

She walked along behind them, trying to keep an eye on all of them, calling a word of warning now and then. Suddenly five children who were further ahead grabbed hands and started to run. It happened very quickly. One child lost his footing, pulling the other four along with him into the turbulent water.

Without a thought for herself, the teacher ran forward and plunged into the water after them. One by one she pulled four out, fighting against the swirling stream. She drowned in the attempt to reach the fifth child.

Those who would serve others as teachers, government workers or in any other sphere of influence that vitally affects the destiny of others have a rare opportunity to fashion a better future for everybody.

True they must make a sacrifice. More often than not they are forgotten, unappreciated, misunderstood and receive little recompense in this world for their valiant work. But they can have great consolation that the greatest of all teachers, Jesus Christ, paid the same price. It is a small sacrifice for the peace of eternity.

"He that shall lose his life for my sake shall save it."
(Luke 9:24)

&§ Cost what it may, let me reflect Thy love in all I do, O Lord.

A COSTLY APPETITE

In New York, a 54-year-old saleslady was recently charged with stealing $5000 from her employer for "lunch money."

For two years this woman had daily stolen small sums of money by making out false refund slips and sending them up through the department store's pneumatic tube to the cashier who would unwittingly send back the amount asked for.

The woman was apprehended when she sent in one of her "slips," signing another saleslady's number to it, as usual. The cashier called to check a small error on the slip, and discovered that the saleslady of that number didn't know anything about it.

When the thief was finally apprehended, she told police that she stole because she didn't make enough money to buy the kind of lunches she liked.

A little self-discipline usually suffices to nip in the bud any evil tendency. On the other hand a failure to resist such beginnings is an open invitation to trouble. Whether it is food, drink, money, dress, social ambition or sex, all goes well so long as the attraction is kept in its proper place. But let it become the master, and it quickly degenerates into a consuming passion that nothing will satisfy.

Self-denial is a never-ending task for all of us if we would overcome our human frailties.

"If any man will come after me, let him deny himself, and take up his cross daily, and follow me." (Luke 9:23)

◄§ Help me to overcome my weaknesses, O Lord, by doing good.

THIS ABOVE ALL

Not long ago, Oklahoma A & M College made an unusual survey. They were interested in finding out what were the greatest likes and dislikes of the freshmen. Too, they wanted to know what gives this age group the greatest cause for worry. They felt that such a survey would help them arrive at some meaningful conclusions.

To their great surprise, none of the expected answers were given. The average freshman, they found, was not primarily concerned about examination, classes, athletics, dates or money. The biggest worry turned out to be finding a place to park his car!

Finding a spot to park one's car often tries the patience of the most stalwart souls. But things may be a bit out of balance in your life if that or any other minor preoccupation becomes a major issue in your life.

Never forget for one moment that you are on a brief voyage through life and that your one big job here below is to save your immortal soul and to help others to do the same.

Miss that, and everything else adds up to nothing more than a handful of ashes. No matter how successful you may have become intellectually, socially, businesswise or in any other worldly manner, if you have failed to fulfill your chief purpose for being alive, then your greatest triumph is merely a bubble which quickly bursts.

"What doth it profit a man if he gain the whole world, and suffer the loss of his own soul?" (Matthew 16:26)

Let me never forget, O Lord, why Thou didst create me.

EVERY THOUGHT, WORD AND DEED

In 1916 a British soldier was tossed off a mule. He broke his wrist in the fall, but it healed and he thought no more about it.

After the war, the soldier went to Canada and got a job there as a barber. He worked at this for nearly 30 years, when suddenly his wrist began to stiffen. The condition grew worse,—so much so that he could no longer use that hand to work with. He had to quit his job.

He filed a claim with the British Army for compensation. When they asked for proof of the accident he wrote his regimental association with this unusual request, "Please find me witnesses who saw a mule throw me in 1916." Unbelievably, the association found not just one but two witnesses.

It is often difficult for any of us to recall accurately what happened in the past. But God knows. Keep ever before you that one day you will answer to God for every thought, word and deed of your life.

It should be more than a sobering thought. It should remind you that every hour of every day presents countless opportunities to do something positive and constructive that will be for the glory of God and the good of your fellowman.

"Nothing is covered that shall not be revealed; nor hid, that shall not be known." (Matthew 10:26)

&3 Keep my vision clear, O Lord, that I may always seek first things first.

HE SET FIRE TO FIVE SCHOOLS

In New Orleans, police went on a determined search for a crazed firebug who seemed to have a fanatical hatred for schools. By the time they had caught up with the culprit he had set fire to five public schools, causing $85,000 damage.

When the man was questioned as to why he wanted to destroy these school buildings, he gave a strange reason. He said he had only gone as far as the first grade himself, and that he didn't want to see anybody else get an education.

Whoever harbors bitterness within him not only embitters himself but constantly runs the risk of letting his venom express itself in some ugly way.

Merely trying to hide one's resentment is not enough. No matter how much it is restrained, it is still in the heart and can explode at any time.

On the other hand, if you develop the habit of filling your heart with love, if you learn how to rejoice in the success of others, if you are able to take obstacles and set-backs cheerfully, regardless of where the fault lies, then will you find that what you think, say and do will be a happy expression of your inward peace and joy.

"Out of the abundance of the heart the mouth speaketh." (Matthew 12:34)

&§ Let me so fill my heart with Thy love, O my Redeemer, that it may overflow into the world that needs it so much.

151

TRIBUTE INDEED

Recently, a series of articles has been appearing in "Komsomol Pravda," the newspaper of the Communist Youth League in Moscow, calling for an intensified drive against religion among Russia's youth.

In spite of all efforts to stop what Red officials regarded as an outrage against communism, many young people are taking up religion, attending churches, and even participating on the altar in religious ceremonies.

The paper called upon the League to wake up and put an end to what it calls, "these prejudices and superstitions."

One of the greatest consolations that anyone working on God's side can have is that reverence for his Maker is so deeply imbedded in every human being that it can never be completely eradicated.

Even the most violent atheist, therefore, can never entirely succeed in banishing from his mind, heart and soul the deep-seated conviction that God exists. His very fury in ridiculing God and in waging an incessant battle against religion is perhaps his greatest tribute to the fact that he has within him at least a lingering knowledge of the truth.

"I am with you all days even to the consummation of the world." (Matthew 28:20)

Keep me ever mindful, O my Savior, that I can never lose while working for Thy Truth, regardless of how many difficulties there may be.

THE GOOD IN THE WORST

Last January, four convicts in a Boston prison staged a revolt and held five guards and six fellow prisoners as hostages in a demonstration against what they called "bad prison conditions."

Prison officials finally persuaded the desperadoes to negotiate with them. Entering the cell block where the convicts were holding out, they began their talks.

One of the leaders and spokesmen for the prisoners was Theodore Green, a bank robber. He dramatically presented his side of the controversy, but broke down halfway through.

"I've done a lot of bad things," said Green, whose 16-year-old daughter earlier appealed to him to give up and not to harm the hostages.

"Evil things," he continued, his eyes filled with tears. "My only wish is that some time I might do a good thing. Like giving my eye so that a blind child might see, or my body so that men could understand disease better. Isn't there some way I could do something good?"

Deep in the heart of every human being is the haunting desire to be creative and constructive. God Himself put it there. No matter how low a man, woman or child may sink, regardless of how much he may belittle or ignore his nobler side, this yearning to do good can never be completely eliminated. That is the hope of mankind. That is why you can never completely fail in trying to reawaken the good in the worst.

"Whatsoever you would that men should do to you, do you also to them." (Matthew 7:12)

🙚 Inspire me, O Lord, to do good and avoid evil.

FOR JUSTICE' SAKE

In Pensacola, Fla., a woman indignantly called the Traffic Bureau to make a complaint. She went shopping one day, and parked her car in a zone where there were no traffic meters. When she returned to her car there was a meter in front of it—and, adding insult to injury, a parking ticket stuck in her windshield. She informed officials that she didn't know what had happened, but that she was sure of her sanity. There hadn't been any meter there when she parked the hour before!

It all seemed very strange, but at the woman's insistence, there was nothing to do but investigate. To their surprise they found that the woman had been right. The meters had been installed while her car was parked, and a passing policeman, not knowing this, had given her a ticket.

This mistake was quickly corrected and the good lady forgave the overzealous police. But many just grievances are not so easily adjusted. On the contrary, many go through life as the victims of unfair persecution, cheated out of what is their due or deprived of an advancement that rightfully belongs to them.

You can do much to right such wrongs and also to urge those victimized never to lose heart. One day they will receive their just due. Recall for them the words of Christ:

"Blessed are they that suffer persecution for justice' sake for theirs is the kingdom of heaven."

(Matthew 5:10)

❧ Strengthen me, O Lord, to fight for the just rights of others.

154

18 YEARS OF BAD CONSCIENCE

Eighteen years ago, an 11-year-old boy was rabbit hunting in the woods with a 7-year-old playmate, when the two boys began to quarrel.

The younger boy taunted the older about being such a poor shot. In a passion of anger the bigger boy shot his little friend, killing him instantly.

Terrified at what he had done, the boy invented a clever lie when the police arrived, laying the blame on a mentally retarded 16-year-old boy who had nothing to do with it, but who hadn't the wits to defend himself.

The case was dismissed, but the young murderer's conscience wouldn't let him rest. For eighteen years he lived with his guilt. Recently, he confessed to the authorities what he had done. He said, "The other guy has had a black mark on his record all these years. But I've been living with the actual guilt."

There will always be great hope for the world, no matter how degraded men become. In the very worst is an element of good that can always be revived. That man is always capable of rehabilitation is a constant and stimulating challenge to anyone who would be a Christopher or Christbearer.

The more that you specialize in bringing hope to the hopeless, the more true joy you will bring into your own life. Remember that it was Christ Who said:

"I am not come to call the just, but sinners."

(Matthew 9:13)

🔊 Inspire me, O Lord, to show a special love for sinners.

STARVING IN THE MIDST OF PLENTY

Recently, in Bethlehem, Pa., police were called upon to investigate the whereabouts of an elderly couple who lived in a mountainside home. Neighbors who hadn't seen the couple for some days had begun to worry about them.

On arrival, the police found the couple alive in their house, but huddled in a corner of the bedroom, slowly dying of starvation. No one knows how long they had stayed there in their weak condition, but the surprise lay in the fact that in the old man's hand was clutched a bag containing $2800. And although there was no food in the house, they found the deeds to four lots in the city and a bankbook showing a deposit of $1000.

A case such as this is unusual to be sure. But far more frequent than most realize are the instances of those who are spiritually starved, despite the fact that God has provided abundant ways and means to nourish and sustain them.

You can be God's instrument in relieving the hunger, physical as well as spiritual, of those who live in the midst of abundance and who either do not know how or hesitate to reach out for it.

"The Son of man is come to save that which was lost."
(Matthew 18:11)

FIRST THINGS FIRST

An Indianapolis mother raced for the telephone to call a doctor for her three-year-old son who was dying of meningitis.

When she picked up the receiver the party line was busy. Frantically Mrs. Oran Chastain tried to break in to explain that this was an emergency call. But each time the persons using the line ignored her plea and continued talking.

Mrs. Chastain ran back to see if her baby was still breathing. He was, but it was hardly perceptible. Hoping the line would be clear in the intervening minutes she tried again but the two parties were still talking.

The hysterical woman tried to cut in four times in half an hour but without success.

The boy died minutes after the neighbors hung up.

If these "party-liners" knew they were causing the death of a child by conversing at length on the phone they certainly would have stopped. No doubt, at the moment they thought nothing could be quite as important as the conversation they were having.

But we must be constantly on guard to keep first things first. Insistence on minor issues or issues which touch us personally, when bigger issues are at stake, can cause great havoc in the long run.

In fact, it has been promised us that if we keep first things first that the other things we need will be given us also.

"Seek ye therefore first the kingdom of God and his justice, and all these things shall be added unto you."
                                                                (Matthew 6:33)

ENCOURAGE, DON'T DISCOURAGE

In Milwaukee, Wisc., last winter two policemen were on their beat when they came upon a man shoveling his sidewalk. It was 3:30 A.M. and the policemen took a dim view of this early morning activity even though it was done quietly and without bothering anyone.

The policemen, anxious to fulfill their duty, booked the man on charges of disorderly conduct. But they were in for a surprise when the case was brought before the judge.

Instead of penalizing the man for shoveling his walk, the judge severely reprimanded the officers, and released the man. "What's disorderly about shoveling your sidewalk?" he asked. "A man can shovel his sidewalk anytime he wants to. The city sends out shovels and snowplows at all hours."

Take great care lest you discourage people who are trying to do the right thing simply because they are a little out of step with normal procedure in the way they tackled their task. Belittling or finding fault with others for their tactless methods often stops them from trying at all.

It is far better to praise them for their good will and honest effort—to give credit where credit is due. A kindly Christlike approach frequently helps them to overcome minor defects in reaching a good goal.

"Let the peace of Christ rejoice in your hearts."
(Colossians 3:15)

◄§ Give me the good sense, O Lord, to encourage those who are trying.

TEEN-AGERS' ENTERPRISE

Towards spring of this year the city of Buffalo was suddenly the victim of a severe snowstorm. Traffic moved along at a snail's pace . . . the citizens' spirits fell.

But there were eight youngsters who decided to turn this dismal weather to their advantage. When the snow finally stopped, motoring was difficult. These boys made their way to a notoriously steep incline at the height of the rush-hour, and approached skidding drivers with a grinning, "Push your car for 50 cents, mister?"

Their enterprise paid off for the youngsters. They made an average of $6 every half hour.

Everybody is gifted by God with imagination and resourcefulness. Unfortunately very few take the time and trouble to bring into play this power for good. Taking the line of least resistance, they tend to avoid many opportunities that would improve their lot in this life.

Strive conscientiously to develop the bit of greatness that the Lord has entrusted to you. He has given it to you for a purpose. He has assigned to you a mission in life. He expects you to use your head and heart to find it. If you make a real effort, He will generously aid you.

"And every man shall receive his own reward, according to his own labour." (1 Corinthians 3:8)

❧ Help me to be up and doing for Thy sake, O my Jesus.

MILLIONS OF YEARS AGO

Twenty million years ago a tremendous explosion took place far away in the galaxy of stars creating a new star. So large is this star that it is what scientists call a super-nova. But because of the great distance from the earth, this star, born 20 million years ago, is only now visible from the earth for it has taken that long for its light to travel to earth.

The discovery of the "new" star was made by a Swiss research assistant, Paul Wild, with an 18-inch Schmidt telescope at Palomar Observatory, and has excited scientists the world over.

To give an idea how far away the explosion occurred, one light year is the distance light travels in a year which is six million million miles. Figure for yourself how much distance is equivalent to 20 million years.

The greater our knowledge of the universe becomes, the humbler we should be. Seeing we are a pinpoint in space and a moment in time, we should see more clearly that without God we are nothing.

Our age needs a renewal of humility and a deeper faith in God which shows us our proper significance.

Pray that our leaders will gain this insight and thus lead us aright.

"What is man, that thou art mindful of him; or the son of man, that thou visitest him?" (Hebrews 2:6)

&5 Without Thee, O Lord, we can do nothing, with Thee we can do all things.

HE GAVE THE WRONG ANSWER

In downtown Manhattan, a patrolman who had just gone off duty was making his way home, when he noticed a boy running blindly down the street.

He stopped the youth and inquired where he was going in such a hurry. The boy looked frightened. He replied that he was running to catch the subway. The patrolman's suspicions increased. There was no subway station in that direction.

"Where is the subway?" he asked. At length, the boy had to confess that he didn't know. He looked desperate.

Just then a man came panting down the street. "That's him!" he cried. "That's the one who robbed me of $51." The patrolman took the thief to the nearest police station.

Those who resort to evil pay a high price for the little they gain. Also they seldom have a moment's peace. Only those who are true to God, to themselves and to others know true peace of mind, heart and soul. Christ Himself stressed this when He said:

"The truth will make you free." (John 8:32)

◄§ Grant me such a devotion to Thy truth, O Lord, that I shall suffer anything rather than betray it.

HELP YOURSELF BY HELPING OTHERS

A woman in Springfield, Mass., took her small son to the doctor for a routine check-up.

In the course of the examination, the doctor tried to get the child to open his mouth wide so that he could examine his tonsils. But suddenly junior balked. For some reason he positively refused to open his mouth. Neither pleas nor threats made any impression on him.

Finally the mother tried a little psychology. "Look, dear, it's very easy," she said. As she opened her mouth wide to show the child the doctor couldn't help but see her tonsils. Then he frowned. "Hmmmm," he said to the boy's mother. "Your tonsils will have to come out, too!"

Keep trying to help others regardless of what handicaps or faults you personally may have. All through the Gospels you can read of persons with many defects whom Jesus Christ used as his instruments in reaching others.

But at the same time take care that you make a sincere and continued effort to make yourself a more effective Christopher or Christbearer by removing your defects. One of the best ways to do this is to be generously interested in the shortcomings of others. It is one of many blessings that God bestows on those who strive as best they can to put into practice His command:

"Thou shalt love thy neighbor as thyself."

(Matthew 19:19)

&5 Grant, O Lord, that I may help myself by helping others.

HE NEVER HAD A LICENSE

A policeman in Tulsa, Okla., was prowling around in a squad car, when his attention was attracted by the unusually good driving of a certain motorist. He noticed how deftly the motorist handled his car in the unwieldy traffic. Admiringly, the patrolman followed him for about three blocks, becoming more and more impressed with such good driving.

Finally, he pulled up alongside and stopped the car. He congratulated the man on his driving and asked to see his license. He was curious as to how long this man had been driving. Imagine his great shock when he discovered that the man had been driving for seven years without a license!

Many persons who lead seemingly faultless lives fail to fulfill responsibilities that are vital for the well-being of all.

They feel that little harm is done, for instance, if they do not vote. They do not realize that the stability of a country is weakened just that much by the failure of even one person to live up to the privilege of freedom that God has entrusted to us. Many a country has lost its freedom because too many individuals have evaded their duties. You have it in your power to fulfill your responsibilities.

"There is no power but from God." (Romans 13:1)

᭟ Give me the grace, O Lord, to fulfill all my responsibilities.

THE DEVOTION OF A DOG

A three-year-old boy lives with his mother near the edge of a thick woods in Palmyra, Ill.

One day, his mother gave him permission to play with some of the older children who lived close by. The youngsters started into the woods, the little boy with them. His collie followed at his heels.

It was much later when it was discovered that the small boy had become separated from his companions and was evidently lost. The mother was frantic. To make her fright worse, heavy rains began to fall and gave no sign of stopping.

A search party set out to find the child and his dog. For eight hours they combed the woods in the relentless downpour. When they finally found the boy, he was lying exhausted on the ground. His faithful dog was lying on top of him trying his best to shield him with his body from the cold rain.

The loyalty and devotion that the Creator has put in animals is often a powerful reminder to human beings. Even the least among us have been gifted by God in a far more generous way. Assist those who have a right to our interest and devotion, regardless of the inconvenience or suffering that it may cost.

"Cast thy bread upon the running waters: for after a long time thou shalt find it again." (Ecclesiastes 11:1)

&§ Let me learn, O Lord, to inconvenience myself for others.

PRACTICE WHAT YOU PREACH

There was a touch of irony to a robbery which recently took place in Leicester, England.

Two men entered a movie house one evening and sat through a double feature—"You Can't Get Away With Murder" and "This Side of the Law."

When the two pictures were over they hid themselves while the manager locked up, and then blew the safe open and made away with $3000.

It is understandable that thieves are seldom moved by any amount of moralizing. It is part of their shady business to cultivate a hardened conscience.

But it is a matter of surprise that those who believe in God's truth are so slow in blending it into the mainstream of modern life that needs it so much. They enthuse over books stressing the necessity of applying truth to all spheres of influence. They agree heartily with stirring talks that the followers of the Crucified Savior should seize every opportunity to imitate His sufferings. And yet they will give all sorts of limp excuses for not filling one of the 100,000 teaching posts that are still open in the country.

Those who use the classroom to undermine a nation never complain about "hard work" or "poor pay." Strangely enough they often *practice* the self-sacrifice we *talk* about.

"So *faith also, if it have not works, is dead in itself.*"
(James 2:17)

◄§ O my Savior, let me suffer for Thee, not just talk about it.

THE EVIL SHOW IMAGINATION

From Muncie, Ind., comes the report that jail officials have banned the delivery of hard candy to prisoners.

This unusual ruling was made after it was discovered that someone had sent a prisoner a piece of a hacksaw blade inside a large piece of hard candy.

Those bent on mischief can seldom be charged with apathy or lack of imagination. They are ever on the alert to find ways and means to reach an evil objective. Nothing daunts them. They scarcely notice any difficulties and setbacks. Again and again they push on with new attempts after repeated failures that would discourage anyone else.

Whether the objective is cutting through prison bars or spreading the hatred of God from one end of the globe to the other, the followers of the Devil invariably work like the Devil!

The reason that most good people show a lack of imagination and daring is that they have little or no objective in life beyond avoiding trouble. Leading such a negative existence prevents anyone from touching the bit of greatness that God has put in every human being.

Stir up the power for good within you. You will surprise even yourself. You will find that it is much easier to be a missionary of good than a missionary of evil!

"*Knock and it shall be opened to you.* (Matthew 7:7)

⋙ I believe, O Lord, help Thou my unbelief.

ALERTNESS IS NEEDED

The receptionist at the desk in the outer office was very busy indeed. The want ad for an office boy had brought in many applicants. She would be glad when the position was finally filled.

An alert looking little fellow approached the desk. "If you're applying for the job of office boy, I'm afraid that you'll have to wait your turn," she said with a smile. She pointed to the long row of young men lined patiently outside the door.

The boy smiled back at her. "Oh, yes. I'll wait," he said. "But please, will you give this to the boss right away for me? It's very important." He handed her a note.

The receptionist complied and the note won the boy the job, for it showed the boss that he could use his head. It read, "I'm the last kid in the line. Don't do anything until you see me."

Once those who are for God show as much initiative in making their voices heard for good as those do who are dedicated to disloyalty and corruption, a refreshing change for the better will take place all over the world. The Lord blesses in a special way those who are alert and daring out of love of Him and their fellowman.

"The children of this world are wiser in their generation than the children of light." (Luke 16:8)

ð O Lord, grant me the grace of being daring in all that concerns Thee.

MISSING THE MAIN ISSUE

In Denver, Colo., the members of the police force are photographed annually to be sure that accurate files are maintained.

Not long ago the time came for the photographs to be made, and one by one the policemen sat for the camera. It was only at the end of the week, when all the pictures were made that someone thought to check the camera. It wasn't working—and hadn't been all week.

In our busy, modern world it is easy for most of us to become so preoccupied with incidental details that we forget the main issues.

Some even go through a whole lifetime and yet miss the very purpose of life. It can be a very dangerous hazard to be so taken up with the gadgets of comfortable living that one completely overlooks that this life is merely a stepping stone to eternity.

In your conversations, your letters, articles, classroom work or business discussions, you can perform a valuable missionary service by touching on this subject. If you do no more than help one person to keep first things first, it will count for all eternity.

"In all thy works, remember thy last end and thou wilt never sin." (Ecclesiasticus 7:40)

&5 O Lord, fire me with a desire to help all people to attain the eternal reward Thou hast prepared for them.

DON'T WAIT FOR EMERGENCIES

Last winter near Winona, Minn., two boys, twelve and sixteen, were hunting in the deep woods, when by accident the younger one was shot in the head. The bullet lodged in the lad's brain, and blood gushed in a heavy stream from his forehead.

It was freezing weather, and they were far from any signs of human life. The frightened 16-year-old did what he could. He sat cross-legged on the ground, holding the head of his unconscious victim in his lap. The temperature was 25 degrees, but he stripped himself to the waist and laid his clothes over his friend. Then he sat there for 24 hours holding his thumb against the bullet hole, and praying for help.

A search party found them the following morning. The wounded boy was still alive. His friend's thumb had kept him from bleeding to death.

Emergencies bring out a bit of the greatness that God has put in every human being. Think of the resourcefulness, generosity and nobility that this teen-ager displayed when he realized that the very life of his companion was in jeopardy.

Don't wait for an emergency to bring into play the greatness that is in you. There is something that you can do today, in God's name, to change the world for the better.

"Greater love than this no man hath, that a man lay down his life for his friends." (John 15:13)

❧ Deepen in me, O Lord, the desire to help others.

169

WHEN MEN CORRECT THEMSELVES

A sheriff in Goshen, Ind., was mildly surprised when an old farmer walked into his office and announced that he had come to give himself up. Occasionally criminals voluntarily surrender, but it is the exception rather than the rule. Moreover, this man did not seem to be like the ordinary criminal.

"What have you done?" the sheriff inquired. The man explained that he had stolen a car in 1924.

"Why have you waited so long to come and give yourself up?" the puzzled sheriff queried.

The farmer spoke slowly. "You see, it's this way," he said. "I just became converted to the Lord, and my conscience is beginning to hurt."

Those who strive honestly to live up to God's law make some minor mistakes, it is true. But seldom if ever are they to be found in the ranks of those who make a business of crime, immorality and disloyalty.

One of the chief reasons why there is a trend today toward brutality, corruption and a general moral breakdown is because millions, one by one, have been getting away from religion. You, whoever you are, can do something to bring at least one of them back to God. You will make a big contribution to the peace of the world if you do.

"He must know that he who causeth a sinner to be converted from the error of his way, shall save his soul from death, and shall cover a multitude of sins." (James 5:20)

◁§ O Lord, let me be an apostle of Thy love.

MORE THAN TALK IS NEEDED

A couple of years ago, a department store in London held a widely advertised exhibit on crime-prevention methods conducted by Scotland Yard.

Hundreds of interested citizens crowded the store to watch this world-famous detective force demonstrate its infallible crime-stopping tactics.

During the exhibit a young man calmly walked up to the store's cash register, removed the day's receipts in money, and walked out before anyone was aware of what had happened.

There is more talk today about peace than there has probably been in all history. But for some strange reason, while most do little more than "talk" peace, others who are dedicated to evil are working with the zeal of apostles to spread crime, hatred and death—and right under our very noses. Those beset on mischief are short on words and long on action. They make it their business to concentrate their attention in a very practical way upon the areas of influence that touch the lives of practically everyone: education, government, communications, entertainment and labor relations.

If you make it a point to be a "doer" rather than merely a "talker" you will be blessed by God and man.

"Be ye doers of the word and not hearers only."
(James 1:22)

✿§ O Lord, let me learn once and for all that actions speak louder than words.

A TEEN-AGER SAVES HER MOTHER

A 13-year-old girl in New York found her way to the nearest police station and requested tearfully that they "please stop those people from selling dope to my mother."

The child had connected the strange state her mother sometimes was in with the visit of an unknown man and woman who came to the apartment at regular intervals. She noticed, too, that after they left, it always seemed that something valuable had disappeared. She concluded that these strangers were harming her mother and thought they should be arrested. She was right. The police apprehended the pair and found a great deal of heroin in their possession.

The initiative that this teen-ager took to rehabilitate her own mother is a touching example of the power for good that God has implanted in every young person. Strange circumstances often bring it out, as happened in this case. But the very fact that young people show a deep solicitude in helping others in their own family circle or in the world as far as they can reach, has a double effect. It is God's way of seeing that such a one helps himself by helping others.

"Bear ye one another's burdens and so you shall fulfil the law of Christ." (Galatians 6:2)

⇜§ Inspire teen-agers, O Lord, to be Christbearers in every way they can.

FAME AND FORTUNE CAME AND WENT

A wasted and penniless little old man named Oscar Matthew Nelson died of lung cancer in a Chicago charity ward. "Battling Nelson," they used to call him—and he was one of boxing's finest, a former lightweight champion.

Born in Denmark, he fought his way up from obscurity to win his title in California, July 4, 1908. From that time on he fought 300 fights and made a great deal of money. He said that he gave away much of it, and lost more in bad investments. However it was, this man who had scaled the heights now made a steady descent into poverty and obscurity.

Filled with despair, Nelson went from bad to worse. When he died at 71, there was only the pitiful little collection of newspaper clippings to show that this man had once been one of those who had known world-wide applause.

Most of those who seek fame and fortune realize the painful emptiness of their quest. Think of what a different world we would have today if for everyone with such ambition there was one other person who would strive with equal devotion and singleness of heart to bring God's peace to all mankind. Far from dying in disappointment or despair, such a man would live a rich life here, and a far richer one for all eternity.

"Many that are first shall be last, and the last, first."
(Mark 10:31)

            (Mark 10:31)

⚜ Let me seek only the glory that lasts forever, O Lord.

SANCTIFY THE NEW AND MODERN

A 93-year-old man died recently in Columbus, Ohio. Although he had seen many changes in his long lifetime, he had refused to accept modern methods.

He was suspicious of everything that was new. He used an old-fashioned cistern and hand pump for his water supply. He lighted his small frame house by gaslight. He rode a bicycle until he was 90. But he was well able to afford himself every convenience and comfort, for on his death it was discovered that he had left an estate of well over $100,000.

It was ironic that he should be killed by a "new-fangled contraption." He was run over by an automobile.

Rather than run away from the many new inventions of modern science, we should thank God for every one of them that is good. And we should use them in every way we can for the spread of His love, peace and truth throughout the world.

You can play the role of Christopher or Christbearer by doing whatever is in your power to sanctify twentieth century education, government, literature, entertainment and labor relations.

"The Lord hath given me a tongue for my reward: and with it I will praise him." (Ecclesiasticus 51:30)

✧ Help me, O Lord, to bring out the good in every person and in everything that Thou hast made.

SAFETY FIRST—BODY AND SOUL

The home is the place where the second largest number of fatal accidents occur, according to a recent report by the National Safety Council.

The Council listed these precautions which it would be well for everyone to put into practice:

1. Take extra care of the kitchen. This is the most dangerous room in the house.

2. Keep a window open when using gas appliances.

3. Watch out for slippery floors, rugs, stairways, etc.

4. Watch out for rotting window frames and loose screens.

5. Be careful with cleaning mixtures.

6. Be careful with accessible poisons.

7. Never underestimate your child's curiosity, or agility.

As such precautions can contribute to the physical well-being of the family, so can the spiritual laws of Christ and His Church safeguard the immortal souls of each member of the family for time and for eternity.

The more concerned you are with your spiritual welfare, the more likely you are to show a sensible concern for the body. You then realize that it is the temple of the Holy Spirit.

"Fear ye not them that kill the body, and are not able to kill the soul: but rather fear him that can destroy both soul and body in hell." (Matthew 10:28)

◄§ O God, let me always think, work and pray from the point of view of eternity.

175

WHAT ABOUT THEIR RIGHTS?

A few months ago, the water-works superintendent of a town near Cincinnati was arrested on a disorderly conduct charge.

This 42-year-old man received a bi-monthly check of $136 for his services. For some reason, on one occasion his check did not arrive on time. The man became so angry that he went on a rampage against the city. He turned on every fire hydrant he could reach, completely draining the town's 183,000 gallon supply tank.

People who fly into such tantrums not only make spectacles of themselves, but worse still, they behave in a way that is very unfair to everyone else.

This superintendent had a right to expect his check on time. But certainly, one who is so sensitive about his own rights, ought to be particularly conscious of the rights of others. Instead, he deliberately caused inconvenience and discomfort to many blameless persons who had even more title to their rights than he did to his.

Loving your neighbor as yourself, as Christ commanded, means that each of us should show the same respect and solicitude for the just rights of others as we expect for our own.

"All things therefore whatsoever you would that men should do to you, do you also to them." (Matthew 7:12)

⤐ Keep me, O Lord, as mindful of the interests of others as I am of my own.

HOW IT HURT HIM

In Portsmouth, Ohio, a 35-year-old father felt compelled to spank his small son. He deplored such harsh methods, but he felt that this time it was the only course to take.

Wishing to make his son see that this was a well-deserved punishment, and that he didn't relish doing it, he said, "Son, this is going to hurt me more than it will you."

Little did he realize the truth of this statement. In the middle of the paddling, the father suddenly dislocated his shoulder, and had to be taken to the hospital to have it set!

Many of us make off-hand remarks that we don't expect to be taken too seriously and yet how surprised and shocked we are when our words are taken literally.

It is easy indeed to protest that we love Christ so much that we will suffer anything for Him. And yet, a moment afterwards, we act as if we meant the very opposite, by being impatient with those around us, by dodging responsibility that is rightfully ours or by constantly seeking the creature comforts that quickly bog down anyone who would play the role of a Christbearer.

Let your words come from your heart, not merely from your lips. You will do far more for God as well as for your fellow man, if you do.

"This people honoureth me with their lips: but their heart is far from me." (Matthew 15:8)

&⸱ Let me say what I mean, O Lord, and mean what I say.

THE DUCKS LED HIM TO DEATH

A two-year-old boy was playing on his grandparents' farm in Oklahoma when he delightedly spied a flock of ducks waddling their way to the pond.

The child had never seen ducks before, and he was entranced with the way they walked one behind the other. Playing "follow the leader" he joined the line, gleefully waddling behind them.

The ducks walked into the pond and began swimming. It never occurred to the child that he couldn't do the same. When he tried to swim too, he sank. He drowned before anyone could get to him.

The tragedy of this little tot is being multiplied many times over in different ways throughout the world today. Little ones, lacking the mature judgment that comes only with full development must look to their elders for true guidance. This is as God intended it.

But if those who should care for them fail to give them the right patterns, they are thereby abandoning their impressionable minds and hearts to the deceits of those who would lead them astray.

There is something that you can do to see that millions of children are provided with their God-given right to proper home life, teaching, literature and entertainment.

"He that shall scandalize one of these little ones that believe in me, it were better for him that a millstone should be hanged about his neck, and that he should be drowned in the depth of the sea." (Matthew 18:6)

⊷ Let me show a special solicitude for children, O Lord.

THE FOOTPRINTS OF GOD

A traveler was sitting outside his tent in the Sahara Desert one evening talking with his young Bedouin guide about the meaning of life. The guide was convinced that the universe was designed and ruled by an all-wise Being. The traveler objected: "But nobody can know for certain that there is a God."

Pointing to a track of footprints in the sand, the lad asked: "What would you say made those marks?" "Why a man, of course," the traveler replied.

"Well then," the boy said, pointing to the starry sky. "When I see the sun and the moon and the starry heavens in their beauty, I know for certain that the Creator has passed this way. They are the footprints of God."

The Creator of the universe has filled the world with wonders. And yet it is easy to go through life without appreciating them.

Make it your business to see the beauty and goodness that God has put in both men and nature. See in all of it a reflection of His truth, beauty, and goodness. Let each bit of it be a continuing reminder of the reward that will be yours for eternity if you do God's will on earth.

"Eye hath not seen, nor ear heard, neither hath it entered into the heart of man, what things God hath prepared for them that love Him." (1 Corinthians 2:9)

᠊ᣟ Let me share with others the joy that is mine in knowing Thee, O Lord.

PREVENT THE WRANGLING

A police officer in St. Louis was invited by the parents' association of a local high school to give a talk on the problem of juvenile delinquency. Anxious to be of service, he carefully prepared what he felt would be a constructive discourse.

When he arrived at the meeting, he was asked to wait a few minutes so that the group could elect officers. But the few minutes lengthened into an hour as the election became a heated dispute, with much table-pounding and wrangling.

"What about my speech?" the bewildered Corporal asked timidly. But no one paid any attention to him. In their stormy quarrelling, the parents had completely forgotten the scheduled talk.

Many splendid organizations defeat the very purpose for which they were started by allowing their meetings to degenerate into controversial gatherings instead of focusing attention on a positive, constructive program.

If this failing prevails in some organization to which you belong, don't stay away from the meetings on that account. Let it be added reason why you should attend and do your bit to see that deliberations are kept on a high plane and do not sink to the level of needless bickering that accomplishes little good.

"Watch ye, and pray that ye enter not into temptation. The spirit indeed is willing, but the flesh is weak."

(Matthew 26:41)

≼§ Let me be Thy instrument, O Lord, in bringing peace where there is much wrangling.

THE FAITH OF GREAT SCIENTISTS

The great scientists saw God in their work. Humbled by the truths that were made apparent to them in their laboratories, the best of them were of religious temperament. They themselves attributed this to their scientific work.

Newton, Pascal, Pasteur, Copernicus, Galileo, and many others were men of deep faith.

Kepler, the founder of modern astronomy said: "O God, I am thinking Thy thoughts after Thee."

Pascal kept the New Testament with him as a constant companion and unfailing comfort.

Gauss, one of the greatest mathematicians of all time, said: "There are problems to whose solution I should attach infinitely greater importance than to those of mathematics, for example, touching ethics, or our relation to God, or concerning our destiny and our future."

One of the best ways to keep your own life God-centered is to bring a consciousness of Him into as many other lives as you can reach. By playing the role of a Christbearer you can be the "connecting-link" between God and those who are groping for Him.

Try in a particular way to stir up a sense of reverence for the Father of All among those who are in such influential fields as education, government, communications and labor relations. The more they respect God, the more likely they are to fulfill their responsibilities conscientiously.

"Thou shalt love the Lord thy God with thy whole heart." (Deuteronomy 6:5)

ᴥ Help me, O God, to reach many with Thy truth and love.

YOU WIN BY LOSING

Sophocles, the great Greek playwright, centuries ago wrote a story that shows the courage of one individual in proclaiming a power higher than the state.

The story is about a woman named Antigone, whose brother died in battle, and because of a feud with the King of Thebes was refused a decent burial. Deliberately disobeying the king's orders, Antigone buried her brother herself and so was brought to trial.

"You dared to break my command?" the king thundered at her. But Antigone answered calmly, "Yes, for it was not God Who gave this order. I did not believe that your edicts had such force that you, a mere man, could thwart the unwritten and unchanging laws of God. These are not matters of today or yesterday, but are of all time."

On the way to her death she cried: "Behold, oh Lord of Thebes, how I, the last remnant of a royal race suffer because I am faithful to the Laws of Heaven."

You will find many an opportunity to take a stand for truth when those in high position take it upon themselves to violate the basic moral law. It will not always be easy to speak up for fundamental justice when those in positions of influence flout it. But you will have deep consolation knowing that by suffering as Christ did that truth might prevail, you will be honoring God and rendering a great service to countless individuals.

"He that humbleth himself shall be exalted."

(Matthew 23:12)

◄§ Give me the courage, O Lord, to speak up for truth regardless of the cost.

SEVEN CENTS FOR THE FIRE CHIEF

Six-year-old Barbara Fichandler spent nearly an hour imprisoned in an elevator in a New York apartment before being released by the Fire Department.

Little Barbara had been quite correct in pushing the button to stop at her floor, but for some strange reason the elevator shuttled back and forth several times between the seventh floor and the basement before it finally stuck between the fifth and sixth floors.

In desperation the little girl rang the alarm bell and within a short time the firemen who had been summoned were able to liberate the bewildered youngster.

So relieved was Barbara at being rescued by the firemen that she wanted to show them her complete gratitude. Brushing away a few tears she emptied the contents of her little purse and handed the entire amount to the battalion chief. It was a total of seven cents—one nickel and two pennies.

No matter how small your expression of appreciation may be, make sure to show it as sincerely and completely as you can to those who have helped you.

Giving credit where credit is due does much to bring the peace of Christ into the home, classroom, office, club or among individuals. One day when you stand before God, you will expect Him to do justice to you. You can do the same for others right now.

"The Son of man shall come in the glory of his Father with his Angels, and then will he render to every man according to his works." (Matthew 16:27)

&§ O God, let me always be thankful to Thee and to all who have helped me.

FOUR HUNDRED THOUSAND
BROKEN HOMES

Today, the United States has the highest divorce rate in the world—four hundred thousand each year.

Anything that undermines the sanctity of the home is promoting the results that the Nazis sought years ago and that the Communists seek today. In a free society, the home, the family, has always been the basic social unit. Our form of government depends on the permanence of marriage and the home for its very survival. A mere glance at the sad results of broken homes is a disturbing one:

1. Six million children in the U.S. come from broken homes.
2. A hundred thousand illegitimate babies are born every year.
3. One million children suffer personality disorders.
4. Another four hundred thousand are brought into court each year on charges of juvenile delinquency.

Don't stand by and let this increasing breakdown of the home continue to take place under your very eyes. Do something about it! Discover for yourself some steps that you can take to ward off one divorce, to mend one broken marriage, to take a Christlike interest in some young person who has been deprived through no fault of his own of the proper home influence that God intended he should have.

It is impossible to have peace in the world if the peace and order of Christ does not reign in the home.

"Glory to God in the highest; and on earth peace to men of good will." (Luke 2:14)

THE POLICE CAME TO THE WEDDING

A 21-year-old man in Hagen, Germany, decided to get married. His fiancée had consented, and the day had been set. There was only one problem. He had no money with which to finance a wedding party.

This enterprising young man was not going to let this stop him. He broke into two shops and made away with enough liquor, cakes and coffee to give all the guests a wedding feast. There was only one unhappy incident to mar the wedding festivities. The police came to the party too!

The groom received a three-year suspended sentence.

There is a growing tendency on the part of many to take the property of others whenever they get in a pinch themselves. While people should be protected when, through no fault of their own, they meet with misfortunes, that does not mean that they have any right to take the law in their own hands and violate the rights of others.

Almighty God made it clear that those who have possessions, great or small, have obligations to others less fortunate. That is part of their responsibility as Christians. At the same time, He specified in the following commandment, given to Moses on Mt. Sinai, that one should not have even a lingering desire to take what rightfully belongs to another.

"Thou shalt not covet thy neighbour's house: neither shalt thou desire his wife, nor his servant, nor his handmaid, nor his ox, nor his ass, nor any thing that is his."
(Exodus 20:17)

185

THE HIGH PRICE OF DISHONESTY

A man in Mexico City was approached by a friend with the offer of an unusual bribe. He was asked by the friend to serve a term in jail for him, and offered him the sum of $4 for his pains.

Being very poor, and obviously not very bright, the man accepted the bribe, and went to jail. But soon he found that the price was too high to pay. The term was quite a long one, and he chafed to be free again. So he told the whole story to the officials.

The officials planned to prosecute the true offender, but they told the unhappy inmate that he too would have to remain in jail—serving his own term—for impersonation.

Those who cooperate in the dishonesties of others usually pay a high price. Quite apart from the peace of conscience that they lose, it frequently happens that they find themselves in far more trouble than they bargained for.

In these days when violations of the truth, both small and large, are causing harm to the home, government, education, labor and business, you can perform an important service by championing that basic honesty that God expects of each individual.

It is impossible to have true peace in the world, while dishonesty prevails. So you can be a real peacemaker by striving at all times to replace error with truth.

"A thief is better than a man that is always lying: but both of them shall inherit destruction."

(Ecclesiasticus 20:27)

⋙ Help me, O Jesus, to be true to Thee, true to myself and true to my fellowman.

BE PATIENT WITH THE YOUNG

In a high-school science class one boy asked the teacher, "Don't you think that a hundred years from now science will take the place of religion?"

The teacher's answer was direct. "It never will," she said. She proceeded briefly to show how religion and science were on different planes. "Science tells us a great deal about the world, but it does not tell us *everything*. Science gives us only a *partial* and *proximate* explanation of reality. The information it gives us must be completed by the data of philosophy and religion."

The boy looked thoughtful and murmured, "I think you've got something there." In her letter to us, the teacher said: "A week never passes when there is not an opportunity to guide some child's thought into the right channels."

More often than not, teen-agers respond generously to both parents and teachers who take the time and trouble to listen patiently to their problems and then give them the sympathetic guidance that God intended they should have.

It helps young people sink their roots deep if those in the home, the church and the school instill in them convictions that are anchored in the immutable truths of God.

"Heaven and earth shall pass away, but My word shall not pass away." (Mark 13:31)

◄§ Grant me, O Lord, an understanding love of teenagers.

187

HOPE IS CONTAGIOUS

If at any time we are apt to feel that there is no hope for
our nation and the world, it would be well to remember
that our nation and the world has outlasted many dire
predictions through the years. Here are some samples:

"All is darkness and despair. As a nation we are at the
bottom of the hill." (Detroit Free Press—1837)

"Nothing in this country is safe, solvent or reliable."
(Philadelphia Gazette—1857)

"Collapse is a grim reality. The days of the Republic
are numbered." (New York World—1873)

"On every hand there is depression, wreck and ruin.
We can't go much farther." (New Orleans Picayune—
1893)

"The old ship of state is sinking. Even Morgan is using the subway." (Wall Street Journal—1907)

It is difficult to avoid, especially in our times, the dangers of extreme cynicism and its very opposite—a foolish
optimism that ignores dangers and is an open invitation
to disaster.

No matter how dismal the outlook may be, there is
always hope if you put faith in Christ and do something
in a positive, constructive way to improve a situation.
Merely complaining or criticizing accomplishes little or
nothing. A prayer, a word or a deed to remedy the trouble is a step in the right direction. It is a hopeful sign—
and there is something contagious about the virtue of
hope.

*"In thee, O Lord, have I hoped, let me never be con-
founded."* (Psalms 30:2)

⌇ Grant me the grace, O Holy Spirit, to keep on trying
even when there seems no hope.

SHE FOOLED HIM FOR EIGHT YEARS

Twenty-five years ago a businessman in London hired a woman as typist and bookkeeper. The young woman proved to be so willing and efficient that she won promotion after promotion.

As the years went by, she so won the confidence of her employer that finally she was promoted to the position of managing director of a company branch, and promised further promotions when he retired. It seemed to this man that he had found the "perfect" employee.

Imagine his surprise, when it was discovered that she had taken advantage of his faith in her to make away with $22,400 of the company funds!

For eight years, this woman had been forging checks in her employer's name and cashing them at the bank.

It is possible to deceive those who trust us in small and large things. But it is not so with God. Some jump to the conclusion that because He does not visit them with punishment immediately, they are safely eluding any reckoning for their evil thoughts, words and deeds.

But the day of final accounting inevitably comes. Each of us will stand alone before the judgment seat of God to render an account of our stewardship.

"With him is strength and wisdom: he knoweth both the deceiver, and him that is deceived." (Job 12:16)

⊷ Help me so to live, O my God, that I may be always ready to die.

MARK TWAIN WAS FORGOTTEN

A three-story building which had stood for 114 years in Greenwich Village, N.Y., was recently razed to the ground to make way for a large apartment building.

The old house was a landmark. It was once the home of Mark Twain. Samuel Clemens (Twain's real name) wrote his memoirs there, and Washington Irving is said to have been a frequent visitor. For this reason the Greenwich Village Chamber of Commerce felt that it was worthy of saving for posterity, and they initiated a drive to raise $70,000 to set the house up in another site, and turn it into a historical museum.

But the plan failed. They were unable to raise the necessary funds. When it was necessary for the house to be removed, they had only managed to raise $203, of which only $3 had been contributed by New Yorkers.

Men and women of far less merit than Mark Twain strive over a lifetime to gain a bit of fame that often vanishes into thin air two days after they are buried. They pay a high price for a very flimsy and fleeting reward.

You would do well to pay little or no attention to the very elusive prizes that the world offers and concentrate, instead, on the true, enduring and deeply satisfying rewards that God has promised for all eternity to those who do His will here on earth.

"Lay up to yourselves treasures in heaven: where neither the rust nor moth doth consume, and where thieves do not break through, nor steal." (Matthew 6:20)

⚜ Keep me ever aware, O Lord, that my final destination is heaven.

ADMITTING THE GOOD AND THE BAD

John Holmes, 31-year-old salesman, told the plain truth in a classified advertisement he ran in a Connecticut paper, describing his farm. He frankly told the reader the good and the bad points of the 100-year-old farm.

Holmes said he had several calls from persons who wanted to take a look at the property after reading the following ad:

"Ramshackle farm; for direct sale from the owner (realtors just laugh!) at fancy price, forty acres of pine oak and black snakes. Old World charm includes sagging floors, tortuous stairway and draughty fireplaces. Located in Higganum (ugh) Conn. If you think this ad is funny, wait until you see this farm. Telephone. If a hollow laugh answers, don't hang up—that will be the owner."

There is a great tendency in our day to overplay and exaggerate. But in the end dishonest or slanted advertising defeats itself. True humility and honesty in estimating oneself or one's products are not only pleasing to God but to man as well.

Those in advertising and public relations are in a position to do great good by being honest. Do what you can to use modern techniques to best advantage by always adhering to truth and justice.

"And the publican, standing afar off, would not so much as lift up his eyes towards heaven; but struck his breast saying: 'O God, be merciful to me a sinner' . . . I say to you, this man went down into his house justified."
(Luke 18:13-14)

⊷ Help me, O Lord, to be honest and to avoid deception in my daily life.

CRITICISM USUALLY HELPS

On the wall of a New York businessman's office one may read this interesting sign:

"My competitors do more for me than my friends do; my friends are too polite to point out my weaknesses, but my competitors go to great expense to advertise them.

"My competitors are efficient, diligent and attentive; they make me search for ways to improve my products and services.

"My competitors would take my business away from me, if they could; this keeps me alert to hold what I have.

"If I had no competitors I would be lazy, incompetent, inattentive; I need the discipline they enforce upon me.

"I salute my competitors; they have been good to me. God bless them all!"

Most people make a mistake by dodging criticism. More often than not that is the disguise in which God sends his blessings. It is human of us to want others to see only our good points. But it is a sign that a man is deepening his spiritual roots when he not only takes criticism in stride, but still more, risks it when certain principles are at stake.

If you are sincerely interested in bringing the love and truth of Christ into the marketplace—in being a Christopher or Christbearer—then you will see in every criticism a blessing.

"And whosoever doth not carry his cross and come after me, cannot be my disciple." (Luke 14:27)

Let me see in every cross, O Lord, an opportunity to improve myself.

YOUR HIDDEN POWER

A well-known gasoline company in a recent advertisement told car owners, "Your engine may be 15% more powerful than you think." The ad went on to explain that this undiscovered power, known as "captive power" is "trapped by the steady accumulation of lead and carbon deposits," and that it is possible to release this power so that it will work for and not against the car.

If unreleased, the deposits, we are told, will build up on the spark plugs—sometimes in a very short time—and cause a short-circuit and the engine to miss.

With far more force can the same poignant reminder be directed to practically every individual. There is little danger of exaggeration in saying to you, for instance: "You have a great hidden power that has scarcely been touched."

Many, if not most people, go through life and never uncover the great force for good that God has put in their heart, mind and soul. Furthermore, the failure to put this power to use creates many problems within them. It breeds a stagnation, dissatisfaction, frustration and cynicism, which cuts down even the little power that has been developed.

The best way to overcome this danger is to keep reaching out as far and as fast as you can with God's love and truth.

"I am come that they may have life, and may have it more abundantly." (John 10:10)

Let me learn to help myself by helping others, O Lord.

ADRIFT FOR 46 DAYS

A 28-year-old man set out in a dinghy for a fishing trip off the tip of Cape York peninsula in the northern-most part of Australia. But a storm suddenly arose in which he lost both paddles and drifted out to sea.

Soon he was stranded far out in the ocean, with no way of sending an S.O.S. or of steering his small vessel back to shore.

For 46 days he drifted—farther and farther away from where he started. He was weak and worn, and his hunger was intense. He managed to exist on seaweed and rain water which he caught in a cup. Once he was lucky enough to catch a small shark, and he forced himself to chew the raw meat carefully and swallow it.

Finally, the little boat drifted towards a strange shore. He was found suffering from malnutrition and exposure, on the shore of Cairns, Australia, 930 miles from his place of departure.

The voyage through life often seems as difficult and hopeless to those who are not blessed with the faith that God intended should buoy up one and all from cradle to grave.

Do all in your power to reach those who are drifting aimlessly on the sea of life and remind them of the why and wherefore of their existence. The whole concept of life takes on real meaning when one understands why he is here and where he is going.

"What shall I do that I may receive life everlasting?"
(Mark 10:17)

&§ Let me bring Thy truth, O Lord, to those who are groping for it.

82 SNAKES IN THE BASEMENT

A farmer in Ferrara, Italy, was startled one night to see four snakes crawling along his kitchen floor. It is quite possible that a single snake may find its way into a house, but when four of them suddenly appear it is time to investigate.

The farmer killed the four snakes, and then looked around to see how they could have gotten in. He decided that they must have come up from the cellar, so he pulled away some bricks to see if he could find their place of entrance.

He found more than he expected. When he was finally certain that he had gotten rid of all of them, he had killed 82 non-poisonous snakes, some of them more than four feet long. The snakes evidently had been hibernating in the wall all winter.

Like these snakes, evil has a way of being so inconspicuous that it can throw most people off guard. Serious trouble is often about to break just at the very time that those who would be the most harmed take the attitude: "What I don't know can't hurt me."

The best way to protect the home, church, school and government is to be so active in strengthening weaknesses and in curing defects that there is little opportunity for evil to settle down.

"Take ye heed, watch and pray. For ye know not when the time is." (Mark 13:33)

☙ Let me work so hard for good, O Lord, that there will be no room for evil.

THAT LINGERING GOODNESS

The city police of Fredericksburg, Va., were puzzled by the peculiar antics of a well-dressed man who loitered in front of the police station.

He lit one cigarette after another. He walked around the block again and again. Then he stopped in front of the station, puffing furiously on a cigarette. Suddenly, as though finally having made a definite decision, he put out the cigarette, and walked determinedly into the station. He identified himself, and then explained that he had come to give himself up for a $150 robbery he had committed in a Miami, Florida, café.

There is always hope for even the worst of men so long as the voice of conscience is not completely ignored.

One of the deep satisfactions that can come to parents who have instilled in their children a deep reverence for God and religion is the staying power that it gives them all through their lives. Even though they may drift into trouble, the lingering goodness within them reminds them that they can still cooperate with God in rehabilitating themselves.

"I do believe, Lord; help my unbelief." (Mark 9:23)

A RUNAWAY BALLOON

An 11-year-old French boy was curiously inspecting the apparatus of a large observation balloon at a Paris fair when the wind suddenly snapped the rope holding it to the ground.

In a matter of seconds, the balloon was hundreds of feet in the air and slowly disappearing into the dark clouds. As the boy carefully peered over the side of the basket in which he was riding, he could see the figures of his parents rushing for help.

At ground level it was suggested that the Air Force send up a plane to shoot down the bag. This radical move was quickly voted down.

Just when the boy's parents and police were mapping another way to get the youngster down safely, word arrived that the "pilotless" balloon had landed 20 miles away and that the boy was safe.

There is little chance of young people being spirited away from their parents' hands in this way, thank God. But in many ways their minds, hearts and souls can be taken away from the sound truths of Christ that fathers and mothers strive to nurture in them.

Do what you can to see that young people in America are so rooted in divine truths that they will not be whisked away by any false doctrines.

"He that shall scandalize one of these little ones that believes in me, it were better for him that a millstone should be hanged about his neck, and that he should be drowned in the depth of the sea." (Matthew 18:6)

BEETLES NEARLY WRECK A CATHEDRAL

Tiny beetles, about a third of an inch long, have eaten so deeply into the beams of Westminster Abbey in London, that the roof might have caved in within two years had not the damage been discovered.

The dangerous damage to the rafters was accidentally found by workmen who were repairing stone parapets which had been eaten away by London's acid smoke over the years.

Officials said the beams were riddled with tunnels dug by the beetles which have also bored their way into many of Britain's historical relics.

Westminster Abbey was begun about 1220 and the great nave was completed approximately 300 years later.

This startling example of what little beetles can do is a further reminder of the power of the individual. As they almost wrecked a cathedral, so the individual can wreck a government or any institution he sets his hand to wreck. All he has to do is quietly to get into the vital spots and exert his influence on others there. To work, thus, slowly and "in the dark" is a more effective method than by armies and bombs.

The reverse, thank God, is also true. A nation can be strengthened and saved by the same method. To have good people in government, education and other vital spheres of influence is still more important than cleaning out the "beetles," important as this is.

"He that contemneth small things, shall fall by little and little." (Ecclesiasticus 19:1)

⋙ Reveal to me the power Thou hast put in me, O Lord.

THEY TAUNTED HIM TO DEATH

Nine-year-old Johnny Urso's playmates kept daring him to touch a 23,000-volt transmission wire near his home in Halifax, Nova Scotia. But the spry youngster refused to take such a dangerous risk.

Eventually, he became irritated at the jibes of cowardice hurled at him by his playmates so the youngster agreed to show his daring and scrambled up the spire of steel.

Each step was followed by a cheer and Johnny began to feel quite brave. Soon he was at the top looking down at his buddies. Then without a moment's hesitation he touched the deadly wires. The shock threw his body several feet in the air and it landed on the bed of wires. It took rescuers an hour to remove him from the tower and he died the following day of third degree burns.

One weakness which afflicts most of us from youth to old age is being "afraid of what others think." Once we lose the courage of our own convictions and are dominated by human respect, we betray our best interests. Also we deprive others of the example and inspiration that might help them to take a brave stand themselves.

Stick to your principles and you will be blessed by God and man. You may never know until you stand at the Tribunal of the Almighty the far-reaching good that you may have done by one act of true courage.

"Thou shalt not follow the multitude to do evil."
(Exodus 23:2)

⊷ Keep me ever reminded, O Lord, that Thou art the Judge to whom I must one day render an account of my entire life.

POVERTY AMIDST 5000 SILVER DOLLARS

Even though a 57-year-old St. Paul, Minn., depot gate-man died in a ramshackle $4.50-a-week room, he had enough money to live comfortably for the rest of his life.

An estimated 5000 silver dollars were among the money discovered in the man's dark, grimy room. Fellow employees said he bought all the dollar coins that came into the Great Northern depot in Minneapolis.

Living in extreme poverty, the man also had $10,600 in United States Savings Bonds and some $400 in currency and a container filled with zinc pennies. The dollars were stuffed in coffee cans, cigar boxes and a suitcase.

So great had been the poor man's attachment to his treasure that he deprived himself of ordinary comforts. He had become his own worst enemy.

While few persons would go to such an extreme, many do find themselves becoming slaves to material possessions of one kind or another. Starting off with a very legitimate desire for personal security, more than a few individuals become so engrossed in acquiring physical advantages that they lose a sense of balance and soon become possessed by their possessions.

One of the safest ways to keep a proper sense of proportion is to follow the advice of Jesus Christ to show as much interest in the well-being of others as you do in your own. Here is the way He put it:

"Whatsoever you would that men should do to you, do you also to them." (Matthew 7:12)

◄§ Inspire me, O Lord, to be as concerned for the needs of others as I am for my own.

200

IN THE DEEP STORMY WATERS

An English fishing boat was caught in a storm which sent most of the other boats scurrying for port. Captains of three vessels thought fishing would be bad until the storm subsided.

But there was one captain—Ted Hubbard—who thought otherwise. He told his crew to lower the nets at the height of the storm.

When Hubbard's trawler, the Chrysolite, steamed back to its home port of Grimsby, onlookers were surprised and thought the boat was damaged since it had been at sea only 48 hours. Then the looks of surprise gave way to gasps as a catch of 14,000 pounds of cod was unloaded which brought a price of $1500.

The captain said he filled his ship during the storm and became so loaded down with fish that he had to head back.

Christ often expects us to go into stormy waters as we journey through life. If we refuse, our "take" will be small. Too many, failing to understand this, remain in the "shallows" all their lives and never accomplish very much.

We can be over-cautious or timid when we should be bold and forward-looking. There are some things which will be won only by forceful and courageous action.

Get out into the mainstream of life and the results will always be surprising. You need not fear the cost, for if your purpose is good, God will see you through.

"Launch out into the deep, and let down your nets."

(Luke 5:4)

Lord, give me the strength to be daring in helping others.

FREEDOM'S PRICE

On July 4, 1776, John Hancock, the President of Congress and delegate from Massachusetts, was the first to sign the Declaration of Independence; and he did it with gusto. Grasping the pen, he wrote his name in letters so large and sweeping that since that day "John Hancock" has meant signature.

As Hancock signed he exclaimed: "There! John Bull can read that without spectacles, and may he double his reward of five hundred pounds for my head. That is my defiance!" Then, realizing the gravity of the moment, he added: "We must be unanimous—there must be no pulling apart—we must all hang together."

"Yes," quipped Benjamin Franklin. "We must indeed all hang together, or assuredly we shall all hang separately."

Few Americans today are aware of the bravery displayed by the early pioneers of our nation. Because they dared to risk so much, we enjoy freedom today. And centuries before the founding of America, the Christian martyrs gladly gave their lives that millions yet to be born might be free to fulfill their one big mission here on earth: to know, love, and serve God in this life so as to be happy with Him forever in the next.

"The truth shall make you free." (John 8:32)

SIX SOPHOMORES LEARN A LESSON

When six Rutgers sophomores painted a statue of the Princeton tiger and daubed the door of the Nassau Tavern they never thought they'd be writing thousands of constructive words about their escapade.

Each had to write a 2000 word essay titled, "My own views on the premeditated and deliberate defacement of public and private property." And the assignment wasn't handed out by one of their professors. The judge that heard the case invoked this penalty, plus a $15 fine on each boy.

The school-spirited boys painted the statue and door during a pep rally prior to the Princeton-Rutgers football game. When Borough Judge Paul R. Chesebro asked them why they did it, one student replied, "We thought it was Princeton property."

The judge gave them little over a week to produce the essays which had to be sent in original form—no carbons—to the deans of both schools, the borough treasurer, court, engineers' bureau and the Princeton police department.

It is well for us all to pause and reflect on the obligation to respect rights of others. It is a serious one, for, in effect, wrecking property is the same as stealing or cheating. We ought to remember that any defaced or destroyed property has been paid for by someone—donors or taxpayers.

We would seldom think of defacing property, if we were motivated by a love of all men out of love of God.

"But above all these things have charity."

(Colossians 3:14)

THE BUS DRIVER TOOK A WALK

A driver of an Indianapolis bus was reaching the end of his patience trying to tell his passengers that the bus would not stop until it reached the end of the line.

What perplexed the driver was that the bus was plainly marked as a "North Meridian Express" but the passengers kept buzzing to get off before it reached its North Side stops. Each time somebody buzzed, the driver stopped and explained slowly and emphatically that "This is an express bus."

Seeing that his words were having no effect, the driver stopped the vehicle, turned to the passengers and announced: "I guess this is as good a time as any to quit."

With that he picked up his coin changer and walked off the bus leaving the flabbergasted passengers to change to other buses.

It is easy to place blame in this story on either the bus driver or on the passengers. It can serve us well, nevertheless, to show us how a multiplication of little annoyances and lack of courtesy is in miniature a picture of what is happening on a world-wide scale today. The peace of the world is in danger because of a few who refuse to consider the good of all.

Remember that the peace of the world starts with you. Ultimately, it is nothing but the sum-total of acts of consideration and courtesy shown by individuals at home, in the office, on the street and elsewhere. Start today to add your part to the peace of the world and thus to eliminate these things that destroy it.

"Be kind one to another; merciful, forgiving one another, even as God hath forgiven you in Christ."

(Ephesians 4:32)

AN ALMOST PERFECT FORGER

Many people have natural talents at their disposal but never take time to develop them for good purposes.

A 17-year-old Buffalo, N. Y., boy, for instance, was accused of forging a driver's license so well that the judge told him he was wasting his talent.

The youth forged the State Motor Vehicle Bureau seal on his junior operator's license so exactly that the judge said it was "unbelievable—almost perfect."

"This is a wasted talent," the judge told the boy. "You should be getting money with this type of ability."

The teen-ager also forged a birth certificate to obtain a license under a fictitious name after his original license had been revoked after three violations.

God gives our youth their talents and abilities. But He leaves it to us to supply them with the proper teaching and guidance to use them well. In failing to do this we fail God as well as our young.

Much of our delinquency problem can be reduced to a failure of adults to recognize the energy that lies stagnant in youth and which is looking for a constructive outlet. Outlets must be found for youthful energy or it will seek illicit or destructive channels.

Give our young people vision and proper guidance and they will repay us well in bringing new zest and new ideals to our tired old world.

"Know that your labor is not in vain in the Lord."
(1 Corinthians 15:58)

ENCOURAGE, DON'T DISCOURAGE

It was April Fool's Day in Newton, Mass., and pedestrians glanced with amusement at the old brown wallet lying on the sidewalk. They weren't going to be taken in by it. Around the corner there was sure to be some youngster waiting to laugh at the first one who picked it up.

But along came 15-year-old Donald Burke who hadn't yet acquired the suspicious nature of adults. He picked up the wallet, despite the belittling smiles of onlookers. Their contemptuous looks quickly turned to shocked amazement when Donald opened it up before them and found it contained $78. The wallet was traced to its owner, and the boy was given a $5 reward.

One of the great obstacles met by those who wish to be Christbearers is the "cold water" treatment that they often get from their own family or closest friends. By a smirk, a discouraging or disdainful remark, the beginnings of what might have been a lifetime of apostolic action can be stifled.

Make it your business to encourage the slightest effort on the part of the young or old to take one step in the right direction.

"He that is not with me is against me."

(Matthew 12:30)

SAVED BY AN OLD INJURY

A rattlesnake had just dug its fangs into the leg of newsman Jim Morton as he tramped across a North Carolina field. It was impossible to call a doctor because a hurricane had blown down all telephone lines.

Morton's buddy applied a tourniquet and used what medication was handy in a kit. The next day, the newspaperman was taken to a hospital where he began to recover.

Doctors puzzled over his condition and said it was almost unbelievable that he had survived. Upon examination, though, they found that an injury to the bitten leg during the last war saved his life. The circulation in that limb was so poor that it prevented the venom from spreading through Morton's body.

The story is a good reminder of the part that our handicaps and difficulties can, perhaps not in so spectacular a way as in the case of Jim Morton, be turned into advantages.

Those who see their difficulties as a challenge usually go farthest in life, and do the most good. Some of the "greats" in history have been in ill health, lame, blind, or poor. They probably became great because they were handicapped.

You will find obstacles every time you try to do right. They are not there to stop us but to be turned into accomplishments. Expect some troubles in your undertakings, but trust in God and you will contribute much to change the world for the better.

"Enter in at the narrow gate, for wide is the gate and broad is the way that leads to destruction."

(Matthew 7:13)

GOOD INTENTIONS NOT ENOUGH

Can you imagine anyone seeing a brush fire closing in on a heavily populated residential area and then neglecting for a whole hour to call the fire department?

Well, that is actually what happened. This man, with the best of intentions, saw the fire all right. But for some strange reason he let an hour go by before frantically phoning the fire station. Fortunately, someone else had reported the blaze and the firemen were now returning from it.

Curious about the man's belated hurry the firemen asked him why he had not called sooner. The man replied:

"I intended to call earlier, but I forgot all about it. But I thought you'd want to know."

An old expression reminds us that "hell is paved with good intentions." Good intentions are far from enough. They must be matched by performance.

So many with high ideals and ability are often distracted and lost in their own small worlds. If they took the steps to come back to the big world God had made they would no doubt make a great contribution toward solving the problems that convulse mankind.

There is a point where analyzing and rationalizing should stop and effective action should begin. God will help those who launch out and try. He will make up for their deficiencies.

Begin today to take one step toward making the world a better place because you have been in it.

"Be ye doers of the word and not hearers only."

(James 1:22)

CLOCK WATCHERS HURT THEMSELVES

A Berlin policeman was crossing the street when a robber raced by him with the victimized store manager in hot pursuit.

To the surprise and chagrin of hundreds of onlookers, the policeman didn't make a move. The robber got away and the police department was flooded with calls by indignant citizens.

Called before his superiors, the policeman explained that when the robber rushed by him he had just three minutes of duty remaining that day. He was sure he couldn't capture the robber in that time, so he didn't even try.

This reasoning didn't impress police officials. They jailed the time-conscious cop for seven weeks.

Clock-watchers never accomplish much either for themselves or for others. Usually, they are so busy measuring out what belongs to them—their time, their money, their energy—that they have nothing left for true accomplishment.

Basically, it is a question of being too self-centered. People like this policeman are preoccupied with what they are going to get out of life. They don't seem to realize that the law of life is one of giving.

The truly successful man, the happy man is the one who has learned to give of himself. Those who are generous with God and their fellowman make the best parents, teachers, writers, etc. They are what our nation needs most today—selfless servants of the common welfare of all.

"For he that loves his neighbor, has fulfilled the law."

(Romans 13:8)

THAT FINAL EXAM

A University of Oklahoma law student who took too little trouble to prepare for his final examination fainted after taking one look at the questions.

The questions were too difficult and the shock too much. This student had skimmed over the material in preparing for the test, hoping that the usual questions would be asked. But the unusual ones appeared much to his surprise.

The student had coasted along all year and made the mistake of pre-judging the exam. Instead of preparing for every possible question he took what he thought was the easy way out. And it was—he passed out.

Life, short or long, is a preparation for a "final exam" before the Master of all life. We have to prepare for this examination by day to day application to our duties and tasks. Letting things go till the end in the hope of "cramming the night before the exam" will not work in this case.

If we continue to live carelessly, with no thought of the day of reckoning, a big and unhappy surprise is awaiting us on the last day. And we will not be able to "faint away."

The best guarantee of a favorable judgment is a life of service of others—for Christ. There is so much everybody can do to lead a useful and Christ-like life. We have only to choose.

"Every idle word that men shall speak, they shall render an account for it in the day of judgment."

(Matthew 12:36)

HE LIFTED 3300 POUNDS

William Backman had enjoyed a picnic with his family in a grove in Harmony, R. I. As he got his car ready for the trip home the scream of his four-year-old son sent him hurtling from his automobile.

He winced with fright when he saw what he had done. In backing up, he had run over his own boy.

Without a pause, the 130-pound man grabbed the bumper of the 3300-pound car and almost miraculously lifted it high enough to free the boy pinned under one of the wheels.

This slightly built father probably never realized that he could perform such a feat of strength. It is a good example of what can be done in an emergency, especially when the motivating force is love. The great psychologist, William James, showed that we all live far within the limits of our capabilities and only in time of stress and emergency even approach what we really can do.

What a wonderful thing it would be if more people could become so strongly motivated by love of God and mankind that they would multiply their energy by ten times and put it in the service of all. Our biggest problems would be solved almost over night.

What a pity, on the other hand, that the majority of good people go through life at a comfortable pace and never, except in rare emergencies, bring out the strength and talents that God has implanted in them.

Start today to try to put to work the great power of love within.

"In this we know that we love the children of God: when we love God, and keep His commandments."

(1 John 5:2)

WATCH THAT IMPULSE

More and more women today are buying articles because they see them and not necessarily because they need them.

A recent nation-wide survey by an advertising agency found that women made 60% of all their purchases only because they saw the item displayed. This is known as "impulse buying."

This survey was confined to drugstores and asked housewives what buying pattern they used when shopping in chain or independent drugstores.

Thirty-two per cent of all purchases tabulated in the 1954 survey were made by housewives who bought one or more items they had not intended to buy before entering the store. These "impulse" purchases were two per cent greater for 1954 than for 1948.

Many of our impulses are good ones, and can be valuable forces in getting things done. But too often we fail to bring our impulses under the control of reason.

Some people become the plaything of their impulses, not only in minor matters like shopping, but in more serious areas.

When prompted by an impulse think it through. Make sure it is a good and reasonable one and serves a useful purpose under God. Once we get in the habit of harnessing our impulses and drives under the sway of reason, we will be able to accomplish much toward the betterment of ourselves and others.

"What is man that thou are mindful of him? . . . little less than the angels thou has crowned him with glory and honor." (Psalms 8:5-6)

HONEST AS A CAMERA

A camera watches toll collectors on the New York State Thruway to detect those few who might be dishonest.

The first camera was placed near Buffalo which is one terminal point of the new highway. A picture is taken of the license plate and the insignia or plate which shows the driver to be a permit holder. Spot checks are made during the day and night.

Officials explained that a dishonest collector could keep the toll and say that the driver held an annual permit on which no toll is collected.

No doubt most toll collectors on our roads are honest men. But for the sake of the one who would take advantage of any opportunity to "feather his own nest," checks and double checks are necessary. It is for this same reason that inventories are taken and audits are made in every business concern.

Unguarded sources of free income are invitations and encouragement for the weak to "make a tidy little sum on the side."

In spiritual and moral living it is the same story. Checks are needed, and God has provided them. The commandments, conscience, judgment, and the like are so many reminders that a complete accounting must be made at the end.

"In all thy works remember thy last end, and thou shalt never sin." (Ecclesiasticus 7:40)

CONSCIENCE WOULD NOT REST

A 25-year-old Augusta, Georgia, woman roamed about the country for three years before she confessed to a "perfect murder." It was likely that police officials would never solve the crime. But this woman had more to deal with than the police. She was followed and hounded everywhere she went by her conscience.

Unable to stand the pangs any longer she telephoned the police and said she "wanted to get something off her mind." She told them she had served a roommate a "roach poison cocktail." Authorities had pronounced the roommate dead of natural causes.

She had killed the woman because the deceased had asked her to move out of the home. The murderess confessed because she could not "forget about it."

Conscience is a thing of extraordinary power. This is true especially when one of God's basic commandments are involved, such as "Thou shalt not kill."

The law of God is not only written on tablets and in books, but in our hearts, that is, our conscience.

It is true that some succeed in stifling their conscience almost completely. But they never succeed fully and even to succeed at all, it takes many years of deafness to its constant voice.

You can perform a real service by taking a stand for God's truth. Merely being against evil touches few consciences.

"Who show the work of the law written in their hearts, their conscience bearing witness to them . . ."

(Romans 2:15)

CHANGE THIS TREND

A 73-year-old man, beaten unconscious by thugs lay crumpled in a dark hallway of a Second Avenue tenement in New York City.

To make matters worse, he had been robbed of $700—all the money he had in the world. Upon recovering consciousness the poor old man was in a state of despair. He had striven all his life to stand on his own two feet, and now suddenly found himself penniless through no fault of his own.

Innocent men, women and children all over the world have suffered at the hands of a tiny minority of unscrupulous fiends, who, like these thugs, live off the efforts and earnings of those who conscientiously try to live according to the will of God and His laws.

How long will the majority stand by and allow this alarming trend toward brazen crime to go from bad to worse all over the world?

Are we not allowing the evil to take the initiative and doing little more than trying to restrain the evil-doers after they have a head start?

The sooner those with high ideals show the same daring for good that those bent on evil display, the sooner will this trend change for the better. By taking a stand for God's truth you can help shape the future—and help millions of innocent people over the earth.

"For the children of this world are wiser in their generation than the children of light." (Luke 16:8)

NEVER TOO OLD TO DO GOOD

Soon there will be more than 16 million persons over 65 years of age in the United States.

Science has done a remarkable job in extending the life-span of Americans and will probably continue to do so. Yet, while the number of those over 65 increases every day, many if not most of these good people find it difficult to lead useful, worthwhile lives.

Temple University in Philadelphia recently sponsored a conference which encouraged the employment of people reaching their later years. The conference pointed out that many of the arguments employers use against hiring elderly people do not hold water. Not only that, but the attitude of some employers in regard to old people is creating serious social problems detrimental to the economy of this nation.

There is much good left in this large group of individuals. Many of them will be in their prime, excelling in ways that younger people cannot. If they are forced to retire they will not only lead unhappy lives but also will be a burden to themselves, their families and the state.

The hopeful thing is that they themselves want to be independent and contribute their part. For this they need some help from us.

Our job is to find work or outlets for their abilities and talents. Take upon yourself the Christ-like task of seeing that at least one person is given a job where he can be of use.

"Honor thy father and thy mother . . . that it may be well with thee, and thou may be long-lived upon earth."
(Ephesians 6:2-3)

HOW TO GO ABROAD ON 17 CENTS

Eleven-year-old Eugene Hart had every intention of being back for lunch. After all, his grandmother had given him his orders: "Don't go far, and be back in good time for lunch."

To make a long story—and trip—short, he didn't make it. In fact, five days later he was in Southhampton, England.

And he had a very plausible explanation.

"I had only 17 cents and thought that a movie would be a good place to spend the morning. I then saw in the paper where the S.S. United States was in port, so I thought I'd have a look."

The youngster had no trouble getting aboard, it seems, and several hours later found himself on the high seas, en route to England.

"Mom told me she'll be waiting at the pier," he explained, after receiving a telegram from home. "I guess I'm going to get in trouble."

A certain amount of curiosity and daring is a healthy sign in a youth and adults should not completely discourage it. Only extremes should be avoided.

Youth needs guidance and discipline tempered with kindness. In this way a youth's God-given energies are channeled into constructive paths. Today our world needs leaders with energy and imagination that are rooted in changeless truth.

"The kingdom of heaven suffereth violence, and the violent bear it away." (Matthew 11:12)

TURNING THE TABLES

Not every student is able to cross swords with his professor and come off the winner. It takes special courage to face up to one who is accustomed to run rough-shod over things which many of his students hold sacred.

But there always comes a day when profs like these meet their match. This particular one knew that the young man he was addressing was sincerely religious.

"I'll give you a dollar if you'll show me where God is," the professor said in a surly voice.

The boy, we might say, had the professor's number and was ready for him. Without a moment's pause, he replied:

"And I'll give you two dollars if you'll show me where He is not."

Today more than ever we need those who will stand up for the truth and the right. While this young man's refutation was superficial, he could easily have held his peace and then gone out to complain about education in general. He chose to do what he could when it would count most.

The best way to defeat error is to "push" the truth. The best way to defend it is to take the initiative. The best way to follow the right path is to lead.

You will be surprised to find that it is easier than you think to "turn the tables" on those who would tear down rather than build. Make your influence felt even when it requires more than average courage and initiative.

"It shall be given you in that hour what to speak."
(Matthew 10:19)

NO ONE TO THROW THE STONE

Three boys, accused of stealing watermelons in Ripley, Tennessee, nervously faced the judge when brought to court. They expected the worst.

The judge, an experienced man, knew well the need of discipline, but he also knew how to temper it with mercy when necessary. He was particularly cautious in the case of young offenders. They were at the beginning of the road of life; giving them a "record" or throwing them in with hardened criminals could be the start of a life of crime.

"Anybody in here who never stole a single watermelon when he was a boy, raise his hand," he asked with a rap of a gavel. He waited for an answer, but all was quiet. Court officials, patrolmen, spectators, all kept their hands at their sides.

The judge dismissed the case.

Much wisdom and insight are required in dealing with youth. Whether they flower into mature and balanced personalities or pursue a road of indifference or destruction depends a great deal on the measure of both discipline and understanding they receive at crucial moments.

A balance of discipline and kindness must be struck, if the best is to be brought out and the worst kept in check.

You can do something to help to guide our youth onto proper and useful paths where they will be able to dedicate their energies and talents in the constructive manner intended by God.

"Suffer the little children and forbid them not to come to me." (Matthew 19:14)

ACCENTUATE THE GOOD

For three years taxi driver Don Bivens of Sydney, Australia, drove a seven-year-old crippled girl to and from school. He was always at the girl's beck and call, in all kinds of weather, and managed to find time for his steady customer even during his busiest hours.

Then the faithful cabbie did something to brighten the future of the handicapped youngster. He returned all the fares she had paid him in those three years. The gift totaled $450.

Some are tempted to be frustrated and cynical because of man's weakness, disloyalty and brutality. They can recover their sense of balance by recalling that the majority of human beings lead good, simple lives, despite their minor shortcomings.

You would be surprised and heartened to find how many individuals in your community there are like this Sydney cab driver who show extraordinary generosity to those less fortunate.

What each of them do is often known only to God, who will reward for all eternity such acts of charity done in His name.

Encourage your newspapers, radio and television stations, magazines and movie companies to present more articles and programs about the good side of mankind and less about the seamy side of life.

"Be not overcome by evil, but overcome evil by good."
(Romans 12:21)

&⸏ Let me encourage the good in every man, O Lord, and thus help him overcome evil.

LESS HONKING IN PARIS

Some time ago, Parisian motorists were ordered to use their brakes and gears instead of their horns. As a result, the accident rate has dropped considerably.

A French magazine, "France Actuelle," reports that in one month there were 2607 auto accidents in Paris. But in September of 1954, the magazine points out, there were about 100,000 more cars on the streets and only 1712 accidents.

Andre Dubois, Paris police chief, is responsible for the change. He was appointed to muffle the noise in Paris—primarily the excessive horn blowing. Dubois made it a violation of the law to blow a horn except in cases of extreme emergency.

If you belong to an organization where there is much talk and little action, you may do much to increase its effectiveness by taking a stand for fewer words and more tangible achievement.

There is a strong temptation for all of us to be long on talk and short on performance. It is a danger that requires constant watching.

God expects each of us to put our ideals to work and not just talk about them. As Paris is better off with fewer honks of the horn and more careful driving, so will the world be benefited when more become "doers" instead of mere "talkers."

"Be ye doers of the word and not hearers only."
(James 1:22)

Inspire me, O Lord, to be so busy doing things for Thy glory that I will have little time left to talk about it.

ONE WAY TO FRIGHTEN THIEVES

A man entered Max Soufer's diner in Philadelphia and showed a paper bag to the proprietor. A pistol was sticking from the bottom of the sack.

"What's the matter with you? Are you kidding, holding up a fellow this early on a Sunday morning?" Soufer asked in a perturbed voice.

"Go ahead and get it yourself," Soufer told the bandit when he asked for the money. Seeing the man scoop up $23 in bills and coins, the owner, very much annoyed, said: "The least you could do is leave me some change to conduct my business."

The robber complied with this latest request but ordered Soufer to lie on the floor until he escaped.

"I can't serve food the rest of the day with my clothes all dirty," the vexed man answered and boldly stared at the thug. The bandit allowed this plea but was so unnerved by this time that he turned and fled.

While avoiding anything reckless, it is important that each one take a firm stand in facing up to evil-doers of our day. More often than not there is more bark than bite to them. Being cowards at heart, they can be easily taken off guard by those who show the courage of deep convictions.

If you wish better government, education, entertainment, literature or labor relations, you must make your voice heard and exert the power for good that God has entrusted to you.

"If God be for us, who is against us?" (Romans 8:31)

✑§ Help me to face Thy enemies, O Lord, and not be frightened by them.

SHOPLIFTING COSTS $75 MILLION

A New York psychologist recently pointed out that thefts by shoplifters have reached the almost unbelievable total of 100,000 a week in stores throughout the country, costing merchants about $75,000,000 a year.

Dr. Fabian L. Rouke, chairman of the department of psychology at Manhattan College, said these figures might be reduced by as much as 25 per cent if every offender was given the proper treatment.

Dr. Rouke said only 10 per cent of the offenders could be classified as professionals. He added that many stole to make a living, while less than five per cent actually used the goods they stole. Nearly 87 per cent stole because of some emotional conflict.

The inherent weakness in each human being manifests itself in a variety of ways. It reveals a lack of inner security or stability that can be satisfied only by the truth and strength that comes from God.

Rather than merely bemoan the trend to crime that is spreading over the country, try to do something positive and constructive to solve the problem.

If you did no more than reach out to one of these unfortunates who is the victim of his own weakness, you may, with God's help, do much to rehabilitate him. It would be a big step in the right direction.

"I am the way, and the truth, and the life."

(John 14:6)

&§ Help me to help others, O Lord, when they are inclined to evil.

223

RISKING EVERYTHING TO COME HERE

An 18-year-old German stowaway, without food or water for 11 days in the locked hold of a New York bound freighter, lost 60 pounds before he was found by a crew member.

When the ship sailed from Bremen, Germany, Alfred Oestmann, who always dreamed of coming to America, slipped into the hold. But before the ship docked in New York, a longshoremen's strike had been called and the hold where he was hiding would not be unloaded until a week later in Baltimore. This meant the stowaway would starve.

Then a seaman remembered he had stored a coil of rope in that particular hold and unsealed the hatch. He and his companions heard the stowaway scratching and moaning from the deck 65 feet below.

Upon closer observation they saw Oestmann struggling to climb the ladder. Weakened by hunger and thirst, he fell back into the hold.

He was covered with dirt and the light made him squint. His lips were so dry he could hardly talk and he collapsed when lifted to the deck. Under a doctor's direction, the young man rallied and soon began to gain weight.

If men will suffer so much to obtain the freedom and abundance of America for the fleeting years of this life, how much more should they endure throughout life to reach the never-ending happiness of heaven which was intended by God Himself as their eternal reward.

"That eye hath not seen, nor ear heard, neither hath it entered into the heart of man, what things God hath prepared for them that love him." (1 Corinthians 2:9)

FAKE CANCER CURES

Cancer quacks who claim they have sure cures for this dreaded disease are "filling our cemeteries with tombstones as monuments to the inefficiency of their treatments," is the claim of Dr. Alfred M. Popma, president of the American Cancer Society.

Dr. Popma said his society is trying to check claims of "cures" by so-called cancer specialists. "But efforts have not been enough," he said.

"It therefore becomes our responsibility," Dr. Popma declared, "to use every means at our disposal to combat the vicious quackery which is slowly infiltrating throughout the country. . . . It is our obligation to the public which supports our activities to wage an increasing battle against such men or groups of men who are exploiting the cancer patient. . . ."

False remedies for the ailments of the body deceive many an unfortunate person who is looking desperately for a cure. But we fear that far more are duped by those who falsely claim they have the remedy for the ills of the mind, heart and soul.

You can be a committee of one in reaching out to those who are confused and troubled and show them how they can obtain the spiritual aid they seek. Especially in knowing why they were created, where they came from and where they are going. You may help them obtain eternal happiness if you do.

"A brother that is helped by his brother, is like a strong city." (Proverbs 18:19)

INVITING TROUBLE

A woman in New York City discovered that a glib tongue and perfect manners aren't always the sign of honest people only after she was robbed of $12,000 by a "nice couple."

This unfortunate woman met the thieves at a gathering and struck up a conversation. She invited them to visit her apartment.

The visit was pleasant and formal at first. Then the man cautiously remarked about her material advantages. She was flattered. He then expressed an interest in seeing her rings and bracelets.

When the woman obliged but first opened the closet door to show them a new dress, the couple pushed her in and began searching the room for the jewelry. Terrified, the duped woman remained in the closet afraid she would be harmed if she called for help. She fell asleep there and awoke several hours later to find the thieves had made away with cash, furs and jewels totaling $12,000.

The confidence that people place in chance acquaintances about whose background they know nothing, in reports and articles which are not substantiated by fact and in teachings which are seldom checked for their truthfulness, is ample proof that many are ready to believe, however misplaced their faith may be. It should be a strong reminder that we should show much more speed and zeal in reaching with God's truth those who are taken in by error and deceit, because no one takes the trouble to bring them anything else.

"By their fruits you shall know them." (Matthew 7:16)

WHAT ONE YOUNG COUPLE DARED TO DO

One young couple in San Diego, Calif., has recently started to make an annual gift of $5225 to the American people.

We learned of this from a brief remark in a letter which arrived at Christopher headquarters from a woman in California. She casually mentioned that her husband had given up an $8000 position in business to take a teaching post that pays only $2775 a year. Then cheerfully commenting on this, she wrote: "You see how strongly we both believe in the Christopher cause."

You can figure out for yourself that this means a sacrifice of $5225 in annual income for this one home. Frankly, we think it is a little short of heroic. It ought to restore the faith of any skeptic in human nature to know of individuals motivated with so sincere a desire to work for the glory of God and the benefit of humanity.

Such a sacrifice must mean a serious hardship for this family in its desire to help countless other families. But Christ Himself has told us that the world can be saved by means of sacrifice and suffering. We firmly believe that once a million individuals are sparked by this daring missionary spirit in working for the peace of Christ their effort may prevent millions from dying for peace.

"Fear is not in charity: but perfect charity casteth out fear ... And he that feareth is not perfected in charity."
(1 John 4:18)

PARENTS KNOW BEST

When the mother of a sleeping 10-year-old Wilmington, Calif., boy decided not to move him to his bedroom little did she realize that she was indirectly saving his life.

The boy fell asleep while reading in a bedroom at the rear of the home. His mother thought she might wake him if she moved him to his own room. This decision saved his life, for later that night a car smashed into the front of the house, killing the family dog, asleep on the boy's bed.

God gives special graces to parents. When they earnestly strive to fulfill the responsibility of caring in every way for the precious young lives entrusted to them by Almighty God, they instinctively and habitually do a good job of rearing their children. Often, without being conscious of it, such fathers and mothers do something for their sons and daughters by giving them the preparation for life that they need and deserve.

Rearing children is far from an easy task, especially these days when there are so many distractions that compete with the sanctuary of the home.

But for parents who conscientiously try to give of their best to their young ones there is the deep and lasting reward of having done a job well—of having fulfilled the mission assigned to them by God Himself.

"And beware of thy own children, and take heed of them of thy household." (Ecclesiasticus 32:26)

 Instill in me, O Lord, a love of children so that I may be truly interested in helping them.

FIFTY HOURS IN A WRECK

With both arms and a leg broken, a 61-year-old salesman in Macon, Ga., was pinned helpless in the wreckage of his automobile. In desperation he blew the horn until the battery was dead. Then he yelled himself hoarse. Fifty hours later he was found near death.

This salesman said he blacked out while driving and his car careened across a field. It finally settled in a crumpled heap behind a heavy stand of trees and underbrush which hid it from the highway.

For two nights in near-freezing weather the man laid in the twisted metal suffering great pain. He later said his agony was so severe he could not feel the cold. Finally an unidentified man found him and brought him to a hospital just in the nick of time.

The ordeal that this poor man went through was, in one sense a miniature of the spiritual and physical plight in which hundreds of millions of helpless human beings find themselves today. They are in a struggle for their very survival in the wreckage around them—wreckage created by a few of their fellowmen.

Do all in your power to reach out to them in their misery and help their tortured souls and bodies. Better still, take every step you can to prevent a repetition of the terrible catastrophe that afflicts such large portions of mankind today.

"Which of these three, in thy opinion, was neighbor to him that fell among the robbers? . . . Go, and do thou in like manner." (Luke 10:36-37)

✍ Inspire me, O Lord, to something to prevent the wrecking of the world rather than wait until it happens.

A THIEF'S STRANGE EXCUSE

A man in Manila was recently sent to prison for eight years for a $250 robbery committed two years ago. He gave a strange alibi to police for his life of crime.

"Had I been arrested earlier, I never would have had the chance to commit so many crimes," he told the judge. His police record listed 24 crimes at the time of his last arrest.

One human weakness that affects most of us is our tendency to lay at the door of others responsibility for trouble we have brought about ourselves. It is so easy to blame someone else for our negligences and faults when it would be so much more to the point to do a little soul-searching ourselves.

However, whether it was justified or not, this particular thief made a point that deserves attention. If he had been either properly corrected or punished long ago, he might have been leading a worthwhile life today.

There is plenty of evidence that there has been a softening of essential discipline in the home and school as well as in the courts and corrective agencies of government. But at the root of it all is the letdown in self-discipline that God gave each individual to exercise over himself.

Do something to bring about corrective measures that are firm, prompt as well as constructive in helping others as well as yourself.

"If any man will come after me, let him deny himself and take up his cross and follow me." (Matthew 16:24)

◄§ Let me learn how to help in the discipline of others by first practicing self-discipline myself.

230

POWER FOR GOOD IN YOUTH

A fast streamliner was bearing down on Fletcher, North Carolina, when an 11-year-old boy wandering along the Southern Railway tracks discovered a flash flood had washed away a portion of the track.

The boy, Quentin Dill, sprung into action and told his older brother Jimmy to report the damage to railroad officials. Meanwhile, the train was rushing closer to the treacherous spot.

Jimmy and Quentin ran as fast as their legs would carry them and when they reached a telephone Jimmy was so winded he could hardly talk. A message was quickly dispatched to the train and it was held up in Fletcher, while the track was repaired.

It is heartening to see the power for good in young people. If more could be done within the home and under the encouraging eyes of sympathetic parents to bring out the bravery and daring that God has placed in every one of them, the problem of juvenile delinquency would diminish rapidly.

The first and most important school is the home. God planned it that way. But be sure that it is the center of inspiration and stimulation along positive lines to guide energy and talent into constructive channels instead of being merely a restraining influence, important as that is.

"And the child grew, and waxed strong, full of wisdom, and the grace of God was in him." (Luke 2:40)

Grant me the opportunity, O my Savior, to enthuse young people to do good rather than merely dampen their spirits.

231

KEEP YOUR EYES OPEN

Curiosity killed a cat but it made Ernie Pizzuto $75 richer.

Pizzuto was walking home from work on a much traveled Philadelphia street when he noticed a small parcel on the sidewalk. Scores of pedestrians were stepping over the bundle and others kicked it out of their path. But Pizzuto decided to pick it up and see what was inside.

To his surprise, he found the bag contained uncut diamonds, several watches and a card with the name and address of a neighborhood jeweler. Pizzuto took the jewelry to the owner and was rewarded $75 for his honesty.

The more preoccupied people become with their own little lives, the less they seem to observe and enjoy the wonders with which God has filled the world.

Those who seek happiness by concentrating on self usually end up by becoming so shortsighted they cheat themselves more than anyone else.

The more you reach out of yourself with love of God and love of everybody, the more you will experience the real joy of living. You will find opportunities opening on all sides of you to add a little joy and brightness to the world. And in so doing you will be garnering for yourself a reward here below that God reserves for those who live for Him and others—not merely for themselves.

"All the earth is full of his glory." (Isaias 6:3)

&§ Grant me the grace, O Jesus, to experience a foretaste of heaven by working for Thee and others.

THE GOOD IN THE WORST

A 49-year-old murderer had his fellow inmates at a Tennessee prison farm in a dither with his sudden outburst of ambition.

Although under the death sentence, this prisoner worked seven days a week to earn overtime pay which doubled the normal wages. His fellow inmates became more puzzled when he gave up smoking and stopped buying other luxuries.

It was obvious that the man was saving for something which he wanted very much. Otherwise, he wouldn't put so much zest and time into a job which paid a pittance of $2 a month.

Then the day he had been waiting for was here. He gave his savings of $7.71 to a polio fund.

"It isn't much," he said, "but if it helps some kid, I'll be glad."

Due to the innate weakness and inadequacy of men, there will always be a certain amount of crime even under the best conditions, even as there will be some sickness despite the healthiest surroundings.

Rather than get cynical or frustrated about this continuing problem, it is much more sensible to find the element of good in the worst criminal and work on that to rehabilitate him as a doctor carefully cultivates the spark of life still remaining in a disease-ridden body.

"As long as you did it to one of these my least brethren, you did it to me." (Matthew 25:40)

  Encourage me, O my Savior, to be more interested in helping mankind than in criticizing it.

SHE REFUSED $200,000

A 52-year-old Long Beach, Calif., woman recently refused to accept a $200,000 legacy from her grandmother because she felt she did not deserve it.

After being informed that her grandmother left her acres of vineyards and a small inn in Gostingen, Luxembourg, Mrs. Clemontine Cardula Hess said:

"I never had anything to do with the vineyards. My uncle deserves the land. My husband and I and our two children could use the money, and I'd accept it if I felt I deserved it."

Mrs. Hess and her husband work seven days a week in a delicatessen located in a market they own and live in a modest home.

It is refreshing these days to hear of someone who is so detached from material things that she has the courage to refuse a real fortune in favor of another.

If more were motivated by such a high ideal it would do much to preserve harmony in many families. Avarice and greed on the part of some results in endless squabbling and bickering that hurts everyone involved.

Cultivate a detachment from worldly possessions in order to prepare better for the rewards of eternity.

"Blessed are the poor in spirit for theirs is the kingdom of heaven." (Matthew 5:3)

⇜§ Keep me, O Lord, from being possessed by my possessions.

"POOR JOHN" HAS $150,000

Friends thought he lived near poverty and called him "Poor John," but when he died they discovered he had a hidden fortune of $150,000.

The man was John Nelson of New York City who lived in a $16-a-week room for the past 17 years, while his safe deposit vault contained a $150,000 hoard in stocks, bonds and cash.

A bachelor, Nelson kept his savings so secret that friends and relatives thought he was very poor. They offered advice and tried to find him jobs.

The 68 year-old man was living on a pension at the time of his death. He never drank or smoked, never went to a movie, never listened to a radio or watched television. His landlady said he did not have a visitor in the 17 years he rented the small room.

Since "Poor John" left no will his entire savings were to be claimed by seven distant cousins who scarcely knew him.

Men show meticulous care over a whole lifetime to accumulate honors, prestige or a little wealth, yet they all quickly vanish at death. One wonders how much richer and more satisfying their existence here below might have been if they had striven even harder to prepare for the unending years of eternity.

"Lay not up to yourselves treasures on earth: where the rust and moth consume, and where thieves break through, and steal." (Matthew 6:19)

❧ Let me be ever conscious, O Lord, of where my lasting destiny lies.

18 YEARS IN AN IRON LUNG

When 44-year-old Fred B. Snite, Jr. died not long ago after 18 years in an iron lung, he completed a mission in life which will count for all eternity.

Completely paralyzed by an attack of polio in Peiping in April, 1936, young Snite lay near death in a Chinese hospital for several months. He recovered sufficiently to be moved to his home in Chicago.

Despite the fact that he was destined to spend the rest of his days in an iron lung, Mr. Snite decided that he would live as full and purposeful a life as possible.

In 1939, he married and had three children. In addition, he tried to hearten and inspire others who were likewise stricken with polio.

Difficult as it was in the beginning to adjust himself to his condition, he gradually regarded it as a blessing. "One matures very quickly when an illness strikes," he once remarked. "Your sense of values change. Religion and my family have become the important things in my life and that is as it should be."

Just a few months before he died, he said to a friend: "You will be happy so long as you follow God's will."

You too will enrich your own life as you follow God's will.

You too will enrich your own life as well as the lives of countless others if you see a hidden blessing in every cross that you must bear.

"And whosoever doth not carry his cross and come after me, cannot be my disciple." (Luke 14:27)

⋘ O my God, let me draw joy from suffering, not bitterness.

236

BLIND MAN BECOMES JUDGE

A 31-year-old Auburn, N. Y., man recently became a city judge—21 years after he lost his sight.

Joseph Namisniak was an assistant corporation counsel until his election by the city council to fill a vacancy on the bench. He attended the state school for the blind and was graduated from Cornell University law school in 1951.

Thousands of other physically handicapped persons have shown, as this blind man did, that they can lead lives that are of advantage to others as well as to themselves.

There is something that you can do to open doors for one or more of the 30 million physically handicapped in the United States today.

Most of these people prefer to work out their own problems rather than to be dependent on public welfare. Instead of being supported by others, they long for the chance not only to earn their own way, but to make a contribution to society through their own effort and enterprise.

It is a Christlike act, therefore, to help such individuals to help themselves. You may be surprised one day to see what far-reaching good has come of it.

"Amen I say to you, as long as you did it to one of these my least brethren, you did it to me." (Matthew 25:40)

⇝ Grant me the grace, O Lord, to help others to help themselves.

11-YEAR-OLD BLACKMAILERS

A 10-year-old boy in England was blackmailed for $50 by five boys who threatened to tell his parents he was smoking.

Two of the boys took the money from the lad over a period of months and used it to hire taxis and to buy air pistols, jackknives and cigars. They used the rest of the money to buy lemonade and candy for their friends.

Three of the boys were placed on probation, two were granted conditional discharges and all had to repay the money.

Every human being born into this world is capable of great good or great harm. The better side of young people is often neglected or taken for granted with the result that soon they slip into evil habits that handicap them for life.

Our aim should be to bring out the good implanted in the hearts of men. There God has written the law He expects all men to follow.

Above all else, God wishes us to love our fellow beings, not to fight with them or to take revenge on them in any way. Jesus Christ was sent from heaven by His Father to teach this lesson anew to men of all nations. Much remains to be done before His mission is completed. There is something that you can do as an instrument of His love.

"A *new commandment I give unto you: that you love one another, as I have loved you.*" (John 13:34)

O Lord, instill in the young a special love for each other.

A COSTLY MISTAKE

An interne's refusal to treat a 62-year-old Long Beach, N. Y., man was termed a "mistake" when the man died two days later.

The deceased, refused admission to the hospital, was found dead in his bedroom. An autopsy showed the right side of his chest was filled with pus and the right lung was collapsed. The physician who performed the autopsy said the man would have died anyway but should have received treatment.

Doctors and internes as a rule show great concern when a life is at stake. Many of them risk their own lives in order to save that of another.

This unfortunate exception can be a reminder to all of us that in some circumstance or other we may fail to show the proper attention to those who are broken in body or spirit.

The best way to avoid making such mistakes is to adopt a positive and sympathetic policy of seeing Christ in everyone we meet. If we do, the Master will never say of us:

"For I was hungry, and you gave me not to eat. I was a stranger, and you took me not in; naked, and you covered me not; sick and in prison, and you did not visit me. . . . Amen, I say to you, as long as you did it not to one of these least, neither did you do it to me."

(Matthew 25:42-45)

O Lord, let me suffer anything rather than hurt others.

·DEATHLY DARING

A young Canadian Air Force pilot thought he'd take a ride in his training plane and dip low over the farmhouse of the girl he was going to marry in two days.

He swooped the aircraft down and as close to his fiancée's home as he could and waved to her. But when he attempted to pull up the plane it would not respond and crashed in a nearby pasture before the eyes of his fiancée.

Dashing through fields and over fences to the crumbled mass, she found her betrothed was dead.

Those who are in love will do daring things to show their affection and devotion. At times they take needless chances, as this young flier did, and thereby substitute tragedy for what might have been, with a little restraint, the blissful joy of a happy marriage.

But those who display an excess of love are few and far between. On the contrary, there seems to be an increasing lack of love for anyone outside of self among too many today. And those who focus upon themselves the love they should give to God and others rarely show any imagination, daring or enterprise, even in helping themselves.

Use every opportunity to develop within you a Christ-like charity to one and all without exception.

"If I speak with the tongues of men and of angels, and have not charity, I am become as a sounding brass and tinkling cymbal." (I Corinthians 13:1)

DRIVER GETS 17 TICKETS

A fleet of police cars zoomed down a busy Chicago street in hot pursuit of a fleeing sedan.

The car they were chasing zigzagged through a tangle of traffic just like a midget racer trying to make the rail on a turn. It was touch and go and for a while it looked as if the police were going to lose the race.

After 10 miles of clipping along at speeds near 90 miles an hour, the chase ended, when the sedan piled into two cars. As the driver emerged from the wreck, he looked surprised and asked police: "What did I do?"

He got a very specific answer in the form of 17 tickets for traffic violations among which were drunken driving, speeding 90 miles an hour, running through 14 red lights and one stop sign.

Even though evil people often say: "What did I do?" when they get into trouble, they usually try to convince themselves that there is no difference between right and wrong. Then they frequently develop habits of carelessness or deliberate evil which show they have the same disregard for others that they display for their Creator.

Spread as far as you can a respect and reverence for the sublime standard laid down by Jesus Christ when He said:

"Thou shalt love the Lord thy God with thy whole heart, and with thy whole soul, and with thy whole mind, and with thy whole strength. This is the first commandment. And the second is like to it: thou shalt love thy neighbor as thyself." (Mark 12:30-31)

FOR BETTER OR FOR WORSE

A Buffalo, N. Y., county judge, after sentencing a larcenist, said he was amazed that the man's wife showed such extraordinary patience despite her husband's bad behavior for such a long time.

Judge Jacob A. Latona, who sentenced the man from two to four years for cashing a worthless check, said he had had too many chances.

"I have had a number of letters from people," Judge Latona said, "speaking a good word on behalf of this man, including one from his wife and it is amazing to me how any woman can take as much as she has had to take in heartache and sorrow and still find room in her heart to forgive him.

"He has gotten away with things for which he was never prosecuted, large thefts from employers who did nothing about it because his family and friends intervened."

There is a widespread tendency today for married persons to "run away" when their partners in matrimony develop evil habits, make serious mistakes or persist in crime.

They seem to forget that they are abandoning ship when they are needed most. They forget very quickly the significance of the second half of their marital promise to be loyal and faithful to the other party "for better or for worse," and "until death do us part."

God must have a special blessing for husbands or wives who spend a whole lifetime trying to reclaim or redeem the partner who has failed in marriage.

"What therefore God hath joined together, let no man put asunder." (Mark 10:9)

FOUR BOYS IN A SEWER

Four boys were exploring a storm sewer in Columbus, Ohio, when a sudden downpour sent a rush of water swirling through the large pipe and sent them cascading into the Clentangy River.

The boys screamed for help as they were swept through the pipe and attracted the attention of two off-duty firemen who had been fishing. Just before the firemen ran for help, one of the boys was thrown out of the pipe into the river. They pulled him to safety. Still no sign of the other boys.

Several seconds later the trio—holding on to each other—shot out of the pipe and managed to clutch a partly submerged tree. Firemen tossed them a rope and pulled in the shivering boys just before they started floating down the river.

Curiosity in young people is a valuable asset. If properly directed, it can develop the power of imagination, originality and enterprise that God has put in every human being. But, if misdirected, curiosity can cause many complications. Those who choose the "sewers" of pleasure, greed or ambition as the scene of their inquisitiveness are inviting trouble. They can easily be sucked in and swept away by their unleashed passions.

You may save the soul of some young person by encouraging him or her to look for pleasure and inspiration in good rather than evil.

"Seek the things that are above." (Colossians 3:1)

THIEF HANDS BACK MONEY

A woman who felt sorry for a hold-up victim talked her accomplice out of the robbery and returned the money to the St. Louis, Mo., gasoline station attendant.

Joe Johnson, the attendant, told police that a car drove up to his station and the driver poked a shotgun out of the window. He demanded that the day's receipts be handed to the woman sitting next to him.

Johnson gave the woman about $30. For a moment she hesitated to take it. Then she quickly handed the money back to Johnson.

"This isn't right, honey," the woman said to the driver. And with that the car sped away.

No matter how bleak things become around you or over the world, there will always be hope. Why? Because the sense of right and wrong that the Creator Himself has implanted in every human being can never be completely extinguished.

Men will go to desperate lengths to debase themselves or others. At times they seem to have succeeded so thoroughly that it appears foolish even to try for a change for the better.

Fortunately, in the most evil and degraded of human beings, there always lingers at least a faint trace of the nobility with which each of them was originally endowed by their Father in heaven. Make it your business to encourage and nurture that spark or remnant of goodness in even the worst.

"Whatsoever you would that men should do to you, do you also to them." (Matthew 7:12)

A 26-YEAR-OLD MOTHER GAVE HER LIFE

As the dark sedan bore down on Mrs. Eunice Repta of Chicago she could only think of one thing: to save her child in the stroller she was pushing.

Just before the speeding car hurled her body 100 feet, she shoved the stroller containing her two-year-old daughter to the sidewalk. Mrs. Repta died 10 hours later.

The 26-year-old mother had been Christmas shopping with her two daughters. As she crossed the street on her way home, the hit-and-run driver swerved around several cars that had stopped to allow pedestrians to cross, and hit her just as she pushed her child to safety.

It is thrilling and inspiring to see the heroic generosity that women show in times of emergency to protect their husbands, their children or anyone who is near and dear to them. They gladly give their very lives to save those of others.

What a transformation would take place in modern life if the 42 million wives and mothers in the United States would apply some of this extraordinary devotion to correcting the evil influences that worm their way into public life and which have an even deadlier effect on the minds, hearts and souls of the young. It is difficult to do this continually, on a day to day basis. But the benefits would be tremendous.

"Greater love than this no man hath, that a man lay down his life for his friends." (John 15:13)

RUNNING AWAY IS NO SOLUTION

For 11 years a former prisoner lived as a hunted man, always suspicious of anyone who asked too many questions, always checking first to make sure it wasn't a trap.

The 45-year-old man broke out of a Rome, N. Y., jail 11 years ago by sawing the bars of his third-floor cell. He jumped to a nearby telephone pole and slid to freedom, after serving one year of a two-year sentence for burglary.

The fugitive came to New York City and got a job at a hospital. Here he stole $200 and disappeared. Recently he surrendered to police. His reason:

"I'm tired of running away."

In many circles today it has become a vogue to show a disdain for moral principles and to claim that there is no such thing as right and wrong.

But even those who are most brazen in such attitudes never seem to quite convince themselves. Their very way of protesting is often an indication that they have uneasy consciences. Deep in their hearts they believe the very things they so loudly deny.

Try to impress on the young the value of being faithful under all circumstances to the voice of a good conscience. Remind them at the same time of the inner conflict that all sooner or later suffer who try to run away from God's law.

"For our glory is this, the testimony of our conscience."
(II Corinthians 1:12)

HEALTH INSURED
FOR A HUNDRED MILLION

More than 100,000,000 Americans—approximately five out of eight—are protected by voluntary health insurance today.

This is the largest number ever insured in history, according to John H. Miller, chairman of the Health Insurance Council.

Total benefits paid in one year exceeded two-and-one-half billion dollars, Miller said.

The extraordinary lengths to which Americans go to protect their health is a credit to them. All that is needed now is to balance this off with a like concern for the mind and spirit of man.

As things now stand, the accent on bodily health, comfort and pleasure and the increasing neglect of the nobler side of the human being are resulting in so many unbalanced individuals that a major problem is fast confronting society.

Great care should be taken of the body. God expects that. After all, it is a temple of the Holy Spirit. But far greater attention should be paid to man's spiritual side which distinguishes him from the beast.

A sound mind in a sound body is most important. But at all times, keep first things first. If you think it important to invest in health insurance, keep ever aware that it is far more essential to have the soul insurance that God has provided.

"What shall a man give in exchange for his soul?"
(Mark 8:37)

CHECK BEFORE YOU INVEST

If you plan to invest money in securities first make sure you are not being defrauded.

The president of the New York Stock Exchange recently said a large number of people are being fleeced by "rathole salesmen" who are selling them worthless Canadian securities, or as he called them—"dreamboats."

Keith Funston, Exchange president, said these salesmen are running "Operation Sucker" from Montreal and defrauding thousands of people. Mr. Funston added that the uranium boom is also dangerous to speculators who invest first and check later.

He found nothing irregular about investing in gold, uranium or oil stocks, but cautioned people to beware of smooth-talking salesmen who promise everything and deliver nothing.

Before investing your money, Mr. Funston said, investigate the stock through reliable authorities.

It is surprising to find so many persons who have worked long and hard to gather a "nest egg" for their later years show such carelessness and gullibility in the way they invest it.

It is far worse to spend a lifetime accumulating the fleeting treasures of this life and give little or no thought to spiritual investment which would last for all eternity.

In all that you say and do, be ever mindful of your eternal destiny. You have only one life to prepare for it.

"Lay up to yourselves treasures in heaven."

(Matthew 6:20)

⊷§ Help me to be doubly cautious, O Lord, about all that concerns eternity.

THEY THOUGHT SHE WAS DEAD

Have you ever been told that you were dead by a person who really believed it?

A New York City woman was informed of her death. She went to the bank to take something from her safe-deposit box but when the clerk looked at her name he thought she was an impostor. Occasionally it happens that someone will impersonate a dead person to gain access to his safe-deposit box.

"I almost dropped dead," the amazed woman said. "I got so sick I almost fainted."

There had been a mixup. Another client with the same name had died, the box was opened, and the contents were confiscated by a public administrator.

It was small comfort to the furious lady that the bank had made an unfortunate mistake. She proved how very much alive she was by suing the bank for $25,000.

The day must eventually come for each of us when we will have finished our course in this life. None of us can escape death. It can be a very gloomy thought for some. For others, it is a stimulating reminder that one must make the best of every opportunity in life to prepare for eternity.

Those who make it their business to fill every day with good works as to be well prepared to appear before the judgment seat of God with full hands usually lead the happiest and most satisfying lives.

"Remember thy last end, and thou shalt never sin."
                                                      (Ecclesiasticus 7:40)

❧ Fill my life, O Lord, with accomplishments for Thee.

249

11-YEAR FIGHT
TO CLEAR HUSBAND'S NAME

A woman in Manchester, England, who cleans offices for a living, recently won an 11-year legal fight to prove her husband did not desert from the British Army in India in 1943.

Mrs. Louisa Devine carried her determined battle to the High Court which reversed an army finding and ruled that Devine did not desert but was killed by fanatics.

"I did it to clear the name of my very fine husband, and for my son, Bobby, who was terribly hurt because his playmates called his father a coward," said Mrs. Devine. "I'm going to fight to get my husband's name put on the city's war memorial."

This determined lady has given a stirring example of devotion to her husband and a persevering insistence in behalf of truth.

In our day when the truth is treated so lightly and even deliberately ignored in so many phases of life, you, whoever you are, can play an important role by insisting without let-up on what is right and just.

Show a particular interest in seeing to it that truth prevails in such vital fields as education, government, labor relations, literature, and entertainment.

It is impossible to have freedom without truth. The more truth we bring into every facet of life, the more peace and liberty everyone enjoys.

"The truth shall make you free." (John 8:32)

⋘ Inspire me, O Lord, to show courage when Thy truth is at stake.

LESS EMPHASIS ON CRIME

Glorification of criminals in movies and television was soundly condemned by a staff director of the United States Senate Subcommittee to Investigate Juvenile Delinquency.

Richard C. Clendenen, addressing the Congress of Correction, sponsored by the American Prison Association, said "too frequently we see the gangster in movies or television riding in a long, sleek car. He goes up to his palatial apartment in his private elevator.

"At the end of the program, there's supposed to be some kind of message that crime does not pay. But it paid off too well during the first 45 minutes of the program. Somehow, it sort of petered out in the last two or three moments of the picture."

Clendenen added that "study after study reveals that most youngsters, teetering on the edge of delinquency, can neither be caught nor pulled back by a new recreation center, a child guidance clinic or a boys' club."

He stressed the need for training youngsters' correct moral values. This means, of course, that parents and others who undertake the formation of young people's lives devote the time and effort to deepen in each of them a respect for God and their fellow men as well as for their own personal dignity.

"Suffer the little children and forbid them not to come to me." (Matthew 19:14)

&& Inspire, O Holy Spirit, those entrusted with the training of the young to be ever aware of their privilege.

CLEAN UP COMIC BOOKS

Public opinion has been called upon to help enforce a code by which comic books will be judged either good or bad for the youth of this country.

The administrator of the new cleanup code said the publishers who have agreed to abide by its rulings "mean business." The code grew from "public clamor," the administrator said, and will need the support of the public to insure its success.

Some major items in the code are: Good shall always triumph over evil; criminals shall never be treated as "glamorous"; the "unique details" of a crime will never be revealed; scenes of "excessive violence . . . brutal torture, excessive and unnecessary knife or gun play, physical agony, gory and gruesome crimes" are not allowed; the word "crime" shall never appear alone on a book's title.

Precautions such as these are certainly a step in the right direction. But merely avoiding extremes is far from an adequate solution.

Young people have a right to the best quality in comic books and all other forms of entertainment just as they have a right to pure food, not merely to that which is not quite poisonous.

Encourage more persons with a high sense of purpose to get into the creative end of comics and other forms of literature and entertainment that are directed to the young.

"Woe to him by whom scandal cometh."

(Matthew 18:7)

FOUR-YEAR-OLD
GIVES LIFE FOR SISTER

Four-year-old Thomas Leamy Jr. of Ballston Spa, N. Y., was playing on the bank of a creek near his home with his seven-year-old sister.

Out of curiosity she toddled onto the ice which coated the creek and just as she reached the middle, the ice cracked and she plunged into the freezing water.

Thomas tried to save his sister but fell through the same hole.

Then the children's father heard the girl's cries and came running. He pulled out the little girl safely but the young Tommy was carried under the ice. He had given his life to save his sister.

It often takes an unfortunate mishap such as this to reveal the goodness, generosity and bravery that is hidden in little children.

God has instilled in even the youngest a desire to reach out to others in love. It is a quality, however, that needs encouragement and development by parents, teachers and all others who are entrusted with the care of children.

If the power for good in the young is allowed to remain dormant, it is not only a great loss, but worse still the weaknesses and evil tendencies of human nature may soon begin to assert themselves.

Bring out the best in youth and there will be little room for juvenile delinquency.

"Whatsoever you do to the least of mine you do unto me." (Matthew 25:40)

COURTESY CAN SAVE LIVES

More people are killed each year in auto accidents than all those who die from polio, cancer and tuberculosis combined.

More than 38,000 persons lost their lives in auto accidents on the highways and byways. Yet, many of these could be living today if they had abided by the basic principles of safe and sane driving.

Highway accidents are actually more preventable than death from the above named diseases. But it seems that the effort to curb auto accidents has not been great enough. People take these accidents for granted much as they do other plagues to society.

If everybody observed the letter and spirit of all traffic regulations and practiced more courtesy to other drivers and pedestrians the number of deaths and injuries would surely decrease. The life you save may be your own.

Every time you drive a car or walk across a busy street, you have an excellent opportunity to put into practice the second commandment: "Thou shalt love thy neighbor as thyself." In short, you can do something to sanctify your own workaday life by showing the same consideration for others that you would expect of them.

Being motivated by such a spiritual ideal will inspire you to be a better driver or pedestrian than will the mere fear of being hurt or killed.

"Thou shalt not kill." (Exodus 20:13)

✑ Keep me ever reminded, O Lord, to respect the rights of others.

HOW A BABY AVOIDED DROWNING

When a Long Beach, Calif., mechanic dived into a channel to save his 18-months-old daughter, his only hope was that he could reach her before she disappeared beneath the surface.

But when 43-year-old Donald C. Newton reached the baby after a 50-yard swim, he found Pamela floating on her back and apparently undisturbed by her precarious position. Newton had left Pamela in his car with three other daughters who ran to him crying that sister had fallen into the water.

"She was floating on her back, looking at the sky," the thankful father said. "She wasn't even crying."

If most of us could acquire the complete trust that is a special gift with which God has endowed all little ones, we would do a much better job of meeting the complicated problems of our day.

Those who are confused, frustrated or bothered by a variety of mental troubles might learn how to relax if they would study children. True, youngsters have little or no idea of what the responsibilities are that harass older people. But, nevertheless, they start off life with a tremendous asset of confidence that if preserved and cultivated could buoy up anyone through the years and prepare him for everlasting happiness of eternity.

"Suffer the little children to come unto me, and forbid them not. For of such is the kingdom of God."

(Mark 10:14)

◄§ Grant me the grace of remaining a child at heart, O Lord, through all the days of my life.

A POOR RICH OLD LADY

A little, 84-year-old lady thinking she might die some day without a penny, left an estate in Philadelphia of $170,119, including $168,119 in cash.

When she died Oct. 27, 1954, this "poor" rich lady was living in a house valued at $2500. Her only worldly possessions were furniture and furnishings worth $96.75 and clothing and personal effects valued at $12. She had denied herself every ordinary comfort and kept putting money in savings funds accounts allowing the interest to accumulate.

In her will she even made a similar arrangement so that her lifetime savings and the money she inherited from the family poultry business might last longer for her beneficiaries.

Executors found $4291 cash in her home, $63,994 on deposit in one Saving Fund Society, $56,732 in another, $39,363 in a third, and $3106 in a trust company.

It is amazing to see to what lengths some people will go to protect themselves against poverty or to bequeath their earthly possessions to others.

An enormous amount of time, thought and personal sacrifice is devoted to accumulating a little treasure that is soon scattered for better or for worse. In His Sermon on the Mount, Jesus Christ gave us this pointed reminder:

"Lay not up to yourselves treasures on earth: where the rust and moth consume, and where thieves break through, and steal. But lay up to yourselves treasures in heaven: where neither the rust nor moth doth consume, and where thieves do not break through, nor steal."

(Matthew 6:19-20)

PRIVILEGES ARE COSTLY

Seven fire trucks wended their way through a tangle of New York City traffic in answer to a fire alarm. Pedestrians thought an inferno was raging out of control in the business district.

But when firemen arrived on the scene they could find neither smoke nor flame. They did find a 48-year-old Brooklyn brewery worker who had turned in the alarm.

"There's no fire," he explained to a fire lieutenant. "I just wanted you to help me get the bird."

The man said his canary escaped and flew behind a panel in a barroom. Charged with malicious mischief for turning in a false alarm, the man pleaded that he "tried repeatedly to catch my bird but the bartender finally put me out."

Those who seek special privileges for themselves from the government rarely realize that they may be putting others to great inconvenience or danger.

One way in which every individual can apply Christian principles to everyday life is not to seek any preference or privilege at the expense of others. On the contrary, each and every one could do a positive and constructive service by respecting and protecting both the material and the spiritual welfare of others.

"Whatsoever you would that men should do to you, do you also to them." (Matthew 7:12)

TO SAVE ONE GIRL'S LIFE

In order to save the life of a 20-year-old Egyptian girl gravely ill with a heart disease, two nations, an American University and a famous doctor teamed up in an all-out battle against death.

The girl, Fiaza Abdel Aziz, was penniless and officials of the United States and Egypt temporarily forgot international problems to help her come to this country when they learned she must have "immediate surgical intervention to save her life."

Egyptian doctors said she had a damaged heart artery and that only certain American doctors could perform the delicate operation. So the U. S. State Department contacted Dr. Charles A. Hufnagel of Georgetown University who had developed an operation to replace injured heart valves with plastic valves. The Egyptian government flew the girl from Cairo to Washington.

Dr. Hufnagel said he would perform the operation without charge, while Georgetown University said it would not charge for the girl's care.

It is refreshing and inspiring to see what both men and nations can do when they focus attention on the value of a life. In doing so they pay tribute to the fact that each and every human being is made in God's image.

If that same reverence could be extended to all mankind, if everyone could realize that all of humanity are creatures of God, a great advance would be made towards that peace for which all men yearn and which God wills for us even in this life. You can do something to make that dream come true.

"Let us make man to our own image and likeness."
(Genesis 1:26)

WHAT TEEN-AGERS NEED

Five boys between the ages of 12 and 14 wrecked the interior of an $85,000 Long Island, N. Y., home because they said they had "nothing else to do."

Police said the 15-room home located at Kings Point was a "shambles." The vandals found nobody was home while hunting snow-shoveling jobs.

"Every room was entered," police said. "Bedroom furniture was wrecked, clothing was torn, drawers were emptied, kitchen cabinets pulled down, sugar and cereal and food provisions were strewn on the floor, china and glassware were broken, bedding was ripped."

One of the boys is 12, three are 13 and one 14. Police pointed out that three came from homes where parents are divorced.

It is a frightening thing to read of the increasing number of teen-agers who are drifting into the ways of brutality, immorality and destructiveness. Thank God that most of those who cause deliberate mischief are only a fraction of all teen-agers. Too seldom is it pointed out that the vast majority of young people are basically good and more than a little ashamed of the way a few are misbehaving.

However, the trend is still in the wrong direction. Rather than merely bemoan what is happening, it is far more urgent to get at the heart of the trouble; to restore the love and influence of a happy home life.

"His bones shall be filled with the vices of his youth, and they shall sleep with him in the dust." (Job 20:11)

CLEVER THIEVERY BY TWO HOUSEWIVES

Two housewives in Oldham, England, worked out an ingenious scheme whereby both qualified for jobless insurance benefits by doing each other's washing.

They employed each other and met every Monday to exchange laundry. For six months—the minimum time required to qualify for compensation—they stamped each other's cards to show that they worked. Then they fired each other.

The next six months the women collected jobless benefits totaling 26 shillings ($3.64) a week and rehired each other to start another cycle.

One Labor Ministry official commented: "I don't think there's anything we can do about it . . . it is probably going on all over the country."

When one considers all the time, thought and cleverness of execution that those bent on material gains put into working out their evil objectives, he can find a powerful lesson without probing too deeply.

To carry out any sort of crime requires thinking things through. Patience and perseverance are essential to avoid the many risks of being caught. Extraordinary vision certainly had to be employed by these two housewives to figure out the big scope of their dishonesty.

All of this adds up to only one thing: in this as well as practically every instance, it is simply another case of God-given talent being used in the wrong direction. What great hope for the world once more if we try to channel this power in the right direction!

"Every idle word that men shall speak, they shall render an account for it in the day of judgment."

(Matthew 12:36)

A VERY BUSY BURGLAR

A 36-year-old hotel clerk in New York City was recently arrested for 300 burglaries netting $75,000 to $100,000—all committed in little over a year, according to police.

The clerk was sitting in an expensive car outside of his hotel when detectives approached to question him. He tried to flee but was captured three blocks away in midtown Manhattan.

In his car, detectives found a $3000 mink coat and later discovered $15,000 in loot in his room. This included 18 watches, 25 rings, 15 necklaces, 25 brooches, pins and earrings and six labels torn from fur coats.

Those who become deeply involved in theft, falsehood, immorality, bigotry or any other pernicious vice usually make their biggest mistake when they fail to check the small beginnings of these vices. Sooner than they realize, a deep-seated habit is formed that takes such a grip on them that they can scarcely resist temptation.

It is a safe and sound law of the spiritual life that one of the best ways to prevent moral disaster is to "resist beginnings." This is an important lesson to get over to young people in particular. A little friendly advice and encouragement can help shape their whole future.

"Be sober and watch: because your adversary the devil, as a roaring lion, goeth about seeking whom he may devour. (I Peter 5:8)

GRANDMOTHER SHOWS HOW TO
PUT OUT FIRE

Construction workers in Charlotte, N. C., were burning scrap and before they realized it the flames were out of control and spreading in every direction.

They called the fire department but at the same time saw a little old lady dash across the street with her garden hose. The woman closed in on the fire and with the help of children quenched the blaze before fire trucks arrived.

The workers later discovered the woman, Mrs. S. A. Van Every, was the mother of the city's mayor.

God has endowed every human being with talent. Most go through life without ever realizing the great power for good buried within them. Because they tend to lead self-centered lives, they neglect to develop the imagination and enterprise that are stimulating factors in the lives of all that strive to reach out of their own little worlds into the big world.

Life can be very dull and boring when we concentrate on self. But whole new vistas open up when we honestly try to reach out as far as we can with the love of God and our fellowmen.

Whether you are young or old, you will find endless opportunity to display the initiative and resourcefulness with which God blesses those who love Him above all things and their fellowmen as themselves.

"And I will make ye to be fishers of men."
                                    (Matthew 4:19)

&⸱ Inspire me, O Lord, to be ever alert in all that concerns me.

THIRTY MILLION HANDICAPPED

In the United States today, more than 30 million persons are afflicted with physical handicaps of one kind or another. Most of these partially or totally disabled persons can be helped to become useful, productive citizens. The more effectively they develop and use the God-given abilities that all of them possess, the more we will all benefit.

You may be able to find a disabled person and do something in a Christlike way to help him to rehabilitate himself. Remind him that his abilities are far more important than his disabilities.

Here are three suggestions that may help you to be a "participant" rather than a mere "spectator" in regard to this great need.

1. Find a job for at least one handicapped person.
2. Encourage young people to take up a career in social work.
3. Pray for the handicapped who are lonely and discouraged.

"Bear ye one another's burdens; and so you shall fulfill the law of Christ." (Galatians 6:2)

⇘ Allow me, O Lord, to supply what others lack.

MIDGET SAVES AERIALIST

A Barnum and Bailey midget circus clown, Alvin Schwartz, four feet tall and weighing 105 pounds, saved the life of a woman aerialist when he broke her fall with his body after she slipped from a rope 30 feet above the ground.

Miss Gladys Rimmer was practicing an aerial act on a rope at Sarasota, Fla. and Alvin Schwartz was holding the end of it while standing on the ground 30 feet below. While doing a spectacular movement, Miss Rimmer's foot which was in a loop in the rope, slipped out and she plummeted earthward. Schwartz saw what happened, braced himself, and took the full force of the falling body.

He suffered broken ribs, while Miss Rimmer escaped serious injury.

Those who are alert and sympathetically interested in the welfare of others have abundant opportunities these days to put their good will to work.

A circus midget, despite his handicap, risked his life in order to save that of a fellow entertainer and has given inspiring example to others. Those who are blessed by God with many greater advantages, should be willing to go to considerable inconvenience to see that their fellowmen are protected from the debasing and corrupting influences that are undermining society today.

"Greater love than this no man hath, that a man lay down his life for his friends." (John 15:13)

❧ Inspire me, O Jesus, to work hard for the good of others.

GOOD GOVERNMENT
OVER THE AIRWAYS

The management and staff of a local radio station in Southern California is striving to make the best of every opportunity to live up to its responsibilities. One of their objects is to keep the public informed concerning their local political obligations. The reaction to their efforts has been most encouraging. One appreciative listener wrote the Christophers: "Just two years ago only a handful of citizens realized what our city council was for and how their decisions affected each and every one of us directly. Citizens' eyes have been opened, citizens are acting, and our town progresses."

Where there's a will, there's a way! When any individual is truly sincere in his determination to raise the level of government, education, literature, entertainment or labor relations, he usually discovers an opportunity to apply his ideals in an effective, practical manner.

Needless to say, there will be plenty of difficulties and obstacles. Moreover, many if not most of those who should encourage the slightest effort in the right direction, will often throw cold water and offer countless reasons why a thing can't be done. God blesses the efforts of even one individual who rises above such cynicism and shows single-handedly why it can be done.

"Behold I am with you all days even to the consummation of the world." (Matthew 28:20)

⊷ Assist me, O Lord, to persevere despite all difficulties.

WIFE'S NAGGING SAVES HUSBAND

A 50-year-old Andalusia, Alabama, lawyer said his wife's "nagging" saved his life because it forced him to see a doctor who discovered he had cancer.

Edward F. Reid, 50, said his wife Gladys spotted three danger symptoms in him after reading cancer society literature.

"She got to nagging me," Reid said. "I didn't feel any pain and didn't want to see a doctor. When I did, two of them told me I was all right but it did not satisfy her. So I went to a specialist in New Orleans and he told me I had a malignancy."

After five operations dating from 1942 to 1947, Reid was cured. During this period he had time to think and changed his outlook on life.

"Before cancer, I worked hard for the security of the material things of life," he explained. "After cancer, I found that it is security of character that counts. Somehow if you try to help your fellow man, financial matters take care of themselves."

To help others in matters that concern their temporal and eternal welfare often involves the risk of being misunderstood and even criticized. Even when you make the most tactful approach, you, too may be rebuked for "nagging." But if your love for others is deep and true, you will never give up trying to aid them.

"Which of these three, in thy opinion, was neighbor to him that fell among the robbers?" (Luke 10:36)

ℛ Let me learn to love others, O Lord, as myself.

THIEVES WORK HARD FOR LITTLE

Safecrackers in Omaha, Nebraska, worked feverishly to open the door of a vault they thought held a large sum of money.

For three hours they pounded away at the concrete and peeled layers of steel from the door which weighed tons. It was a hard nut to crack.

Exhausted, they finally tore a hole in the safe and with great expectation looked inside. To their surprise the safe contained only $25 in cash and a $5 check.

But police said they would be really red-faced if they knew how much time and work they had wasted, for on the door of the safe was a piece of paper containing the combination of the vault.

Many people spend a whole lifetime looking for the treasure or fortune that they think will put them on easy street, and they usually go at it the hard way. Yet seldom do they seem to achieve the goal to which they have devoted themselves.

In their pursuit of happiness, too many multiply difficulties for themselves by ignoring the simple, effective formula provided by God Himself. He does not force it on us. But it is ours for the asking.

"But seek ye first the kingdom of God and His justice, and all these things shall be added unto you."

(Luke 12:31)

⊷§ Grant me the wisdom, O Lord, to follow Thy way.

BANDIT MEETS HIS MATCH

A holdup man, posing as a messenger, pushed a pistol into a Brooklyn, N. Y., home after the door had been slightly opened. Minutes later his gun hand looked as if it had been caught in a meat grinder.

The bandit thrust the gun into the crack when the door was opened by a housewife. When she saw the gun she quickly slammed the heavy door and pinned the man's hand in the door jamb. The 132-pound woman called her daughter and the two of them threw their weight against the door.

The thug howled with pain and dropped the gun. But the women still applied pressure. By now blood began to run down the door jamb and a fingernail was torn off. With a final, desperate pull, the gunman freed his hand which was severely lacerated.

With things moving as fast as they are over the world today—and so often in the wrong direction—it is important that every individual seize every opportunity to show the courage of his convictions. Even a slight delay in standing up for good and against evil may cause considerable harm.

To be sure, God expects us to use common sense and caution and not to take needless risks. But at the same time, we must avoid favoring ourselves and being over-cautious. Make it your business to avoid both extremes.

"For you have not received the spirit of bondage again in fear." (Romans 8:15)

> O Lord, help me to be fearless where Thy truth is at stake.

EAGER BANDITS GET ONLY PENNIES

Two young bandits who recently held up a Long Island City, N. Y., bank learned that crime doesn't pay.

Armed with a shotgun and pistol, the gunmen lined 14 employees and two customers against the wall. As one of them headed for the open safe he jerked a telephone from the hands of a clerk who had just dialed a number. This so unnerved the bandit that he grabbed a bag from the safe and fled with his partner to a waiting car.

And what did the heavy bag contain? Twenty dollars in pennies. The bandits worked so fast that they missed $25,000 in bills on an adjoining shelf in the safe plus $18,000 distributed among eight tellers.

Those who defy the laws of God, even in small matters, usually try to put on a brave front. But in one way or another they reveal the lack of security within themselves.

The old story that a coward dies a thousand deaths certainly applies to everyone who is trying to take advantage of his fellowmen.

Some seem to succeed for a while but not infrequently they show poor performance at their own trade. In their hasty greed they fail to reach their own objectives.

Life is so short and eternity so long that it is to our lasting advantage always to play the game of life squarely as God intended everyone to do.

"Lay not up to yourselves treasures on earth: where the rust and moth consume, and where thieves break through, and steal." (Matthew 6:19)

Deepen in me, O My Savior, a reverence for Thy law.

SHE RAMMED THE POLICE CAR

Two Omaha, Nebraska, patrolmen were driving down a one-way street when suddenly a car rounded a corner and headed in their direction.

They flagged the car to a stop and told the woman driver that she was driving the wrong way on a one-way street. But instead of taking their advice, the woman became exceptionally angry.

The policemen watched as she slowly backed her car. Then her anger exploded. She stepped on the gas and purposely rammed into the police car.

All of us are tempted to get impatient at times. But the more that we are able to control our feelings, the more we act like children of God and intelligent human beings.

Rather than merely avoid losing our temper, which is a negative procedure at best, we should strive to show a friendly understanding and a consideration for others, even when they have done things to irritate us.

This does not mean being overly soft. It merely proves we are capable of being agreeable without being disagreeable.

In your home, your office, driving along the road, getting on the bus, shopping in the super-market, or in a hundred daily circumstances you have countless opportunities to show that you can rise above the temptation to be impatient, complaining or sarcastic. You will be a real witness of Christ if you do.

"By this shall all men know that you are my disciples, if you have love one for another." (John 13:35)

Help me, O Lord, to be kind when it would be so easy to be impatient.

ONE WAY TO STOP A MOTORBIKE

A young lady in London, Irene Karison, started out for a ride around the block on a borrowed motorbike and got off 50 miles away.

Irene just wanted to take a short spin but once on the machine discovered she did not know how to stop it. She had no choice but to wait until the machine stopped itself.

She rode down the highway to let it run out of gas. Fifty miles later the bike sputtered to a stop and Irene boarded the first train for home.

Many of us are like this young lady on a motorbike which she didn't know how to control. We are carried along by the trends of modern day life at such speed and to such lengths that we often despair of being masters of our own lives.

But do not lose heart at your seeming inability to cope with all the problems that sweep you along with them in any direction they take.

Almighty God has given you personally and individually a power to change the world itself for the better. There is much you can do by prayer and work. But always remember that you change the world or the world will change you.

Look for ways and means to shape and control the trends of the day and urge others to do likewise. You may play a decisive part in restoring sanity to the world.

"I have overcome the world." (John 16:33)

&ε Grant, O Lord, that I may influence more than I am influenced.

SHE SHARED WITH EVERYBODY

Nearly everybody in the tiny town of Hoo St. Werbergh, England, received part of a $270,000 fortune left by a 95-year-old spinster.

Miss Emmeline Pye meticulously measured out the money in her will to the last cent. Local school children received seven cents each; neighborhood children 90 cents apiece; $15 to each postman and a newspaper deliveryman; from $1.50 to $2.80 for church choir members; $750 to a favorite servant and $2800 for a nearby hospital.

The woman, who lived frugally in a Victorian-style villa, also provided money to buy Christmas blankets for the poor and the remainder went to needy professional people.

Few people would think of going into such detail in sharing their earthly possessions with those who survive them. On the contrary, many think and act as if they were actually going to "take it with them."

God entrusts all of us with some talent—spiritual and intellectual as well as material—which He expects us to share with others. He merely sends it to them through us. He leaves it to us to "deliver" it to them. If we fail we cheat ourselves even more than we do others.

Do all in your power while you are still alive to play the role of a Christbearer by bringing His love into as many lives as you can.

"It is a more blessed thing to give, rather than to receive." (Acts 20:35)

⌒§ Open my eyes, O Lord, to the countless ways in which I may honor Thee by serving others.

PEACE BEGINS WITH YOU

Police were dumbfounded when they found who the man was they arrested for five traffic violations. His job: a state safety engineer.

The 34-year-old motorist was arrested on charges of drunken driving, speeding, driving without a license, driving with inadequate lights and failing to change the address of his registration.

It is easy to criticize a man like this but in all sincerity each one of us can probably say in one way or another: "There but for the grace of God, go I."

For instance, we all talk much about peace and its advantages. But how many of us work against peace by our thoughts, words and deeds.

Yes, we want peace in the world but we often overlook the fact that peace in the world begins with each of us. If we accomplish nothing more than bringing the balance and harmony of Christ into our own private lives that would be one big step toward peace.

Significantly enough, the more we strive to bring the truths of God into the lives of others, the more conscious we are that we should practice them in our own lives.

Almighty God has placed in your hands a share of His peace. He expects you to keep a bit of it for yourself. But the rest of it you should share with others.

"Peace I leave with you." (John 14:27)

◦§ Help me, O Lord, to be true to Thee and others by being true to myself.

WHAT WE FAIL TO DO

Someone in Reading, Pa., breathed a sigh of relief upon dropping a bundle of Christmas greetings into the post office slot.

There were 125 envelopes in the bundle and it was quite a job to address them. But this labor of love was all lost.

It seems this well-wisher forgot to include one very important ingredient in his missives—the Christmas cards. One hundred and twenty-five to be exact.

A clerk discovered the oversight as he untied the bundle to run the envelopes through a cancellation machine. Each envelope was properly addressed and carried the correct postage stamp.

Some people tend to comfort themselves by the thought that they have done no wrong. This is to their credit, to be sure. But God put us on the earth to do more than avoid sin and evil. He expects us to do something positive and constructive—to do good rather than merely avoid evil.

It is easy to lull ourselves into a sense of smugness if we ignore or overlook what we should have done and failed to do. Few people admit their sins of omission.

By constantly seeking opportunities to do as much good as possible in Christ's name, you will not only grow spiritually but you will protect yourself against the danger of not doing enough.

"O God, *be merciful to me a sinner.*" (Luke 18:13)

ᪧ O Lord, allow me to do as much as I can for Thy glory.

BLAMING OTHERS ACCOMPLISHES LITTLE

A Buffalo, N. Y., steel worker, whose 16-year-old son was killed in an auto accident, claims the boy's death was caused by society.

In fact, the man went to court in a battle to have this inscription on the boy's tombstone:

"In memory of our beloved son—a victim of the present social system and conditions it creates."

This parent maintained that the social system in the United States *"has ended parental authority over their children."*

The father's attorney admitted that there were indications that the boys had been drinking and were racing when the fatal accident happened.

Many are tempted to place the blame on others when trouble strikes. It may be partially justified in some instances. But merely placing blame solves little or nothing.

Parents today face many influences that offset the good training that they strive to instill in their young. After they have done their best a child may still do something to break a parent's heart.

But it is more the exception than the rule that youngsters seriously misbehave when fathers and mothers have conscientiously devoted the thought, time and energy to the training children need and deserve. Instill in boys and girls an adequate reverence for God and their neighbors as well as themselves, and there will be little to fear.

"His bones shall be filled with vices of his youth, and they shall sleep with him in the dust." (Job 20:11)

 Remind me to do my part and not blame others, O Lord.

DEATH STRIKES LIKE LIGHTNING

A 56-year-old Kernersville, Ky., woman was waiting for the pilot to warm up an airplane which would take her to Norfolk, Va., for an all-day shopping trip.

Mrs. Everett W. Berry, Sr. was making the flight in the four-seat, single-engine plane with her husband and 17-year-old grandson. Everybody was in the plane waiting for Mrs. Berry.

As the pilot idled the motor, Mrs. Berry walked to the right side to board the craft, but finding her husband sitting in that seat started to cross to the other side.

The pilot was checking his temperature and when he looked up, Mrs. Berry's head was no more than five inches from the whirling prop. She did not notice how close she was walking towards the spinning steel.

Quickly the pilot threw the switch but it was too late. The blade struck the woman's head and she died instantly.

None of us know when death may overtake us. But it is one thing that every one of us, without exception, must face. We may linger on with a long illness, be hit by a car on the street, suffer a heart attack or be summoned in any of a hundred ways. But, come as it will, death ushers each of us before the judgment seat of God to render an account of our lives. The record of our lives is an open book on that day and determines our future for eternity.

"If then thou shalt not watch, I will come to thee as a thief, and thou shalt not know at what hour I will come to thee." (Apocalypse 3:3)

A $29,000 JEWEL KICKED AROUND

While dancing at a New York charity ball for the blind, a young girl stepped on what appeared to be an expensive diamond pin.

Her escort said it was junk, but the girl thought it genuine. Other men supported her escort's claim.

A waiter "wouldn't be bothered by it," and the press table called it worthless. The publicity chairman of the ball gave it to a hotel employee, who turned it over to the first woman who claimed the jewelry.

Meanwhile, the owner, a Chicago lady, petitioned the hotel management to help her find an 82-diamond clover leaf pin valued at $29,000, which she claimed she had lost at the ball. A thorough search failed to locate it and a statement was given to the press announcing the loss and offering a reward.

Within a few days the hotel manager received an anonymous letter containing the pin with a note that the reward be given to the blind for whose benefit the ball was held.

When man does not realize his divine worth, he usually abuses his fellowman. One of the most effective ways to counteract the growing crime wave is through a positive constructive approach. When men show disregard for their fellowmen—when they rape, murder or trample on them, it is usually because they do not know or have forgotten the precious worth of even the least individual. They are like the dancers who kicked around the expensive pin and even referred to it as junk, when they were unaware of its true value.

"And God created man to His own image."

(Genesis 1:27)

277

TWO WOMEN AND A SHOE

A shoe salesman in Denver, Colorado, was in a dilemma: two of his women customers wanted the same pair of shoes.

They refused to give ground and glared at each other for 15 minutes. The salesman left for lunch and other clerks entered the mediation.

One of the women—Solomon-like—suggested that since one of her feet was larger than the other she would keep one shoe and give the other one to her opponent. Two and one-half hours later when a reporter and photographer walked in the woman who had taken the shoe from the counter left in a hurry.

"You know something," the salesman said, "that shoe didn't fit either of them."

Quibbling over matters of little consequence, when no principle is at stake, is usually a waste of time. Worse than that, it is a device used by the devil to divide otherwise good people when they should be united and friendly.

Make it up for the lack of kindness on the part of others rather than go down to their level.

"By this shall all men know that you are my disciples, if you have love one for another." (John 13:35)

O Jesus, let me help others, not hurt them.

278

THIEF ROBS BLIND WOMAN

The thief who stole the purse of Mrs. Sylvia O'Brien of Chicago had an easy time making away with the $40 it contained. She didn't see him because the woman is blind.

Mrs. O'Brien operates a candy counter in the Criminal Courts Building and the thief grabbed the purse from behind the candy case. This money meant very much to this middle-aged woman since her husband was sick and confined to his home for a year.

It wasn't long before word of the woman's misfortune circulated through the building. A collection was taken and $67.50 was donated by everyone from judges to clerks. Then she was called to a courtroom for the presentation.

The fact that people in general show a generous helping hand in times of emergency should be a source of deep and lasting consolation to those who are tempted to lose faith in mankind.

Headlines reporting crime, brutality, corruption and disloyalty sometimes give the impression that civilization is fast going on the rocks and it is practically hopeless for the average person to do anything about it.

It only makes a bad situation a bit worse for even one individual to succumb to such a defeatest attitude. No, the vast majority of people, despite their weaknesses and failings, are basically good. Their power for good often goes unnoticed except in times of emergency, but it is always there, thank God, waiting to be developed.

". . . *God saw all the things that he had made, and they were very good.*" (Genesis 1:31)

⊷ Inspire me, O Lord, to stir up the good in every man.

DANGLING AT 15,000 FEET

A dozing Army officer got a rude awakening on an air flight from Chicago to New York recently. He suddenly found himself dangling outside the speeding plane held only by his safety belt.

The four-engined plane was cruising about 300 miles an hour 13,000 feet above Indiana when a two-foot emergency door next to Lt. Col. James Greenway became loosened and was torn off. In a flash, the tremendous air suction pulled him out of the airliner. Fortunately, his safety belt was buckled and held him by his knees. In a matter of moments fellow passengers grabbed Greenway by one leg and arm and pulled him to safety.

It is difficult for the average person to realize how close disaster is in these times of extraordinary speed. Naturally, we don't like to think that, with atomic warfare and the H-bomb now a frightening reality, we may be plunged into a catastrophe in a matter of moments.

But rather than let the thought of such terror paralyze us into cynical inaction, let us all be up and doing in a relentless quest to control these man-contrived horrors. While avoiding the extreme of being oblivious of the fact that we are sitting on a powder keg we must not allow ourselves to be so paralyzed by fear that we retreat into cynical inaction.

God will always help one to rise above his stupid excesses and mistakes if he shows a sincere desire to do so and has the good sense to depend more on help from on high than on his own weak limitations.

"It is I, fear ye not." (Mark 6:50)

DON'T WAIT TILL YOU DIE

In 1952 a smog took the lives of 4000 Londoners.

To prevent a similar tragedy, a 46-year-old English chimney sweep recently willed his body after death to scientists for research on the killer which is a combination of smoke and fog.

The man, Samuel Baker, whose family has been cleaning chimneys for 174 years, said sweeps swallow much more smoke, fog and soot than other people and should be a big help to scientists.

Rather than wait till you die to do something about the "mental" smog that is crippling the spiritual side of millions of human beings over the world today, take a few positive and constructive steps right now.

See that "the truth, the whole truth and nothing but the truth" is taught at all levels of education. That should always be the noble aim of the classroom. But wherever nations have been undermined and eventually destroyed, the beginnings of the breakdown are encouraged by a small minority who strive to eliminate God from all phases of teaching. The result is an atmosphere of half truths, questionable opinions and dangerous errors presented in the name of truth.

Rather than complain about or merely fight against this deadly "smog" which affects the mind, heart and soul, make it your business to restore to education the "whole truth" that is the rightful heritage of every person.

". . . *And the truth shall make you free.*" (John 8:32)

DISILLUSIONED BY COMMUNISM

Richard Tenneson of Alden, Minnesota, one of 22 American soldiers who remained with the Communists after his capture in the Korean War, indicates his dissatisfaction in letters written to his home.

In a letter to his 17-year-old brother Nathan, he wrote:

"Don't leave home yet . . . you don't know the security home offers until you are away from it. How important education is you realize after the lack of it has led you into a blind alley.

"Every night I look at your picture and I feel remorseful. What more can I say?"

What a tragic disillusionment for a young American. And yet how difficult to remind others that the same penalty awaits them if they take to heart the rosy but false promises made by those who are enemies of God and country.

The best place to offset this betrayal of youth is to be found in the words of young Tenneson himself when he warns his younger brother: "Don't leave home yet . . . you don't know the security home offers until you are away from it."

Do all in your power to encourage the sanctity of the home. Bring into it the love, warmth and affection that will make it so attractive to young people that they will always regard it as the center of their lives—rather than find this out after it is too late.

"He went down with them, and came to Nazareth, and was subject to them." (Luke 2:51)

⊷§ Help me, O Lord, to strengthen the influence of the home.

A NINE-YEAR-OLD TAKES REVENGE

A nine-year-old Philadelphia schoolboy, reprimanded by his teacher, decided to get revenge one way or another.

He hit upon the idea of setting fire to the school and went about planning the scheme step by step. First, he made sure a school window was left open so that he might enter the building over the weekend. Then he waited for an opportune time to slip out of his home without telling his parents.

The youth climbed a drain pipe to the open window, dropped into a classroom and tossed lit matches into paper-filled waste baskets. After each basket was blazing, he ran out the front door of the school and was seen by residents who called the police. An alarm was sounded but three classrooms were wrecked before the fire was put out.

"My teacher," the fourth-grade pupil told the fire marshal, "was always picking on me."

Punishment is often necessary. But if carried too far it can cause needless trouble. It is difficult to estimate the great harm done in homes, schools, offices, shops and organizations of all kinds when those in authority abuse their position by being habitually harsh or sarcastic. Those who make mistakes, whether they be young or old, usually understand correction that is justified, but they have a right to expect that it should be done in a kindly manner.

"Cast out first the beam out of thy own eye, and then shalt thou see to cast out the mote out of thy brother's eye." (Matthew 7:5)

Help me, O Lord, to be able to disagree without getting disagreeable.

HOW TO SHORTEN SPEECHES

To limit speeches to a reasonable length of time, a group of scientists devised an "electronic lectern" which lets a speaker know when his time is up and routs him with a smoke bomb if he exceeds his limit.

The gadget flashes an amber warning light from the lectern when the speaker has two minutes to finish his talk. A red light tells him his time is up. But if he rambles on then fumes from a smoke bomb force him to retreat from the platform.

Technicians made the speech squelcher so that more than 50 long research papers could be read at their convention.

Those who are long on talk and short on action often defeat the very objectives they are striving for.

More often than not, those who make long-winded talks, or who constantly make resolutions or ask for more proclamations are trying to ease their consciences for their own failure to put into performance the very recommendations they make.

You can do a great service to any organization to which you happen to belong by encouraging a policy of deeds more than words, of actual performance rather than mere lip service.

Discussion is important if it is positive rather than negative, hopeful rather than cynical. You can do something to see that words are translated into action.

"Be ye doers of the word and not hearers only."

(James 1:22)

HER LEG WAS AMPUTATED

Because she refused to see a doctor for fear of losing her place as a high school drum majorette, a 16-year-old Northampton, Mass., girl had to have a leg amputated.

Pretty Elizabeth Eason, according to her mother, bruised her leg against a fence at a fair three months before. Her family urged her to see a doctor. But Elizabeth would not listen, thinking that the doctor might order her to stay off the leg. If so, it would end her career as a drum majorette.

Finally, the family's persistence won out and Elizabeth went to a physician. But it was then too late. The doctor found cancer of the bone and had to amputate to save her life.

The extraordinary risks to which many people will go to gain some passing honor or pleasure is at least a proof of a dynamic drive within them. However poorly or mistakenly it may be directed, it could have been channeled in the right direction.

God intended that the power entrusted to each of us, be it little or great, should be put to work in a manner which rebounds to His glory as well as to the well-being of all His creatures—including ourselves.

You would do well to encourage young people to deepen their sense of true values and to guide them to channel their energy along constructive lines. This takes time and patience, but it can have results for generations to come.

"From thy youth up receive instruction, and even to thy grey hairs thou shalt find wisdom." (Ecclesiasticus 6:18)

ONE LADY FOILS A THIEF

"Get out!" was the reply tiny Sylvia Schippers gave a 35-year-old holdup man who pointed his .25-calibre foreign automatic at her face.

A supermarket bookkeeper in Levittown, Long Island, N. Y., Miss Schippers was taken by surprise. But she in turn surprised the gunman when she shouted "holdup." The robber tried to run away but his path was partially blocked by shoppers who overturned pushcarts in the aisles.

He forced his way to a getaway car but it stalled and one of his two accomplices tripped him as both tried to run. Two policemen heard Miss Schippers' call for help and dived at the bandit as he swung his gun at them. Then angry bystanders joined in the melee and almost mobbed the thugs, who were later charged with assault and robbery.

While it is not practical for most people to take such a daring stand, there are countless ways in which the average person can at least make his voice heard in shaping the trends of our day.

Good government, good education and good everything else depends for its vitality on an articulate public. Each person has a responsibility before God and man to see that the vital spheres of influence which affect the destiny of everyone are maintained at a high level.

Not to make one's voice heard, not to take a stand, may be to give approval by silence!

"He that shall deny me before men, I will also deny him before my Father who is in heaven." (Matthew 10:33)

SHERIFF THINKS MOTHER KNOWS BEST

The sheriff in Webster, N. Y., answered his telephone and almost had his ear drums pierced by a loud scream for help. Some scuffling sounds followed, a sudden crash, then the line went dead.

Sheriff and deputies raced to the address with drawn guns and slowly opened the front door. Facing them was a seven-year-old boy in tears with his mother standing beside him.

In between sobs, the boy explained that he called the sheriff to help settle a dispute. His mother, he said, wanted him to eat his turkey giblet soup but he refused. When she began to scold him he ran to the telephone and summoned the law. The crash the sheriff heard was the boy's mother intercepting the call.

But the lad's efforts were all in vain—the sheriff agreed with the mother.

At the very foundation of law and order in any country is the training that can be given in the home. All sorts of substitutes have been tried down through the centuries but nothing has been or ever will be found to replace the family.

In these days it is difficult for parents to inculcate a respect for the authority given them by God. But their task, trying as it may be, is more necessary than ever before. Peace in the home must be firmly established before we can have peace in the world.

"Honor thy father and mother." (Matthew 15:4)

GOOD PLANNING BUT POOR PERFORMANCE

A City Planning Commission in Virginia decided to turn over a new leaf and take steps to improve the attendance of its members at meetings.

So at the following meeting the first business on the agenda was *"how to improve the attendance of members."* Then there was a pause, while a count of members present was made. After the count, the commission moved on to other business. It could not act for lack of a quorum!

Many people think that forming an organization is automatically the solution to a problem. For some reason they over-simplify matters by jumping to the conclusion that all that is needed beyond that is to "join" and "to pay dues"—and then do little or nothing.

There are hundreds of thousands of worthy organizations over the country that are virtually crippled in carrying out their excellent programs because their members do not act like members.

You can do a real service by acting as a *"committee of one"* and stirring up individuals 1) to attend regular meetings of their organizations and 2) to participate in deliberations and activities. Fulfilling one's obligation of attendance is a big step in the right direction. But more than that is needed: Playing an intelligent and active role and furthering the just aims of the organization.

"Be ye doers of the word and not hearers only, deceiving your own selves." (James 1:22)

⍋ Help me to be a participant, O Lord, not merely a spectator.

BOTHERED BY CONSCIENCE 7 YEARS

Mrs. Chris Nelson of St. Anthony, Idaho, couldn't imagine who would be sending her $60. She didn't lend anyone that amount, she thought. And she hadn't appealed for any money.

Then she read this unsigned note attached to the three $20 bills: "*Here is the money you lost. Sorry I kept it so long.*"

Seven years ago, Mrs. Nelson lost her bankbook containing three $20 bills.

It is incidents like this that help to restore faith in mankind among those who take too dim a view of the trends of our day.

It would be foolish to blind ourselves to the breakdown of morals, the increase in brutality and the sordidness on all sides. The direction is not a healthy one, to be sure. But doing something to change it for the better is far more hopeful than merely bemoaning the situation.

If things were twice as bad as they are, there is still hope for the very good reason that the worst of men cannot completely obliterate or eliminate the last vestige of goodness within them. Try as they may to stifle that tendency to decency that God has embedded in each human being, they never completely succeed.

That is the everlasting hope of mankind: that man is redeemable, that the sinner can be a saint, that men will do good despite all.

"He that is without sin among you, let him first cast a stone at her." (John 8:7)

◄§ Remind me to show hope, O Lord, even in the most hopeless cases.

A $2.80 SPY

A 27-year-old unemployed clerk in London, accused of giving away highly secret information about anti-aircraft defenses, was a do-it-yourself spy who spied on his own, by his own methods and at the cut-rate price of $2.80.

The Crown charged that this young man had information about anti-aircraft defenses in northern Europe and knew the code word which would mobilize them. He gave this to Soviet Russia and received an occasional pound sterling, something less than three dollars.

Pleading innocent, the former clerk said he would conduct his own defense. He indicated his plea would include mental instability and a claim that the information was obtained from non-secret sources for an article he planned to write.

Yet, no one in court could understand how anyone seeking to prove he was not completely sane could at the same time conduct a complicated defense and cross-examination.

Those who put a cheap value on life and their own individual worth usually show a cheap disregard for the rights of others.

It takes more than restraints and prison bars to cope with such a problem. The only lasting solution is to instill in such an individual before it is too late some idea of his own priceless worth in the sight of Almighty God.

"For what shall it profit a man, if he gain the whole world, and suffer the loss of his soul?" (Mark 8:36)

AN UNFORTUNATE CHARGE

Roswell Woods of Norwich, N. Y., bravely answered a false charge of driving while drunk, according to an Associated Press report.

"It has been testified your eyes were glassy," the attorney said, as the jury looked on. 47-year-old Woods pointed to his glass eye which had replaced the one he lost in World War II.

The lawyer said testimony accused him of having a thick voice at the time of arrest. Speaking with difficulty, the defendant said he had partial paralysis of the throat which resulted from one of 27 injuries received in the South Pacific.

His attorney continued: "It is also testified you failed to pick up a coin placed on the floor."

It was then explained that Woods had undergone an operation in which part of a bone in one leg was used to replace the shattered bone in the other. He was unable to stoop from this battle injury.

Asked why he couldn't blow up a balloon which measures the amount of alcohol in the system, Woods replied: "I lost half of my lungs in the war. I can't exhale very well."

It did not take the jury very long to return its verdict of "Not Guilty" and thus avoid the tragedy of acting adversely on someone's mistaken judgment.

Look for the good in others first rather than their failings and you will never make a mistake!

"With what judgment you judge, you shall be judged."
(Matthew 7:2)

HELP YOURSELF BY HELPING OTHERS

"I think it's gas." These four words were all that a Philadelphia telephone operator heard before the person at the other end of the line gave a final gasp. An ominous silence followed.

Sensing it was a call for help because the line was still open, Operator Lavonne Moyer dialed the number of the home next to the one which issued the mysterious call. She told the man who answered to check his neighbor's home.

The neighbor found a 43-year-old woman slumped over in a chair, the telephone still in her lap. Police called the fire department and the victim was revived with oxygen.

Those who are as alert as this telephone operator to help others in trouble usually lead rich, interesting lives because they take the time and trouble to share with others the spiritual or material security they themselves possess.

It is part of God's divine plan that each of us is entrusted with more of His love than we need for ourselves. He expects us to be on the lookout for those who are in need and to transmit it to them. In short, by fulfilling this responsibility we become God's messengers or transmitters.

And the more one reaches out in this way, the more anxious he or she is to become a Christopher or Christbearer in every way possible. Especially in raising the standards of government, education, labor relations, literature and entertainment.

"Let us love one another, for charity is of God."

(1 John 4:7)

50,000 DOPE ADDICTS IN U.S.

There are more than 50,000 drug addicts in the United States today, according to Dr. Hubert S. Howe, an authority on the subject.

Dr. Howe, writing in the New York State Journal of Medicine, said six to eight of every 10 persons arrested for mail theft in New York are drug addicts. Narcotics are expensive, and Dr. Howe said an addict will turn to crime to obtain money to pay off dope peddlers.

"The United States has the highest crime rate of any civilized country in the world, and the largest black market in narcotic drugs," the article said. Dr. Howe proposed legislation to bar the supply of illegal drugs in the country.

More than laws will be needed for the curbing of drug addiction. They serve as protective measures to be sure, but those who deal in this deadly traffic find ways and means of circumventing laws.

The only hope for a lasting solution of this frightening problem is to get at the roots—at the causes. Most who turn to dope are the victims of spiritual insecurity. A feeling of worthlessness or failure easily degenerates into an attitude of complete frustration. God expects the home, the church and the school to supply the remedy that He has prescribed. If we fail to do this, we are inviting trouble on a bigger scale than we witness today.

"He that hath ears to hear, let him hear."

(Matthew 11:15)

DEATH OVER AN $8 BILL

A Brooklyn, N.Y., carpenter with no previous police record was being questioned by authorities in connection with the slaying of a gray-haired spinster.

He said the woman owed him money for a cellar door. When he asked her for it, she replied: *"I haven't got it— so I just can't pay you."*

"I lost my head and struck her with my fist," the 43-year-old man told police. *"I hit her twice and she fell backward and hit her head on a porcelain-top table."*

And how much did the lady owe the carpenter for the door? Eight dollars!

Losing control of one's self and resorting to violence usually results in making a bad situation considerably worse. But there is a widespread tendency today to jump from a mere misunderstanding to brutal extremes.

This trend is a sign that men are slowly losing an understanding of their true worth before Almighty God. And as soon as one lowers his respect for himself, he inevitably loses his reverence for others.

Urge your schools in particular to lay the foundations in every young person of a reverence for others because each and every individual counts *because* he is made in the image and likeness of God.

"What doth it profit a man if he gain the whole world and suffer the loss of his own soul? Or what shall a man give in exchange for his soul?" (Matthew 16:26)

ONE CRIME LEADS TO ANOTHER

A 40-year-old Philadelphia bookmaker was arrested for the fourth time in four months on charges of selling numbers and taking bets on horse racing.

When last arrested, the suspect was carrying an envelope containing 45 horse bets and three number plays.

"Don't you ever learn?" a sergeant asked him. The bookie said he couldn't stop "trying to make side money because I need it to pay lawyers for defending me."

Those who get into the habit of depending for their financial support on questionable sources, often get so deeply involved that they add one wrong to another in a vain effort to prevent themselves from getting hopelessly enmeshed.

Rather than wait until others have gone so far that it is virtually impossible to extricate them from a vicious circle of crime, do all in your power to help them rehabilitate themselves.

It is within the reach of all of us to give a helping hand to those who are weak in character. More often than not they will respond to the kindness and understanding that is sincere evidence of a Christlike sympathy.

Making such a move, however small, can have a beneficial result for you as well. The very fact that you have revived a sense of ideals in others will probably stimulate you to go further—to make your influence felt in the mainstream of modern life that tends to sink low if most show no interest.

"Be not therefore solicitous for tomorrow; for the morrow will be solicitous for itself." (Matthew 6:34)

NO KNIVES OR GUNS IN SCHOOL

It seems that pupils at Steele Grammar School in Denver, Colo., were carrying knives and guns to school so the principal took positive steps to stop the dangerous practice.

He gave each pupil the following note to pass on to his parents:

"Will you please help to see that children do not bring knives and guns of any kind to school? It has long been the policy of Steele School that pupils not carry knives and guns to school. We are sure you realize the reason for this policy."

The mere fact that such a notice has to be issued by the head of one of our schools is evidence that the trend among some young people is still in the wrong direction.

Rather than sit passively on the sidelines and watch the breakdown of youth taking place in many quarters, it would be far better if each one took it upon himself to do something to supply what is lacking in the training that boys and girls are receiving.

Each new child comes into the world endowed by God with a mind, heart and soul which can be trained to greatness. But much guidance is needed in the formative years to channel that power in the right direction.

"Suffer the little children, and forbid them not to come to me: for the kingdom of heaven is for such."

(Matthew 19:14)

 Help me to show a particular interest in bringing out the good that Thou has instilled in each human being, O Lord.

THEY SUGGESTED WRONG THINGS

City officials in Jamestown, New York, thought it would be a good idea to put a suggestion box in front of City Hall. In this way they would know what the people desired or did not desire.

The idea was an immediate success. Citizens soon filled the box and it was opened for the first time, but Mayor Samuel A. Stroth suggested the box be removed after reading the following suggestions:

"Tear down the jail."

"Fire the police."

"Set up more pool halls."

"Legalize gambling."

"Remove age limits on the sale of alcoholic beverages."

"Get a new city government."

A tendency on the part of most of us is to be *"against"* rather than to be *"for"* something. Little ever comes from vague generalizations especially if they are of a critical nature.

On the other hand some gain is usually made when an individual recognizes shortcomings but makes specific suggestions for improvement in a sympathetic, understanding manner.

God expects us to be doers, not mere complainers. The Christopher slogan *"Better to light one candle than to curse the darkness"* should stimulate all of us.

"Thou shalt not pass by if thou seest thy brother's ox or his sheep go astray: but thou shalt bring them back to thy brother." (Deuteronomy 22:1)

◄§ Let me be positive and constructive in all I do, O Lord.

HANGING BY A HOOK OVER WALL STREET

George Hauser, 26-year-old New York City window washer was humming a tune as he snapped each of the safety belts to a hook on the 12th floor of a Wall Street building.

Then he nonchalantly leaned back to begin the job. There was a crackling noise followed by a desperate scream. One of the hooks had broken and Hauser was left hanging by one end of his safety belt.

"Wall Street on a Saturday morning is practically deserted," he later recounted, *"and I wondered if my screams would be heard—I prayed they would."*

Ten minutes passed before a passer-by noticed him dangling in mid-air and notified the building superintendent who hurried to the 12th floor with a maintenance man. By the time they reached Hauser, he had already held on to the sill for six minutes and was exhausted. But the two men worked cautiously and five minutes later dragged him to safety.

"I was never so glad to see two men in my life," Hauser said of his rescuers. *"I was so excited all I could say to them was 'thank you so much.' "*

While most of us do not take the same risks as those of a window washer on a New York skyscraper, still we are more or less close to death at all times. The important thing is to be always prepared for that last day of our lives that must come sooner or later.

"In all thy works remember thy last end, and thou shalt never sin." (Ecclesiasticus 7:40)

✍ Keep me ever ready, O God, for my final accounting.

BACK TO GOD

The American Legion recently published a handbook entitled "Back to God" which outlines the steps this nation must take if it is to preserve the God-given rights of its citizens.

The "Back to God" movement proposed by the Legion has three objectives: 1) regular public worship; 2) daily family prayer; 3) the religious education of our children.

Emphasis in the handbook is put on the family because it is *"the basic unit of society"* and must be kept from falling apart. In other words, a nation is as strong as the families which form its very foundation.

"As a matter of fact," the handbook added, "it is the only natural unit of society, and as such, it, too, has rights received from God. The family then, as a unit, should also recognize its Creator and be thankful to Him. The family as a unit should express that worship and thanksgiving in prayer. Let us ask God's blessing at meals and be thankful for favors received. Remember, 'the family that prays together, stays together.' "

Great good can be accomplished by the hundreds of thousands of organizations in the United States if they take it upon themselves to restore to the mainstream of American life, a greater reverence of spiritual truths upon which this nation is founded. *You can do something about that!*

"That which you hear in the ear, preach ye upon the housetops." (Matthew 10:27)

◢§ Inspire, O Lord, those who belong to organizations to use them for the greatest good.

THEY THOUGHT HE WAS DEAD

A retired, 78-year-old Chicago painter who was reported dead and buried, shocked friends by appearing a year later as full of life as can be.

Stewart McLean, financial secretary of a painter's union, said he was told a year before by undertakers that they had the body of William "Pat" Wallace. The union gave the undertakers $265 to pay for the funeral, according to McLean.

When union officials went to the wake they were told Wallace had already been buried, McLean said.

"The undertaker told me there was some kind of a mistake but I haven't been able to find out what it's all about," McLean said. "But the Social Security and Old Age Pension people finally took our word for it that Pat is alive."

It must be quite a shock to be taken for dead by friends and acquaintances while one is still very much alive! But it must be a far greater surprise to stand before the throne of God and be completely unprepared for that final accounting of every thought, word and deed of our lives.

Those who conscientiously live for that great day will have the great joy of hearing Our Lord Himself say:

"Well done, thou good servant, because thou hast been faithful in a little." (Luke 19:17)

❧ Let each day of my life, O Lord, be a preparation for the endless years of eternity.

FALLS 1000 FEET—AND LIVES!

Paratrooper Stanley Melczak of Pittsburgh steadied himself for a split-second, then jumped from an airplane 1000 feet over Anchorage, Alaska.

He waited for the sharp snap the chute would give his body when it filled with air. But it never came. He whistled earthward and picked up speed by the second.

Pulling his body together to absorb the terrific shock, he anticipated the crash against frozen ground which would split his body. He hit with a dull thud and all was quiet.

Realizing he was still alive, Melczak staggered to his feet and walked away. He had landed in 38 inches of snow! Not a bone was broken.

We count it a great blessing when we narrowly escape injury or death. But we tend to overlook countless other advantages that are extraordinary gifts of God even though we take them for granted in ordinary fashion.

Yes, count your blessings every day of your life: the blessing of faith, of health, of education, of food and shelter, of leisure and of numerous other special benefits that are not the lot of hundreds of millions of other human beings. Show your appreciation to God by helping others less fortunate in body and soul.

"Not everyone that saith to me Lord, Lord, shall enter into the kingdom of heaven; but he that doth the will of my Father who is in heaven, he shall enter into the kingdom of heaven." (Matthew 7:21)

∽§ Thanks to Thee, my Redeemer, for all Thy graces and blessings.

TAX DODGING UNFAIR TO OTHERS

Income tax collectors in Redruth, England, claimed 58-year-old Archie Hill owed them nearly $10,000 but they would have to risk their lives obtaining the money.

Hill denied owing the money and took strong steps to prevent collectors from doing their duty. He patrolled his property with a loaded shotgun and erected this sign:

"Income tax: any persons employed by the above entering on this property do so at their own risk."

Hill told reporters the collectors "are not going to have my house" and left the officials with a touchy problem to solve.

Very few people show any enthusiasm about paying taxes. But whether they do it grudgingly or not, they realize that one and all without exception have to share the costly burden of running their government. As all have a right to share in the benefits, so all have an obligation to carry their share of the load in supporting it, as well as seeing that it is staffed by capable people.

There are a few, however, who specialize in tax-dodging. In fact, they take a bit of glory in evading their payments through various loopholes and devices. Such a practice, if carried far enough can weaken or wreck a country economically, as has happened in many parts of the world during the past few decades. In addition, it is a form of cheating that is not fair to others, often less fortunate, who must have imposed on them the added burden of taxes others dodge.

"Doth not your master pay the didrachma? He said: Yes." (Matthew 17:23-24)

STICK TO THE FACTS

The town of Clanton, Alabama, was buzzing with news, $440,000—part of it in gold—had been found on land once owned by John Higgins.

One report had it that the Internal Revenue Bureau was interested in Higgins and his new wealth. But it seems that everybody in Clanton heard about the man's good fortune except Mr. Higgins himself.

When asked how it felt to be a rich man, Higgins replied: "Not only did I not get any $440,000, I didn't even get the quarter."

Actually, workmen had found a 25-cent piece on the land, but by the time the story had passed around the Court House, the quarter had inflated to $440,000.

If such exaggeration was limited to harmless subjects, little if any trouble would result. But when under the heading of gossip, the small mistakes of an individual are bandied about and made a little worse as they go from tongue to tongue, the resulting harm can be very serious indeed.

One sure way to increase your love of people is to regard it as an obligation in conscience to spread only what is good about others. You will then run no risk whatever of damaging the reputation of others by exaggerating their faults.

A very safe rule to follow in this regard is the standard set by Jesus Christ Himself:

"Whatsoever you would that men should do to you, do you also to them." (Matthew 7:12)

WHAT TEEN-AGERS NEED MOST

When George Washington left Mt. Vernon to assume the Presidency, his mother, who had taught him a deep respect for religion, said these parting words to him:

"Go, George, go my son, and may the blessing of God and of a mother be with you always."

If every one of the 40 million mothers in America would send their sons and daughters into life with such a fervent blessing, it would do much to instill a greater reverence for God and for parents as well as a much needed respect for authority.

No one is in a better position than parents to deepen in the young a sense of personal responsibility to God and their fellowman. This cannot be done by some passive remark to be sure. It must be a continuing part of training and development from early childhood to the time children launch out for themselves.

In her recent book, "Never Alone," Joan Roberts, who played the first lead in "Oklahoma" gives credit to her mother for giving her a sense of balance that has been a great asset to her ever since. Here is one bit of advice that her mother gave her:

"Always remember, Joan," she said one night after supper, "always remember that whatever talents you have, you got from God; that He made it possible for you to sing so that you can make other people happy. Never, never, as long as you live, ever use your gifts in such a way as to make God regret that He was so good to you."

"For better is one that feareth God than a thousand ungodly children." (Ecclesiasticus 16:3)

MISPLACED FAITH IS COSTLY

A retired Philadelphia carpenter, walking out of his home, was attracted by the shouting of two men who didn't care who heard them.

It developed that one man was a jeweler and the other a Russian seaman. The seaman wanted to sell the jeweler a gold coin and the two were haggling over the price. With the help of this 65-year-old carpenter, who acted as an impartial interpreter, the coin was sold for six dollars.

Then the seaman exhibited a jewel box filled with 10 gleaming stones and offered them for $10,000. The jeweler at this point produced a glass, peered at the stones with a professional mien, and said, "They're real."

"I can raise $5000," he told the carpenter. "Can you raise another $5000? We can sell them for $20,000."

The carpenter, excited with the thought of making a handsome profit, went to the bank to withdraw money. Refused because a two-weeks' notice was needed, he asked for a quick loan and cashed the certified check at another bank.

After the transaction, the men disappeared. Suspicious, the carpenter took the stones to the police. A reliable jeweler was consulted. Breaking the sad news, he said the stones were worth about ten cents.

The confidence that people place in all sort of fraudulent enterprises is a sure sign that they wish to put faith in something. How much better if the trust were placed in God!

"For we walk by faith, and not by sight."
(II Corinthians 5:7)

THE GOOD COMES THROUGH

Policeman J. G. Lamere of Montgomery, Ala., became mighty suspicious when he saw a motorist come to a sudden stop as the light turned green.

Now all would have been fine and lawful if the light were red. But you don't stop for green, Lamere reasoned.

Upon investigation he found his hunch was right. The man was drunk and paid a $200 fine for driving while intoxicated.

It is interesting to note how those who are mixed up in mischief either on a small or large scale reveal in one way or another that they know the truth.

It is, in fact, a real tribute to the truth and to the eternal values of God that the thief likes to appear as an honest man; that the individual who is bent on subversion strives to appear as the most loyal of persons and that he who is given up to immorality likes to pose as a respectable person.

To those who have the faith, hope and charity to push on despite all obstacles, to bring the peace of Christ to the world, it should be a deeply consoling fact that there is some good in the worst of men. No prayer, word or deed, however slight, that aims at redeeming or rehabilitating them, is in vain.

At the same time, keep ever conscious of those who would use good to hide their evil intent. As Christ said:

"Beware of false prophets, who come to you in the clothing of sheep, but inwardly they are ravening wolves."

(Matthew 7:15)

≈§ Grant me the grace, O Lord, to find hope where I see no hope.

COURAGE MAKES THE DIFFERENCE

Jim Wilson, Milwaukee Braves' pitcher, who was chosen the most courageous athlete of 1954 by the Philadelphia Sports Writers Association, was told twice he would never be able to play baseball.

One of the National League's outstanding pitchers, Wilson hurled last season's only no-hit, no-run game. Nine years before, the 195-pound Boston Red Sox right-hander was hit in the head by a line drive off the bat of Hank Greenberg, famous Detroit Tigers' slugger.

Wilson underwent a two-hour operation for a fractured skull and suffered headaches, dizzy spells and convulsions a long time after. Yet, he refused to lay down his glove.

The following year he was back in the minor leagues. Tragedy struck again. He had his leg broken "in six or seven places below the knee" by another line drive.

But the determined Californian didn't take it sitting down. He started from the bottom again and finally made the major leagues again in 1951.

It is amazing, yet refreshing to see what extraordinary goals can be achieved by those who "never take 'no' for an answer." What is even more inspiring is to see what one individual, fortified by the grace of God, will do because his or her heart is set on bringing about better government, better teaching, better literature, better entertainment and better everything else.

"The kingdom of heaven suffereth violence, and the violent bear it away." (Matthew 11:12)

◄§ Give me the vision and strength, O Lord, to persevere in doing good.

THE GOOD THAT CANNOT
BE STIFLED

A sound truck in Montevideo, the capital of Uruguay, was broadcasting Communist election propaganda, and halted to change the record. The weary driver nonchalantly dropped another disc on the roundtable and continued through the mid-town area.

Two blocks later pandemonium broke loose and the driver looked as frightened as a man facing a firing squad. By mistake he had put on the record, "*God Bless America.*"

It is seldom that those who spend their time and energy fighting against God make the mistake of bringing His Holy Name into anything. But we feel even those who are violently opposed to everything that is spiritual have a lingering desire in their heart to work for God.

As a matter of fact, the incessant manner in which they protest is, in one sense, a sign that they do believe. Those who protest too much really show an inner lack of security. Because they cannot stifle the thought of God within them they keep fighting against what they believe in their heart and soul.

Show a great kindness and consideration for such persons. All that is often needed to win them away from hatred and to the love of God is a little word, a bit of attention, and a positive suggestion on how they can do something for God instead of against Him.

"*Lord, what wilt Thou have me to do?*" (The Acts 9:6)

AND STILL NO PEACE

We can rightfully boast of our material advances in this 20th century. But we should not blink at the fact that it has been likewise the bloodiest period in human history, and that modern ingenuity has now made possible universal death and destruction through the atom and hydrogen bombs.

During the past 40 years, 63 million human beings were killed in two World Wars. Countless millions of others were maimed and crippled. The cost in money alone was more than a *thousand billion dollars*.

Within the past few years, 33 thousand Americans were killed and more than 103 thousand wounded in the Korean conflict that cost the American taxpayers almost twenty billion dollars.

Out of a budget of 62 billion dollars to run the U.S.A. for the year 1955-56, nearly 41 billion is for defense against new and deadly conflicts. In addition, four and a half billion dollars must be set aside to pay for obligations accruing from past wars. Therefore, only 17 out of 62 million dollars is being budgeted for the normal functions of government. *And still no lasting peace!*

The defeatist attitude, *"my opinion doesn't count in shaping the policies of our government,"* can be a very harmful one. Those who would undermine our country do everything they can to encourage this point of view. It leaves the field free for them. Play the role which God expects of you.

"The kingdom of heaven is like to leaven, which a woman took and hid in three measures of meal, until the whole was leavened." (Matthew 13:33)

EIGHT YEARS TOGETHER
WITHOUT TALKING

For eight, long, boring years, a Chicago couple communicated to each other by writing notes which they pinned to a bulletin board in the kitchen.

They weren't deaf mutes. Just a husband and wife who didn't get along. The woman was a 44-year-old laboratory technician and her husband a 46-year-old truck driver.

The couple had three children who had to live through this "no-talking" siege. But the silence has been broken. The husband and wife have finally parted company, adding one more broken home to the 400,000 that are split asunder each year in the United States.

It is almost unbelievable that a couple would go to such extremes as not to talk to each other over such a long period. And what a terrible ordeal it must have been for the children who had a right to expect a united front on the part of their parents.

You can make at least one step towards peace by bringing the happiness and joy of Christ into your home circle, classroom, business, or any gathering in which you happen to find yourself.

Take care not to go down to the level of those who tend to be mean, sarcastic or belligerent. Put love where there is no love and you will eventually find love.

"This is my commandment, that you love one another, as I have loved you." (John 15:12)

LIBERTY IS NOT LICENSE

A New York State legislator recently said proposed laws to clean up comic books are meant to make them "funny again" and not to destroy freedom of the press.

Assemblyman FitzPatrick of Plattsburgh, chairman of a joint legislative committee studying publication of comic books and obscene publications, said:

"We have no intention of interfering with freedom of the press . . . But freedom without obligation is anarchy. We feel sure that the responsible elements of the industry agree that we should not countenance any confusion of liberty with license and should move against those who persist in corrupting the minds and morals of children for profit."

The Assemblyman pointed out that his group had found a direct correlation between an increase in crime and delinquency and the horror, brutality and crime depicted in comic books, radio, television and pocket books.

The bill would prohibit the sale of all types of obscene literature to children.

Laws are needed to protect the public against the few who would take unfair advantage of it. But more than legislation is needed to bring about the good literature that most people, young and old, really want. More persons with high ideals and ability are urgently needed in the writing field. Once they are forthcoming and show as much zest and enterprise preparing good stories as a few others do in promoting brutality and immorality, a change for the better is bound to take place.

"Let your light shine before men, that they may see your good works, and glorify your Father who is in heaven." (Matthew 5:16)

NOSE SAVED HIS LIFE

Eleven-year-old Brian Walker walked into a London candy store and asked for a chocolate bar.

The following morning he walked into the store and told the clerk he didn't want the bar he bought yesterday. The puzzled salesman asked why he had changed his mind.

"It smells nasty," Brian answered. "Could I please have a better one?"

When the clerk examined the bar he found he had mistakenly given Brian a bar to kill rats.

God has instilled in young people a fairly keen sense of what is right and wrong and He watches over them with a special protection.

But He expects those who have been delegated by Him to care for their training and development to build up in them a deep sense of values which will exert a strong influence on their entire lives.

To overlook this assistance to the young would be to deprive them of a God-given right. To teach them, as some do, that there is no difference between right and wrong is worse than to tell them that there is no difference between healthy and poisoned food.

Do everything in your power to see that the young are provided with the full measure that God wishes them to have. They should not be shortchanged in any way.

"Suffer the little children, and forbid them not to come to me. . . ." (Matthew 19:14)

&§ Protect in a special way, O Jesus, the little ones whom some would lead astray.

91,000 DIED IN ACCIDENTS

One out of every 17 persons in the United States last year suffered a disabling injury.

Accidents in that year killed 91,000 persons and injured 9,200,000. The economic loss was nearly $10,000,000,000.

Once again the nation's No. 1 accident killer was the motor vehicle, according to the National Safety Council. In 1954, 36,300 persons lost their lives in traffic mishaps, a reduction of five per cent from 1953 and the lowest total since 1950. Traffic accidents last year caused 1,250,000 non-fatal injuries.

The overall death total was a drop of four per cent compared with the 95,000 accidents in 1953.

Accidents in the home took the second largest number of lives—28,000—a decrease of 1000 over 1953. Nineteen thousand eight hundred persons were killed in falls; 6500 died of burns; 6600 drowned and 2300 perished by firearms.

Much if not most of this enormous loss of life and property could be prevented if more people would simply apply to their driving the divine law of "doing unto others as you would have them do unto you."

Letting another person have the right of way, restraining one's speed, showing the numerous little courtesies that everybody would like and too few give is an excellent way of putting into constant practice the love of God and your fellowman.

"Whosoever will force thee one mile, go with him other two." (Matthew 5:41)

❧ Remind me to show respect to others in all that I do, O Lord.

HIDES FORTUNE IN SHABBY HOME

When a 76-year-old Detroit, Mich., spinster was dying, she called her cousin and whispered in her ear: "If anything happens to me, look in the closet off the front bedroom. All my papers are there."

After the woman died, the cousin began searching the shabby, nine-room home inch by inch. They found $150,000 in securities and $100,000 cash tucked in the closet—but no will.

In other rooms they found tobacco sacks, shoe boxes, paper folders and fishing tackle cases filled with bankbooks. Balances ran from $36 to $10,016.31 which were distributed in 10 accounts in five banks. Officials said the secret fortune might total more than $500,000.

Saving for a rainy day is one thing but allowing ourselves to become so possessive that we accumulate far more than we need can turn a virtue into a vice.

It may have been the intention of this good lady to leave to those poorer than herself the treasure that she had carefully gathered and protected over many years.

Death can surprise all of us in the midst of building up treasure on earth and forgetting to lay up treasure in heaven for the endless years of eternity.

One way to keep a sense of balance is to remember what Christ said:

"Seek ye therefore first the kingdom of God and His Justice, and all these things shall be added unto you."
                              (Matthew 6:33)

❧ Keep me detached, O Jesus, from the things of this life.

314

TERMITES HELP EACH OTHER

Termites better be on the lookout for the new electronic "ears" which are so sensitive they reportedly can catch the sound of a termite's footsteps.

And this is important because one entomologist says termites warn each other of impending danger by stamping their feet.

The portable listening device is also expected to help in studies of other insects' behavior. Called the "Microsonic Detector" by its developer, Roy J. Pence of the University of California, it weighs 4½ pounds.

Pence said when they hear wood being tapped, termites stamp their feet to signal the rest of the colony.

The new detector can pick up this stamping through its needle-thin probe which is inserted into the wood and connected to earphones.

God has endowed both man and the least of his creatures with a keen sense of protecting themselves and those depending on them.

Certainly we have no excuse for not being alert to all the dangers that follow in the wake of atheism and godlessness.

Rather than wait for a crisis or emergency to arise, we would do far better to show the enterprise and initiative that will further good and prevent evil.

"Be sober and watch because your adversary the devil, as a roaring lion, goeth about seeking whom he may devour." (1 Peter 5:8)

⚜ Let me use for Thy glory, O Lord, the many powers that Thou hast entrusted to me.

POLICE CANNOT TAKE MOTHER'S PLACE

When a 5½-year-old boy came home from kindergarten in Atlantic City, N.J., and found his mother wasn't there to prepare his lunch, he called the police for help.

Sgt. Albert Wilson, on desk duty at headquarters, answered the phone and heard a high-pitched voice exclaim:

"I came home from school for lunch and Mommy's not here and I'm hungry. Would you please send somebody to 12 N. Main Ave. to get me some lunch so I can go back to school?" He gave his name and hung up.

Wilson figured the boy was the son of a fellow municipal employee, so he sent two patrolmen to the address. They made the boy a sandwich and scrambled an egg. Then they drove the lad to school. His mother had been shopping and forgot it was lunch time.

There are certain functions that government must perform for the people who for one reason or another are not in a position to help themselves. But it cannot take the place of parents. It should be dinned into the minds of all, especially the young, that they should be self-reliant and depend upon others, above all—government, as little as possible.

The home is the most important school of all in which to teach each to be dependent on self as far as possible. God planned it that way. The more time and attention that parents can give to the development of the heart, mind and soul of the young ones, the better for everyone.

"His bones shall be filled with the vices of his youth and they shall sleep with him in the dust." (Job 20:11)

◄§ Remind me, O Lord, to stand on my own two feet.

MAKE THIS TRUTH LIVE

The Lincoln Memorial in Washington, D.C., is a nation's tribute to its martyred Civil War president. This massive shrine pays homage to the greatness of a simple and heroic man whose very life was offered in the cause of liberty.

The gentleness, spiritual power, and determination of Lincoln come to us clearly through the features chiseled in granite by the sculptor. We can almost hear him speak the words that are cut in the wall by his side:

". . . that this nation under God shall have a new birth of freedom, and that government of the people, by the people, for the people, shall not perish from the earth."

It cannot be stressed too often that our country is founded on the concept that all men derive their rights from one Creator and the purpose of government is to protect these God-given rights. Like Lincoln, every President of the United States from George Washington down to the present, has paid repeated tribute to this important fact.

But more than acknowledgment of this fundamental is needed in these critical times. It is easy to fall into a mere lip service attitude on such a vital matter. Do your part to make this truth a living force in every facet of American life, public as well as private.

"Let your light shine before men." (Matthew 5:16)

⁴⁄₅ Let me spend and be spent in spreading a knowledge and love of Thee, O my God, and not keep Thy truth to myself.

A THREE-YEAR-OLD AT THE THROTTLE

Three-year-old Stephen Ford of Hebron, Md., was fascinated by the automobile shift of the family car which his mother left running while she dashed into the post office.

Like any curious child, young Stephen pulled the lever and the car bolted forward. For 12 minutes it careened through the streets.

First, it smashed into the parked car of a city councilman. Then it bowled over an assortment of signs marked "Slow," "Stop," and "No Parking."

Next, the car bumped into several utility poles and mowed down a half-dozen thick oak posts set up to keep cars off the railroad tracks.

With motorists and pedestrians scurrying for cover, the wayward car turned around and rammed into Councilman Smith's insurance office.

Practically demolished in this last encounter, the car limped past a pedestrian who boarded it, climbed through a smashed window and turned the ignition key.

Stephen wriggled out of the heap of metal unhurt.

It is easy to see in a case like this how different things would have been if the little one's mother had taken the proper precaution. But it is not so easy for many to realize how particularly careful one must be in protecting the mind, heart and soul of youth from anything that will debase and defile their outlook.

"He that shall scandalize one of these little ones that believe in me, it were better for him that a millstone should be hanged about his neck, and that he should be drowned in the depth of the sea." (Matthew 18:6)

$15,000 MASTERPIECE FOR $20

A Long Island, N.Y., couple recently bought a painting for $20 without knowing at the time it was a masterpiece worth $15,000.

They bought the oil painting in an old furniture store because the wife was intrigued by its beauty. An amateur painter herself, the woman asked an expert for his professional opinion of the work which was covered with dirt.

He said he was "absolutely convinced" it was the work of Van Dyck, the 17th century Flemish master. He described it as a "penitent Magdalene once in the collection of King William II of Holland."

Few of us will likely make any such discovery as this couple did. But there is not one among us who cannot discover in our own surroundings innumerable opportunities of seemingly small value which when sanctified by love of God and others, take on a priceless worth for all eternity.

Rather than sit on the sidelines waiting for these opportunities to come to you, why not start looking for them? God blesses those who try. And He reserves many wonderful surprises for those who strive in His name to make the world better for their being in it. Stir up others as well to be alert in looking for any and all occasions to enrich the world in which they live.

"Launch out into the deep, and let down your nets for a draught." (Luke 5:4)

SEVEN YEARS SAVINGS STOLEN

For seven years a 57-year-old laborer in Buffalo, N.Y., had been saving his money in $10, $20 and $50 bills which he kept in a closet safe.

But somehow a thief learned where this man had the money hidden and paid a visit to his home. Gaining entrance through an unlocked bedroom window in midday, the thief had little trouble opening the small safe and left $2000 richer.

Some people spend a lifetime gathering together a treasure, small or large, from which they derive little or no pleasure. What a shock it must be, after long years of struggle to see their heart's desire dissipated in a matter of moments through theft, inflation, catastrophe or death.

Man must make some effort to accumulate the material necessities that are essential to his security. But he would do well not to put all of his eggs in one basket. He should strive with even greater diligence to "lay up treasure in heaven."

Make every day of your life count for the endless years of eternity. You must provide for the reasonable cares of this life but don't miss a single opportunity to begin your heaven on earth. To do this you must think, pray and work outside of yourself and work for the material and spiritual welfare of others as you do for your own.

Reflect often on the words of Christ:

"Lay not up to yourselves treasures on earth where the rust and moth consume and where thieves break through and steal. But lay up to yourselves treasures in heaven."
(Matthew 6:19-20)

A TICKET STUB SAVED HIS LIFE

An avalanche buried hunter Evert Stenmark near Tarnaby, Sweden, and for eight days he was trapped under tons of snow.

Each day he grew weaker and his hopes became dimmer. He was so starved that he ate the raw meat of three grouse he had shot.

Stenmark knew a search party would be sent after him as soon as his long absence was noticed. So he had to attract their attention. But how?

Then the idea sprung into his dazed mind. He had a red movie ticket stub in his pocket and attached it to the end of a stick. Then slowly, carefully, he pushed the stick up through the snow and waved it with his remaining strength.

The idea worked! Rescuers saw the red ticket which, small as it was, stood out against the chalk-white snow. In a short time they had dug the half-frozen hunter from what almost became his tomb. Except for frost-bitten feet, he was in good condition.

A tiny piece of seemingly worthless paper was instrumental in saving this man's life, so can little prayers, acts, words and deeds have similar big results for good if done in the name of Christ.

The more your life is dominated by a continuing desire to lead a worthwhile existence, the more you will find a deeper meaning in small details that are ordinarily passed off as being of little or no significance. In the sight of God nothing that you do is insignificant.

"Consider the lilies of the field . . . they labor not, neither do they spin . . . not even Solomon in all his glory was arrayed as one of these." (Matthew 6:28-29)

THE GIRLS LEARNED A LESSON

Girls in the eighth grade of a Dover, N.J., grammar school were wearing blue jeans and saddle shoes to class and the boys resented their informality.

So all the boys in the eighth grade, 70 strong, marched in one day, dressed in gleaming white shirts, ties and shoes polished like mirrors.

The girls quickly caught the point and decided to wear more feminine clothes following the male fashion show.

There are many ways of correcting trends that appear to be unbecoming. The more this is done in a friendly, good-natured manner, the more effective the solution usually is.

Young people in particular should be encouraged to show imagination and initiative in correcting abuses that are creeping up in their midst today. As these boys in New Jersey took it upon themselves to "overdo" in their own dress, they got over a lesson to their girl classmates that might not have been taught in any other way.

The vast majority of young people in America are basically good and decent. If even a few among them showed the courage of conviction, with which they are endowed by God, in taking a similar positive and constructive stand for what is decent and dignified, they might do much to take away the false glamor of juvenile delinquency.

Draw attention to this method among young people. They usually love something with a challenge, especially if it can be helpful to others.

"You are the salt of the earth. But if the salt lose its savour, wherewith shall it be salted?" (Matthew 5:13)

PLAY FAIR WITH THOSE WHO
SERVE YOU

Voters in a New Hampshire town were faced with a dilemma concerning their State Representative who also held down the janitor's job at the local high school.

It seems the 46-year-old man could not regularly attend to his job as custodian because legislative duties were too pressing. Citizens complained and a special meeting of voters was held in this small town to decide his fate as janitor.

The vote allowed him to keep both jobs. As a janitor he receives $3200 a year; as Representative, $200 a year, plus mileage.

It is important in the maintenance of government on all levels to avoid two extremes. We should not allow neglect or corruption in public affairs. On the other hand we should avoid treating public servants with such little regard and providing them with such small recompense that it is difficult for them to tackle their job in a wholehearted manner.

You can render a great service by supporting those who represent you in all levels of government and by providing them with the same fair treatment that you would expect if you were serving in a similar capacity.

This is one important way to put into practical application that important standard Jesus Christ set for all of us:

"Whatsoever you would that men should do to you, do you also to them." (Matthew 7:12)

THE FOUNDATION STONE

James Wilson (1742-1798) commonly referred to as the "philosopher of the Constitution" and one of the few signers of both the Declaration of Independence and the Constitution wrote much about the Natural Law. We quote some of it:

"... that our Creator has a supreme right to prescribe a law for our conduct, and that we are under the most perfect obligation to obey that law, are truths established on the clearest and most solid principles ... (God) being infinitely and eternally happy in Himself, His goodness alone could move Him to create us, and give us the means of happiness. The same principle that moved His creating moves His governing power. What is the efficient cause of moral obligation—of the eminent distinction between right and wrong? ... I give it (the question) this answer, the will of God. This is the Supreme Law. ... The law of nature is universal."

We cannot keep too much in mind that the founders of our nation built our Constitutional form of government on the Natural Moral Law of God. It is well today to recall some of the utterances, especially when we are tempted to listen to those who would guide us in different directions.

Remind people whenever possible of this important fact; that our nation was founded on God's law.

"Moreover, he gave them instructions and the law of life for their inheritance." (Ecclesiasticus 17:9)

&es; Keep us in mind of Thy Law always, O Lord.

NEGLECT CAN BE COSTLY

Melvin Weiss of Queens, N.Y., was busy setting up his camera to take a picture of a store front in Newark, N.J. One camera had been set up and Weiss was focusing another one from a different angle.

The 32-year-old photographer had his head under the black cloth shield of his tripod-mounted camera trying to get the range when someone took advantage of his position. When Weiss took his head from beneath the cloth and started for his other camera he found it had been stolen.

In the busy world of today it is most important that we do not become so preoccupied with one phase of our responsibilities that we take a severe loss in another.

We live in an atomic age. Things are moving fast. The slightest neglect or mistake may be a very costly one. We have no choice but to be alert at all times.

Of far more consequence than any material loss we may take by being caught off-guard is the danger to our immortal souls. Those who hate God are making a greater effort than ever before in history to reduce man to the level of a beast.

Rather than merely take a fearful, cautious attitude toward this danger, do something positive and constructive by prayer and work to champion the sacred worth of the individual.

"Fear ye not them that kill the body, and are not able to kill the soul." (Matthew 10:28)

≈§ Allow me, O Lord, to be an apostle of Thy truth.

WE ALL DEPEND ON OTHERS

Squirrels in Bremerton, Washington, worked like beavers collecting evergreen cones only to have people take and sell them.

About 100 persons sold the fir, hemlock, red cedar and lodge pole pine cones for from $4 to $12 a bag. The seeds are planted and help reforest burned territory.

The squirrels stockpile the cones in the ground or in fallen trees. One cone-picker, lucky enough to find many caches, said he made $40 in one day. Some pickers paid back the animals by leaving corn, nuts and wheat in place of the cones.

An example like this is a forceful reminder that the vast majority of us are more dependent than we realize on God's creatures and His works of nature for our very survival. The food we eat, the clothes we wear, the houses we live in, the autos, trains and planes we fly in and the countless other benefits of life are not the fruits of our own enterprise or imagination. More immediately, we are indebted to our fellowmen who have helped in a variety of ways to put them at our disposal.

But great as their effort may have been, they have done little more than transmit in modified form one or other of the innumerable blessings that a beneficent Creator has placed at the disposal of His children on earth.

The more you play a part in sharing these blessings with others, for their advantage and not merely for your own gain, the more you will realize the privilege of being God's instrument.

"Lord, make me an instrument of your peace!"

(St. Francis)

BACK TO THE SOURCES

On a cold November morning in 1620, a tiny vessel, the Mayflower, approached Plymouth Rock. Aboard, forty-one men, women and children were elated at the sight of land.

Before stepping on firm ground, the men gathered on deck to sign the Mayflower Compact. Long hours of discussion had gone into this record of their crystal-clear purpose, which reads in part:

"In the Name of God, Amen.

"We, whose names are underwritten, the loyal subjects of our dread Sovereign Lord King James, by the Grace of God, of Great Britain, France and Ireland, King, Defender of the Faith etc. . . . Having undertaken for the Glory of God and the Honour of our King and country, a Voyage to plant the first colony in the northern parts of Virginia . . ."

They called upon God to witness the signing.

It is too often and too easily forgotten that our forefathers founded our first American settlements for the Glory of God. It is only of very recent years that a systematic attempt has been made to have us forget or reject our first inspirations. And worse still, those who tend in that direction are those who show most zeal in getting into the vital spheres of influence.

Those who will remind us of our beginning and traditions are sorely needed in these vital fields. Do your part by "getting in" yourself, or encouraging someone else to do so.

"Unless the Lord build the house, they labour in vain that build it." (Psalms 126:1)

43 YEARS IN PRISON

For 43 of his 75 years, a Cranston, Rhode Island, man knew nothing but the lonely, dull life of a prisoner.

He was a convicted murderer and had served 43 years in prison. Worse yet, in all that time he did not have one visitor or one letter.

The lonely old man died recently in a state infirmary where he was transferred in 1951 under conditional pardon. Hopelessly paralyzed, he had spent 26 of those years in bed.

One of the tragic oversights of our day is to neglect those who have made mistakes that necessitate their imprisonment. Regardless of how much they deserve punishment, they likewise should be rehabilitated as quickly and completely as possible.

This is no easy task, to be sure. In fact, in some instances it is impossible to bring about a cure. But because a few do not respond to treatment is no excuse for neglecting the many who are serving short sentences and who could be morally rejuvenated.

Crime correction as well as crime prevention needs your sympathetic interest. While firmness is essential, so is a Christlike understanding and patience.

"I was in prison, and you came to me . . . As long as you did it to one of these my least brethren, you did it to me."
(Matthew 25:36,40)

⇜ Have mercy, O Jesus, on those in prison.

328

THE EVIL EFFECTS OF EVIL

Owners of a Westminster, Md., grocery company found someone had tampered with the safe but could not open it. But after investigating the attempted burglary they would have been happier if the thief had been successful.

And their attitude wasn't unusual. The burglar had jammed the combination of the safe to such an extent, company officials could not get it open. They tried everything possible to find the right combination but to no avail.

At last reports mechanics were surveying the safe which is embedded in a foot-and-a-half of concrete and thinking of blasting out the wall. It looked like an expensive proposition.

Those who violate the laws of God seldom heed the fact that one act of mischief may have far-reaching repercussions. Not until they stand before the Judgment Seat of God will they fully realize the chain reaction effect of one evil thought or deed.

By the same token, those who perform even one act of faith, hope or charity often start an unending series of good deeds without ever being conscious of what they have achieved.

For better or for worse, each and every thought, word and deed of yours counts more than you think.

"Let your light shine before men, that they may see your good works and glorify your Father who is in heaven."
(Matthew 5:16)

Keep me ever reminded, O Lord, of the importance of little things.

THE MISSING $300

Louis Magid, proprietor of a small fruit store in New York City, discovered that he lost $300 and was in no mood to answer the questions of a deputy fire chief who was on the telephone.

That morning Magid had the $300 ready to pay the rent and some urgent bills. He had cashed some defense bonds the day before to obtain the money but suddenly it disappeared.

The store owner finally consented to answer the fire chief's questions about an application he had sent in the day before for renewal of his annual permit to operate a small freezing unit. But he became irritated when the fireman asked him if he had any difficulty making the application.

Magid, despondent at the time, said he had lost $300 and asked to be left alone. Then the deputy chief told him that his worries were over because attached to his application were three crisp $100 bills. The fruit dealer had inadvertently placed the money with his application which called for $3.

Little errors, made in good faith, punctuate the lives of all of us. They should not discourage us, for the important thing is the rectitude of our motives. If we are sincerely trying to do right, God is for us, and "if God be for us, who is against us?"

If our intentions and efforts are good, God will make up for our deficiencies. In the Final Exam it will be the "A for effort" that will help to get us through safely.

"I glory in my infirmities, that the power of Christ may dwell in me." (II Corinthians 12:9)

TELL-TALE GLOVES

A husband-wife burglary team was successfully operating in New York City until the husband became careless with a stolen pair of leather gloves.

While the burglar's wife was bargaining with a pawnbroker, the man stood outside the shop munching on a peach. A detective walking by noticed a pair of gloves protruding from the man's pocket. Knowing that a pair of gloves had been among items recently stolen from an apartment in the vicinity, he questioned the man.

The husband broke down and admitted he had burglarized the apartment in question and led the detective to his wife. It turned out that the wife did all the "work" on the burglaries such as climbing fire escapes, opening windows, carrying off the loot and getting rid of it.

Both defendants told police they were dope addicts and each had to have two "shots" of heroin a day. They stole, they said, to get enough money to keep them supplied with the narcotic.

Few realize how demanding bad habits eventually can become. Slowly but surely they dominate every phase of an individual's life and banish the simple freedom and peace of mind for which all people yearn.

Rather than let bad habits take over your life, cultivate good ones that give glory to God, greater meaning to your own life and benefit your fellowman.

"Labor not for the meat which perisheth, but for that which endureth unto life everlasting." (John 6:27)

KEEP THAT BALANCE

Worry over financial problems caused a Hattiesburg, Miss., worker to so lose control of himself as to shoot and kill his wife, his three small children and his brother. He completed his death spree by committing suicide.

Few would let themselves become so mentally deranged as to go to such a deadly extreme. Yet, too many are inviting serious trouble by allowing the things of this world to dominate their minds, hearts and souls.

God expects us to use ordinary common sense in providing food, clothing and shelter for ourselves and those dependent on us. But, He repeatedly cautions us against letting the comforts and gadgets of life become such a preoccupation that instead of serving us, they become our cold masters.

It is difficult at times to grasp the deep meaning of the divine saying: "Not in bread alone doth man live." But the more we strive to keep the proper balance of the spirit over the body, the greater freedom we enjoy. Then there is little chance of true values becoming distorted—or letting incidentals take on the importance of essentials.

Keeping first things first not only restrains the beast in man, but spurs him on to help others at great personal sacrifice. In a Christlike way, he strives to save others rather than destroy them.

"Not in bread alone doth man live, but in every word that proceedeth from the mouth of God."

(Deuteronomy 8:3)

✍ Help me, O Lord, always to keep a proper sense of balance in my life.

SIMPLE GREATNESS

In Minster, Ohio, a 37-year-old tool-maker and his wife recently made headline news by adopting six children, all in one sweep. The children range in age from 2 to 9. The three oldest are school age, and their new parents are as proud as natural parents of their progress.

Mr. and Mrs. Ben Martin seem quite surprised by the stir caused around the country by their move. The father explains simply, "We wanted some children and it seemed the only way to set about it was to adopt them."

There is heroism in the simplest things, but most people never manage to get near it. Nevertheless, the story of these two people can serve as a reminder of the marvelous potentialities placed in us by God which we can tap once we open up our horizons and reach out to help others. We can all enrich our lives immeasurably just as they did.

"Suffer the little children to come unto me, and forbid them not. For of such is the kingdom of God."

(Mark 10:14)

Give me the vision necessary to move me to assist others, O Lord.

ERSATZ RELIGION

Realizing that men must worship a false god if they do not revere the True One, the Nazis made a supreme effort to set up gods of their own with no standards except those tolerated by the Nazis themselves. Hitler's ersatz religion tried to identify God with Germany. Hitler tried to parody Christ's words when he told his followers: "Let the children come with me, for they are mine." On all sides paganism was imposed on Germans with such expressions as:

"The German Faith Movement acknowledges only one Lord, Adolf Hitler."

"Christ was great, but Hitler is greater."

"To Thee, O My Leader, belong our hearts and our souls."

"Fuehrer, to Thee I owe, alone, my daily bread."

It seems that always when God is eliminated from life someone or something else takes His place. On the political level it is usually a dictator.

But it can happen in our individual lives too. Then God is replaced by money, fame, success, or a thousand other things. Only when God is kept in a central place in life will other goods and values keep in their proper place.

"I am the Lord thy God, who brought thee out of the land of Egypt, out of the house of bondage. Thou shalt not have strange gods before me." (Exodus 20:2)

✍ Help me, O Lord, to keep my life centered in Thee.

CHALLENGING FACTS

Disturbed by the ease with which so many were drifting into agnosticism and atheism, an American scientist, Dr. A. Cressy Morrison, wrote a book, *Man Does Not Stand Alone*. Its challenging message reminded countless people of the power of the Almighty. Here are some excerpts:

"The slant of the earth, tilted at an angle of twenty-three degrees, gives us our seasons; if it had not been so tilted, six vapors from the ocean would move north and south, piling up . . . continents of ice.

"If our moon was, say, only fifty thousand miles away instead of its actual distance, our tides would be so enormous that twice a day all continents would be submerged . . .

"If the crust of the earth had been only ten feet thicker, there would be no oxygen, without which animal life must die. Had the ocean been a few feet deeper, carbon dioxide and oxygen would have been absorbed and no vegetable life could exist."

Then Dr. Morrison concludes: "By unwavering mathematical law we can prove our universe was designed and executed by a great engineering intelligence."

"For from the creation of the world His invisible attributes are plainly observable, being perceived through created things." (Romans 1:20)

⊷ Grant, O God, that millions who do not know You may soon learn to acknowledge You as their Creator.

REACHING FOR THE ROOF

A Chicago housewife didn't know what she was starting one day a few months ago when she took a withered poinsettia plant from the cellar and placed it in the backyard.

With the help of sun and water, several green leaves appeared. Then the lady noticed something sprouting next to the poinsettia. Upon investigation it was found that a hyacinth bean had accidentally fallen into the same flower pot. So the family began to nourish it too. It grew so fast that very soon it began to crowd the poinsettia which had to be transferred to survive. But this was just the beginning for the young giant.

The vigorous vine crawled over the side of the pot and began to scale the side of the house. It snaked its way to the top of the home and down again. By this time it was 25 feet long and still going places.

It is amazing to discover the hidden vitality in persons, places and things—and often where you least expect it.

If you are like the majority of humans it is very probable that you have scarcely touched the power for good hidden within you. God has put a bit of greatness in you as He has in everyone else. If you start reaching for the world by work and prayer you may be surprised at what you can accomplish.

"And other seed fell upon good ground; and being sprung up, yielded fruit a hundredfold." (Luke 8:8)

⋙ Inspire me, O Lord, to make the best of whatever talent Thou has bestowed on me.

GIVE YOUNG PEOPLE THEIR DUE

A six-year-old boy was alone in his Chicago house when a fire broke out in the bedroom where he had been sleeping. He woke to find the curtains by the window ablaze. He was all alone, and he had to do something quickly.

He was frightened. But he sensed that there was something he could and should do in a hurry. He rushed to the telephone.

"There's a fire here," the boy shouted to the operator, trying hard not to sound frightened. But before he could say anything else he was switched to the Fire Department. "Where do you live, sonny?" a fireman asked. But the fire was getting bigger and bigger, and suddenly the boy couldn't remember where he lived and started to cry.

But everything turned out well, because the firemen traced the call and came and put out the fire.

It is understandable that a child would become confused in such circumstances. But it is far more serious when millions of youngsters through oversight, neglect or deliberate omission are deprived of the home life and training that is their God-given due.

Become a committee of one to encourage the idea that the Lord has entrusted to parents the duty of providing children with the affection and guidance essential for their success in this world as well as the next.

"Suffer the little children, and forbid them not to come to me, for the kingdom of heaven is for such."

(Matthew 19:14)

THE COURAGE OF WOMEN

In Scotland, a 39-year-old woman met her death while attempting to scale the frosty top of Ben Nevis mountain.

She and her companions, who followed a few yards behind her, were tied together by a climber's rope. When the two women reached a difficult precipice, the one in the lead suddenly lost her footing and slipped off the narrow ledge, dropping more than 100 feet. The rope saved her from crashing to the ground, but her companion was unable to pull her up.

For 20 hours she hung there swinging in mid-air in the bitter cold while rescue teams toiled up the trails in an effort to save her. But when they arrived, she was already dead from shock and exposure.

The daring risks that women take to perform some feats requiring extraordinary fortitude are proof, indeed, of their capabilities.

There are countless things that courageous women can do in modern life to regenerate the world. And the results can be far more exalting than reaching the summit of a mountain peak, for the tasks will be done for the glory of God and the benefit of others, not merely for self-achievement.

"Behold the handmaid of the Lord; be it done unto me according to thy word." (Luke 1:38)

❧ Grant, O Lord, that enough brave women will be found to consecrate themselves to renewing the face of the earth.

A PIECE OF CORK SAVED HER

A Memphis family out for the day on its 17-foot motor boat decided to have a swim in the Mississippi.

The mother and two of the children, a girl of 10 and her 8-year-old brother, were having a good time splashing around in the shallow water when suddenly in their frolicking they found themselves being swept away by the swift current.

The father dived in and rescued the mother and the boy. But it was three hours later before he was able to reach the little girl ten miles down the river, hanging on to a piece of cork.

Don't ever think you have failed if you do no more than pass along to others only one bit of God's truth. That fragment may keep them from perishing in the whirlpools of modern paganism. Later on they may, in gratitude to God, seek the fullness of His truth.

"He that shall persevere to the end, he shall be saved."
(Matthew 24:13)

⟜§ Grant me the wisdom, O my Savior, to help one and all as much as I can.

THE MISSING $62,000

A 41-year-old woman bank teller was arrested by the FBI for the misappropriation of funds amounting to $62,000 from a bank where she had been employed for 21 years.

Doubling as bookkeeper and teller, she had almost complete control over bank records. An investigation disclosed that she took $22,000 for herself and paid out another $40,000 for bad checks which she cashed for other people.

She explained to the incredulous FBI that she had simply put all bad checks into a safe, because she "felt sorry for their authors and didn't want to embarrass them." As a result, the bank had paid them without notifying the writers.

Those who succumb to little dishonesties gradually lull their own consciences into acceptance of bigger ones. A habit of dishonesty can be formed more quickly than most realize. When that happens, it is easy to become over-sympathetic towards a similar weakness in others, and thus to encourage them in their various thefts.

Strive to be scrupulously honest with your God, your own self, and with everyone who crosses your path.

"What shall it profit a man if he gain the whole world and suffer the loss of his soul?" (Mark 8:36)

Deepen in me, O Lord, a respect for the right of others.

STUDENTS SPEAK UP FOR TRUTH

A Communist high-school teacher in Eastern Germany undertook to prove to his students from the Bible itself that there is no God.

Since most of the students came from religious families, they were not easily convinced. But the teacher held a Bible aloft and cried, "See for yourselves! This is a Lutheran Bible. And on Page 246 it says: There is no God!"

Next day one student, chosen by his classmates to represent them, brought a Lutheran Bible to class with him. He stood and addressed the teacher. "Sir," he said. "It seems that you only read us part of the text." It reads: "The fool says in his heart: There is no God."

Although the students had proved their point, they were all dismissed from school for "having caused a severe disturbance of the democratic order."

Students can do much to see that truth prevails in the classroom. Few teachers deliberately distort the facts. But even one doing that is one too many. It requires courage to speak up for the truth. But failure to do so can jeopardize the freedom of all.

"Woe to that man by whom the Son of man shall be betrayed." (Matthew 26:24)

ᴥᔆ Allow me at all times to defend Thee, O Lord, before those who deny Thee.

341

MANY LETTERS DID IT

Last May, Lincoln's words "under God" were added by Congressional order to the Pledge of Allegiance to the Flag. The measure, passed by both the House and Senate, was signed by President Eisenhower on Flag Day, June 14. The pledge, now recognizing both God and country, reads:

"I pledge allegiance to the flag of the United States of America and to the republic for which it stands, one nation, *under God,* indivisible, with liberty and justice for all."

Upon signing the bill, President Eisenhower said:

"From this day forward the millions of our school children will daily proclaim in city and town, every village and rural school house, the dedication of our nation and our people to the Almighty . . .

"In this way we are reaffirming the transcendence of religious faith in America's heritage and future; in this way we shall constantly strengthen those spiritual weapons which forever will be our country's most powerful resource in peace or in war."

The passage of this measure shows how individuals, each acting on his own, can restore a reverence for God to the marketplace. Hundreds of thousands made it their business to write to Washington. Quick action resulted.

Each letter on its own is a drop in the bucket but multiplied they can have far-reaching effect.

"Be ye doers of the word, and not hearers only."

(James 1:22)

◁§ Help me to be a doer, O Lord, not merely a complainer.

THE WRIGHT BROTHERS DID IT

On December 17, 1953, a unique celebration was held at Kitty Hawk, N. C., in honor of the first airplane flight made by the Wright brothers 50 years ago on that spot.

At the exact moment of day when the first flight took off, the oldest flyable aircraft, a 1912 model, was flown from the same spot. At the same time several sleek modern jet planes joined in the demonstration.

On December 17, 1903, after years of persistent trial and error, Orville and Wilbur Wright successfully proved that man could fly, and altered the whole course of history. They said that they had persisted in trying, because they did not know such an invention was impossible.

Most people don't realize that each and every individual has it within his power to do something that can make the world better for his being in it. It may not be inventing anything like an airplane, as the Wright brothers did. But no matter how insignificant it may seem to you, it may be even more important in the sight of God.

If you persevere in trying to do all that you can, some great blessing is bound to come to you and others as a result of the effort that you have made.

"He that shall persevere unto the end, he shall be saved."
(Matthew 10:22)

> Let me try and keep trying, O my Savior, to change the world for the better.

A LESSON FROM A PARROT

A family in Lentini, Sicily, keeps a pet parrot. Of the many pets which serve a useful function, one would hardly consider the parrot to be such. But recently this bird proved that even a parrot can do something to express its gratitude for kindly care.

One day the three-year-old daughter of the family was playing on the sidewalk with her ball. The ball dropped and rolled out into the street in the path of an oncoming truck. The child, intent only on recovering the ball, ran after it.

The truck driver didn't notice the child and kept coming at the same speed. But suddenly the parrot flew from its perch in the window and fluttered in front of the driver's windshield. The driver was forced to brake, stopping just within a few feet of the child.

The smallest action can, with God's grace, bring results beyond our expectations. For instance, there is something that you, personally and individually, can do to help those who live in terrible dread of such frightful forces as the hydrogen bomb. First of all you can pray that the leaders of nations will realize the tremendous responsibility that rests in their hands. The more they are motivated by a love of God, the more likely they are to take measures to protect all people as well as themselves.

"Watch ye therefore because you know not the day nor the hour." (Matthew 25:13)

Inspire me, O Lord, to do all in my power to bring peace to all men of good will.

OUR GREATEST GIFT

In March, 1953, Soviet Russia held an election to the Supreme Soviet.

The election commission reported that 120,320,192 voters—more than 99 per cent of the eligible voters cast their ballots. Moreover, the report stated that almost every voter to the man supported the bloc of Communist party and non-party candidates. Thus, as the Red newspaper Izvestia put it, "The people's bloc of Communist and non-party members attained a full and undivided victory."

The editor then went on to say: "This is a shining evidence of the great living strength of the people's bloc. There is not in the world a force that can sway the unbreakable unity of the party, Government and people. Our elections are free elections."

When any nation loses its liberty in our times, it is usually due to failure on the part of the average individual to shoulder his part of the responsibility of protecting freedom.

At the last national election in the U.S. only 60 per cent of those eligible to vote bothered to go to the polls. The proportion has been far lower in local and primary elections. It is a human failing to neglect the very means at our disposal to protect our freedom. Do what you can to remind others of what even one person does to weaken our free form of government by failing to vote.

"This people honoreth me with their lips, but their heart is far from me." (Mark 7:6)

&3 I thank Thee, O my God, for the precious gift of freedom.

NO INCREASE IN RENT

Recently 49 tenants in a Chicago apartment building received an unusual notice from their landlord in the form of a letter. He wrote:

"Because this is Brotherhood Week, we should remind ourselves to have proper respect and consideration for our fellow man. This letter is my feeble step to a practical application of brotherhood: to help take some small burden or worry from the mind of a brother man.

"Let me assure you that there will be no rent increase unless a future rise in basic costs forces one."

You may not be in a position to assure anyone that his rent will not be increased. However, there are countless opportunities open to you, whoever you are, to translate into action the love of God and love of man that is in your heart.

One way to do it is to do all in your power to see that everybody is provided with better quality education, government, labor relations, literature and entertainment. Those are vital spheres that touch and shape the lives of all mankind. That is why those who would enslave human beings make it their business to infiltrate into them.

"Bear ye one another's burdens and so you shall fulfill the law of Christ." (Galatians 6:2)

◄§ Grant me, O Lord, the privilege of playing an active role in blending Thy love and justice into the mainstream of life.

IT'S EASY TO FORGET

A druggist in Indiana began saving silver coins to give to his son as a graduation present. As time went by, the sum increased until the bag which contained it could hold no more.

The druggist counted the money and found that he had saved $336. The problem was to find a safe place to hide the money from the rest of the family so that it would be a complete surprise to his son.

After some searching the man found what he considered to be a very good hiding place. He tucked the bag of money behind some cellar pipes.

Not long afterwards it became necessary for the family to move, and remembering his son's gift the druggist went to look for the bag. But to his great distress he had forgotten where he had hidden it. He gave it up as lost. But fortunately the family which moved in after him found the bag of money a year later and returned it to him.

God has entrusted to you a power for good that He has given to no one else. It is up to you to discover it and put it to work for the sake of others as well as for your own. Putting aside the opportunity to play the role of a Christopher or Christbearer until some later date may mean that you will forget the privilege and responsibility that is yours.

"Neglect not the grace that is in thee, which was given thee by prophecy." (1 Timothy 4:14)

⊷ Let me not put off till tomorrow, O Lord, the good I can do today.

FOCUS ATTENTION ON THIS

Firemen in Henderson, Ky., were somewhat puzzled by the behavior of a man whose house was on fire. The fire was a big one, and the heat and noise were terrific. The firemen were doing their best to bring the blaze under control. But the owner of the house kept frantically jumping up and down, trying to tell them something.

His frenzied shouting continued. Finally, understanding that he wanted them to direct their hoses to a certain spot on the house, they complied.

As soon as the fire died in that spot, the man darted through their lines and searched through the ashes and debris. He emerged triumphant. In his hand was a glass jar with $2000 for which he had been searching.

In the hustle and bustle of modern life, never lose sight of the sacred worth of man. Work hard to focus attention on it. Those who are against God will use every opportunity to divert and distract you from that main issue. They know that once they can sidetrack you into confusing petty debatable incidentals with the primary principles, they have nullified or neutralized your effectiveness as a Christbearer.

"Seek ye therefore first the kingdom of God and His justice and all these things shall be added unto you."

(Matthew 6:33)

≈§ Enlighten and strengthen me, O Holy Spirit, to know the difference between essentials and incidentals.

YOUR UNTOUCHED POWER

An American soldier while stationed in Heidelberg, Germany, made friends with a small boy. Captivated by the child, he promised that when he returned to the United States he would send him a toy car.

When he returned, true to his promise, the soldier set about finding the toy car for the boy. Only then did it dawn on him that he had forgotten to get the child's full name and address. All he had was a photograph of the lad that he had taken while in Germany.

He took a chance, wrapped up the car, pasted the youngster's photograph on the outside of the package and mailed it to the nearest town. A resourceful postman found the boy.

Most people are unaware of the untouched power for good within them. The best way to bring it out is to have some worthy goal outside of self. The soldier found a way to get the toy car to the youngster in Germany because he was determined to bring a little joy into the boy's life.

The more you develop within yourself a sincere and persevering desire to share the love of God in your heart with as many persons as you can reach, the more doors you will find opening to you. In a very true sense, you will discover that "where there is a will, there is a way."

"Do good to thy friend before thou die, and according to thy ability, stretching out thy hand give to the poor."
(Ecclesiasticus 14:13)

⊷ Let me enrich the lives of others, O Lord, and thereby enrich my own.

349

WISDOM AND UNDERSTANDING

Throughout our capital city one may find numerous inscriptions testifying to the religious faith of our forefathers. Since these evidences are part of our national history, it would help every student to have his attention called to them in the classroom.

In the Capitol, overlooking Washington from its famous "Hill," we find the lawmakers working in the Senate and House of Representatives. Prominently displayed for all to see is the quotation from the book of Proverbs (4:7): "Wisdom is the principal thing: therefore get wisdom, and with all thy getting, get understanding."

There is a difference between wisdom and mere knowledge or information, and our Founding Fathers knew this well. For one thing knowledge inflates, while wisdom humbles. Knowledge can be used for evil, but wisdom only for good.

Wisdom is knowledge wedded to virtue, to justice, integrity and love.

Our nation was founded on wisdom, let us not try to rebuild it on knowledge alone. Let us send more *wise* people into the careers that count.

"And because they had not wisdom, they perished through their folly." (Baruch 3:28)

⇜ Spread Thy wisdom throughout our land, O Lord.

SIGHT TO THE BLIND

An 81-year-old man in Ottawa, Ill., developed cataracts on both eyes which slowly blinded him.

For two years he lived in darkness, and then he decided to undergo an operation which doctors had assured him would restore his sight.

The operation was completely successful. When the bandages were removed, the old man shouted in his glad excitement, "I can see, I can see!"

Today there are hundreds of millions over the earth who are living in blindness that could be cured if someone would only go to them in Christ's Name.

Suffering in both body and soul, they wait in vain for those who have the truth to bring it to them. Deprived of a knowledge of the True God, vast sections of humanity go from birth to death also lacking the elementary essentials of food, medicine, social life and countless other advantages that would lighten their burdens.

Do all in your power to bring the Way, the Truth and the Life to the countless human beings who live in blindness without Him.

"Go ye into the whole world, and preach the gospel to every creature." (Mark 16:15)

⇜ Let me bring Thy Light, O Lord, to those who are blind.

SCRUPULOUSLY HONEST

Somewhere in LaSalle, Ill., there's a citizen who believes in being honest even in the smallest things.

The Postmaster there recently received a postcard asking that he check the stamp machine to see that it be put in working order.

The postcard read, "I got five three-cent stamps for 10 cents, so I owe the Government five cents. I am attaching three cents, and I spent two cents on this card."

Three pennies were attached to the postcard with gummed tape!

Some might consider this carrying honesty a little too far. On the other hand it is excellent self-discipline to check one's self in regard to little faults. It is easy to slip from little violations of truth, charity or honesty into more serious faults that gradually silence the voice of conscience.

One effective way to keep in God's presence is to examine your conscience each evening. This daily practice, if faithfully followed, will do much to safeguard your eternity.

"It is appointed unto men once to die, and after this the judgment." (Hebrews 9:27)

◄§ O Holy Spirit, let me always live in such a way that I will always be prepared to die.

EVERY IMPROVEMENT COUNTS

In Nashville, Tenn., a proud housewife received a perfect score on a Red Cross first-aid test.

It was a great surprise to her how soon her opportunity came to put what she had learned into actual practice. It was the very next day that she happened to be on the spot when an automobile accident occurred.

Physicians said that the life of a young man, who suffered a deep head wound in the accident, was saved because of the prompt first-aid treatment given by this young housewife.

Anyone can start to be a Christopher or Christbearer. Despite whatever defects he may have, he still retains some power entrusted to him by God to do something to make the world a bit the better for his being in it. No matter how far one is removed from Christ, there is something that he can do for Him, and thereby come one step closer to Him.

But by the same token, each of us is bound to take advantage of every opportunity to improve ourselves and thereby become more effective apostles.

"Love bears everything, believes everything, hopes everything, endures everything." (1 Corinthians 13:7)

◄§ Help me to strive always to improve myself that I may better serve Thee and others.

DON'T BE FOOLED BY DOUBLE-TALK

For 25 years occupants of the city-county building in Pittsburgh, Pa., have been exasperated by the strange perversity in the temperature of the building.

In the winter, when temperatures dropped, naturally they turned the thermostats up to warm the building. But, in each office it was noticed that the higher the thermostat was turned, the colder the office became. In the summer things were no better either. Turning down the thermostats increased the heat instead of cooling the building.

Finally one day a building inspector solved the mystery. It seemed that the whole building had been supplied with defective thermostats. Not that they weren't in good working order, but that the covers had been marked in reverse reading *"hot"* when they should read *"cold"* and vice versa.

This incident is a strong reminder of why much of the world is in confusion today. In the great modern deception that is being master-minded by the Devil himself, his followers find their way into positions of influence in their relentless effort to parade "evil" as good, falsehood as truth, slavery as freedom, treason as loyalty and filth as decency.

This mass deceit can quickly be dispelled if those who are for God show as much daring for truth as others do for evil.

"Jesus therefore said to them: . . . You are of your father the devil, . . . for he is a liar, and the father thereof."

(John 8:42, 44)

§ Grant me the grace, O Lord, to be a champion of truth.

THE EVIL USE THEIR IMAGINATION

One of the biggest fakers in the history of crime was recently exposed by the Minneapolis police force.

After some searching, they arrested a man who had had an astonishing record of success in cashing forged checks. He confessed that his success was due to his rather unique approach.

He would use onions to produce a plentiful flow of tears from his eyes. Then he would rush into some place of business with a check for $25 or less. He would explain to the proprietor that his wife had just died, and that he didn't have enough to pay funeral expenses. The sympathetic proprietors usually handed over the required amount without further question.

One seldom hears of anyone bent on mischief saying "what can I do?" He is usually very resourceful and alert, despite the fact that the odds are usually against him. It is one of the great paradoxes of our day that the very ones who are dedicated to enslaving the world show the most unusual daring, initiative and imagination.

You, personally and individually, can do something to change that!

"Be ye wise as serpents and simple as doves."

(Matthew 10:16)

◄§ Inspire me, O Lord, to show as much imagination in laboring for Thee as others do in working against Thee.

THE BLESSING OF TROUBLE

In Caen, France, a man was having an enjoyable meal of oysters when he suddenly bit on something hard and broke a front tooth.

He was naturally very upset. But when he searched to see what had caused the accident he found a beautiful large pearl.

In great excitement he took the pearl to a jeweler who found that it was genuine and of great value.

You may never find a pearl in an oyster, no matter how many you eat. But it is almost as certain that you will not achieve any worthwhile success, from God's point of view, without some expense to yourself. And it will probably be much worse than a broken tooth.

The reason that many fail to find any real happiness in life is that they work too hard in dodging the very trouble that would help them. When they take a job, they look for only one type of occupation—a job that pays a lot of money, requires little work and provides long vacations.

By the very nature that God gave us we are made to work our way through life in preparation for eternity. Of course, He intends that we should have some pleasure en route. But, what many too many fail to realize, is that He gives the truest and deepest joy to those striving diligently to work for love of Him and others.

"*And whosoever doth not carry his cross and come after me, cannot be my disciple.*" (Luke 14:27)

O my crucified Lord, renew in me an acceptance of life's crosses.

HELPING OTHERS CAN MEAN INCONVENIENCE

A four-year-old boy in Brooklyn is an avid television fan. His favorite programs are those about the fantastic antics of men from other planets who fly through space as effortlessly as breathing. In fact, so greatly was this child impressed that he decided to try it for himself.

One day when his mother wasn't looking, tiny Kenneth Ward climbed up on the window sill of their second-story apartment and poised himself to fly down to earth.

But when he finally reached the outer sill and looked down at the twenty-five foot drop, Kenneth became frightened and tried to make his way back. It was too late, though. There was only room to cling helplessly to the ledge.

Fortunately, a 16-year-old girl who was passing by happened to look up and saw the frightened child lose his grip and drop toward the sidewalk below. She braced herself beneath him, broke his fall, and saved his life.

All of us can learn a lesson from this fast thinking high school girl. It didn't take more than a moment for her to see that she could make up for the judgment that little Kenneth lacked, even though she might suffer a broken back in the attempt. To provide others with good government, good education and good everything else must mean sacrifice for some, but it is far from in vain. It makes for fuller living here and hereafter.

"But I most gladly will spend, and be spent myself for your souls." (II Corinthians 12:15)

✍ Let me suffer here, O Lord, that I may reign hereafter.

THE CORNERSTONE OF OUR NATION

William Penn was a deeply spiritual man. From the moment that King Charles II granted him a Charter in the new world, he was determined that the Commonwealth of Pennsylvania would have spiritual roots.

His purpose was clearly explained in the first paragraph of the Charter of Privilege, written in 1701, as the framework of the Commonwealth. The opening sentence illustrates his abiding faith in God.

"Almighty God, being Only Lord of Conscience, Father of Lights and Spirits, and the author as well as object of all Divine knowledge, faith and worship, who only can enlighten the mind, and persuade and convince the understandings of people . . ."

This prayer of William Penn gives an insight into the religious mentality of early America.

Look for yourself into our country's early history and note how the men who laid the foundations of this nation had, with very few exceptions, a deep sense of reverence for Almighty God. They showed by their frequent and open tributes to Him that they firmly believed that the freedom of this country and its inhabitants was dependent upon our recognition of a Supreme Being and His moral law.

You can help offset the tendency in recent years to drift away from this respectful attitude by restoring a sense of God to every sphere of influence that you can reach. You will be doing much to strengthen your country and to contribute to a true and lasting peace if you do.

"I am the way, and the truth and the life." (John 14:6)

SHE DIDN'T REALIZE IT WAS THE KING

It was a very busy night at the big movie theater in Stockholm, Sweden. The hat-check girl was having a trying time of it. There seemed to be a never-ending line of hands holding out wraps which had to be tagged and systematically put away.

She worked steadily, automatically, without even bothering to look up at the faces. She had to hurry. It was nearly curtain-time.

A tall elderly man put his hat and coat on the counter.

"That will be 25 oere," the girl said. (25 oere is about 5 cents).

"I'm sorry, I haven't any money," the man replied gently. The girl was annoyed. What did he expect? "Well, it will be 25 oere, anyway," she said shortly.

The man turned around and borrowed the coin from someone behind him. Only then did the girl look up. She gasped when she recognized her customer. It was the King of Sweden!

Christ has warned us not to overlook being kind to every human being, whether he be poor or rich, in low station or high, ignorant or educated. In each of them is the resemblance of Christ. To refuse them, therefore, is to refuse Him. Jesus put it very forcefully when He said:

"As long as you did it not to one of these least, neither did you do it to me." (Matthew 25:45)

BE ON YOUR GUARD

A New York policeman was entering a large downtown department store when he met a man who was having quite a bit of trouble getting a large rug through the door.

The policeman smiled at the man's effort, and held the door open for him. "I think you need help, my friend," he said. The man smiled his thanks. "I guess you're right," he said ruefully, setting the rug down on the sidewalk. "And what's more, I still have another one to bring out. Look, I wonder if you'd mind watching this one till I can bring out the other. Then I'll get a cab."

The policeman was glad to oblige. Patiently he stood guard over the rug for five minutes—then ten . . . then fifteen. Bewildered, he went inside the store to investigate. His face was very red when he found that the rug he was watching had been stolen,—and the thief had gotten away!

Any one of us might have been fooled as this police officer was. But it is a terrible thing to realize that in most nations that have lost their God-given freedom in our day, it has been largely due to the fact that well-intentioned but very gullible persons have actually helped the very ones who were out to destroy them.

"Be sober and watch, because your adversary the devil, as a roaring lion, goeth about seeking whom he may devour; whom resist ye, strong in faith." (I Peter 5:8, 9)

↵§ Give me the good sense, O Lord, to know that to stay well is always wiser and cheaper than to try to get well.

IT'S YOUR WORLD

A car was wrecked on a San Francisco highway, and after the routine investigation by the police, a call was put in for a tow truck to haul it away.

In a short time, the truck arrived. The driver got out and looked at the badly smashed car he was supposed to tow away.

"Say! That's a bad one!" he whistled. "Well, I better get started."

Suddenly he stopped, frozen in his tracks, a look of wide disbelief on his face. "Hey!" he breathed. "That's my car."

And so it was. Investigation proved that the wrecked car had been stolen only a few hours before. The owner hadn't even had time to miss it.

Could it be that we are so busily preoccupied with the task of "picking up the pieces" over the world today that we are forgetting that in doing so we are helping ourselves as much as those in distress.

Once you can say to yourself: "This is my world just as much as it is anyone's and I am going to work as hard to save it as others are striving to destroy it," then you will probably do more to prevent world catastrophes and not be content merely with waiting to help when the next "wreck" takes place.

"Go ye into the whole world, and preach the gospel to every creature." (Mark 16:15)

⋙ Help me, O Lord, to extend the faith, not merely to defend it.

AN EIGHT-YEAR-OLD AND TERMITES

An eight-year-old boy in Darwin, Australia, recently tried something entirely new in schoolboy efforts to get out of having to go to school.

He attends a small school, but disliked everything connected with it. One day in class the teacher explained how tiny little termites can little by little destroy an entire building. The boy listened raptly, an idea growing in his head.

Some days later the school superintendent caught the boy in the act of transferring some termites he had found from a bottle to the walls in the basement. The boy explained later that he had hoped that the termites would eat up the school building.

Few would think of going to such an extreme as this youngster did in trying to obstruct education. But many go almost as far by belittling the teaching profession, by discouraging their own sons and daughters from dedicating their lives to the classroom or by neglecting to give the teacher the respect and support that anyone deserves who is actually taking the place of a parent in the training and formation of youth.

It is well and good to be on the lookout for those who use the teaching profession to undermine our school system, but it is far more important to encourage more people with high ideals and competence to enter this vital sphere.

"You are my friends if you do the things that I command you." (John 15:14)

YOU CAN DRIVE TOO SLOWLY

Excessive speeding in automobiles is a good reason for arrest but recently a man was ordered to stay off all freeways within Los Angeles, Calif., city limits for one year because he drives too slowly.

Municipal Judge Evelle J. Younger imposed the sentence after finding the man guilty of driving under a normal, safe speed. Because the man was traveling 10-miles-an-hour slower than he should have, his car interfered with the normal flow of traffic and caused cars to jam up behind him. When this happened eight autos passed him on the right side, a violation of the law.

Judge Younger said this was the third time the defendant had been arrested for slow driving during the past year. At first, a five-day jail sentence was handed down, but was suspended for the more practical punishment.

Many good people go through life at such a slow pace that they are actually doing harm. They hold down positions which a more active and energetic person could use for greater good. It seems that they wish to slow life down to their own pace instead of quickening their own and getting into the thick of things.

If they saw how much the effort of everyone is needed today, and how fast the evil doers are working in every department of life they perhaps would be inclined to step up their pace. Much of our over-cautiousness would be overcome if our enthusiasm for changing our world for the better was increased.

"The harvest indeed is great, but the laborers are few."
(Matthew 9:37)

363

NO ONE CLAIMED THE $10,000 BRACELET

It's seldom that anyone who loses a valuable piece of property doesn't check with the police to see if it has been recovered.

Yet, a 26-year-old New York City salesman was recently awarded a $10,000 diamond bracelet when no one filed a claim for it for more than a year after he found it in a theater.

The police property clerk said it was the most valuable item returned to a finder in the eight years he had been with the department. They are still puzzled why the owner never came round to claim it.

How many really find the marvels and wonders which fill the wide world. God has scattered his treasures with prodigal generosity throughout nature. Men of genius who have realized their God-given talents have added to these treasures. And yet, some go through life unseeing, taken up with their own petty affairs as if they were of sufficient importance for a whole lifetime.

Be on the lookout for the great values and opportunities all about you. Train your eye to see them. Get into the thick of life with a Christlike purpose. Plunge into the mainstream and make your influence for good felt. Do something to raise the level of government, education, writing, labor relations, movies, television or radio.

You may not find a $10,000 bracelet but with God's help you may discover new and lasting ways to help everyone.

"Lord, that I may see." (Luke 18:41)

◄§ Help me, O Lord, to distinguish the true from the false.

POLITE THIEVES

Last Christmas a children's clothes and dry goods store in North Bergen, New Jersey, was the site of an unusual holdup.

A young, well-dressed couple entered the shop and spent about half an hour selecting $200 worth of children's clothes which they then had gift-wrapped. Just as the proprietor and his wife were beginning to be impressed by the nice manners and "elegant taste" of the stylish shoppers, the man thrust his hand into his jacket pocket and said, "Sorry, this is a holdup!"

He took the proprietor's wallet containing $75, and the wife's wedding ring, valued at $100. With $75 more from the cash register, and the children's clothes they had selected, they made their getaway.

On leaving, the man and his woman accomplice called out, "Merry Christmas!"

Many are deceived by a courteous pretense. A polite approach on the part of a thief, a traitor or a defamer of character takes the average person off guard.

How often some people will say of a debasing book or play: "But it was so well done!" They little realize that the more attractively poison is packaged, the more dangerous it can be.

Christ Himself gives you this warning:

"Beware of false prophets, who come to you in the clothing of sheep, but inwardly they are ravening wolves."
(Matthew 7:15)

&3 O Lord, let me not be deceived by appearances.

STEALING TO PAY HIS BAIL

Policemen have heard thousands of excuses—some very logical and others ludicrous. One of the most brazen was that offered by a 21-year-old New Yorker when he and an accomplice were caught prowling on an apartment house fire escape.

"I'm out on $1500 bail," he protested. "I had to get money quick to pay a lawyer."

Protesting one's honesty when actually committing dishonesty is eloquent proof that deep in the heart of every man there is a recognition of a moral law.

During life it is possible to deceive many persons by a pretense at innocence. But there comes a day in the lives of all of us when the entire record of our lives will be an open book.

On that important occasion there will be no "ifs," "ands" or "buts." It will be one time when no one will be fooled, when alibis would be a waste of time even if they could be offered.

Let every day be a preparation for the time sooner or later when you must answer the summons to appear before the judgment seat of Almighty God to give an account of your stewardship. Life will take on a new and truly happy purpose if you strive conscientiously to live as you wish to die.

"Give an account of thy stewardship for now thou canst be steward no longer." (Luke 16:2)

&⸑ Let me be ever mindful, O my Savior, of that day of reckoning when I appear before Thee.

AT THE EXPENSE OF OTHERS

A bank manager in Iowa said he found the cost of living so high that he embezzled $14,500 during a 10-year period to keep pace with it.

The 60-year-old man said he took the money to pay "ordinary living expenses" for his wife and himself. Father of two married children, the man said he was paid $170 a month by the bank.

He first took some of the money in 1939 but told investigators he had not taken any for several years. He added that he took about $18,500, but had repaid several thousand dollars.

When the man first started working at the bank in 1939 he started taking money to make up for his beginner's salary. Taking several hundred dollars at a time, the man said he covered the deficiencies by issuing false statements which showed a depositor had more in his account than he actually had.

The embezzler said he revealed his thefts "Because I think it's the thing to do."

The temptation to live beyond one's means is a serious one in modern life. And yet, if we succumb to it, even if we remain honest while doing so, we never have full peace of soul.

One good way to restrain ourselves in seeking advantages beyond our reach is to show a practical interest in helping those less fortunate to have the essentials of life.

"As long as you did it to one of these my least brethren, you did it to me." (Matthew 25:40)

⊷ Give me, O Lord, a desire to live for others and not only for myself.

115 DAYS AT SEA

A 61-year-old New York seaman, William C. Willis, decided to prove, as he put it, that "a solitary man can conquer the ocean and the fury of the elements with his bare hands and the most rudimentary means of navigation." As a result, he made the longest solo cruise in known history.

Pitting his life against the Pacific Ocean, and the dangers of hunger, thirst, loneliness, storms and sharks, he came out on top. Singlehanded, he navigated 6000 miles of water in 115 days.

Trying to salvage his fish hook from the corner of a shark's mouth, Willis lost his footing and fell into the foaming ocean. His left hand was caught between the mankiller's powerful jaws, and a gash one-half inch deep was torn around his wrist. He stopped the bleeding with a tourniquet and stitched the wound with white cotton thread and an ordinary mending needle.

The brave man sailed on a 34-foot raft made of seven logs. For food, he took along a little corn, sugar, water and emergency rations. Most of his sustenance came from fish and rainwater.

The daring that men show in braving all sorts of dangers for the sake of a worthy but fleeting honor is proof of the great power that the Creator has implanted in every individual.

What a refreshing change for the better will sweep the earth itself once enough individuals apply that God-given power to the improvement of government, education, literature, entertainment and labor relations.

"But who is he that can hurt you, if you be zealous of good." (1 Peter 3:13)

PARAKEET SAVES FOUR LIVES

If a Buffalo, N. Y., family of three didn't own a parakeet they might have all died of carbon monoxide poisoning.

John W. Burt, 27, complained to his wife that he wasn't feeling well and was about to collapse. His wife, Grace, noticed that their 19-months-old son also seemed sick. She soon became ill and after calling the woman who lived in the downstairs apartment, Mrs. Burt observed that the parakeet was lying on its side in the cage.

She hurriedly called firemen who administered oxygen and removed the occupants to the hospital.

Firemen said the deadly fumes were escaping from a defective water heater flue. "By the time I left the parakeet was back on its feet," one fireman said.

God in His great generosity gives us countless warnings of dangers that threaten our lives here below, and, far more important, our eternal salvation. It is easy to ignore them. But invariably we pay a high penalty for neglect.

Carbon monoxide poison is difficult to detect. But as the collapse of the parakeet was a dramatic reminder that all the life-giving oxygen had disappeared from the little apartment in Buffalo, so should increasing rape, perjury, suicide, subversion and murder be sure signs that respect for God's law is fast disappearing from the market place.

You can do something to see that it is restored to every phase of public and private life.

"Fear ye not them that kill the body . . . but rather fear him that can destroy both soul and body in hell."
(Matthew 10:28)

THE PENALTY OF REJECTION

Tokyo police were running down every tip and clue which might lead them to a firebug who had set a match to 17 schools and homes within a period of seven weeks.

Fortunately, quick action by firemen prevented loss of life and heavy property damage in each case. But the big question was; where would he strike next?

Then the break came. Police surprised a 15-year-old boy getting ready to start a fire in an alley. When asked why he had gone on a fire-setting spree, the youth answered that he was "shunned by my playmates and distrusted by my mother."

You probably would be amazed, if you conducted a little investigation of your own, to find out how much of our present day trouble has resulted from ignoring or deliberately disregarding Christ's command: "Love thy neighbor as thyself."

When the young and old are deprived of the love, care and affection that is their due they can easily become embittered and vengeful. Because others have been lacking in a sense of proportion in their regard, they in turn show a lack of balance.

The cure? It is so simple and at the disposal of everyone. Put love where there is no love and you will find love. Reach out to those who are hateful and bitter. You will accomplish far more good than you realize.

"Let us love one another." (1 John 4:7)

FROM BAD TO WORSE

When a Buffalo, N. Y., woman found dirt tracks on her hall floor she became enraged and set out to find the "culprit."

It was a 41-year-old man, whom she wasted little time in telling that she didn't wish to have her home look like a pig sty. He offered explanations and the argument grew hotter.

Then the woman was hit in the eye with the end of a broom handle and had the man arrested on a charge of second-degree assault.

She swore he grabbed the broom and poked her in the left eye. She thought she might lose the sight in that eye. He called it an "accident."

It is amazing to find how many tragedies have their origin in a sharp remark, an impatient action or a lack of common courtesy. Untold harm could be prevented if more people learned to control their tempers in little things.

Far more effective than the mere negative approach of trying to restrain one's anger amidst petty disturbances is the whole-hearted and refreshing effort to show understanding when someone has made a stupid mistake, to display a sincere and serene kindness when others have been gruff or rude.

If you follow this pleasing pattern, you accomplish three things—first, you do God's will; second, you retain your own calm and dignity; and third, you invariably teach a lesson to those who need it without hurting them or anybody else.

"Blessed are the meek: for they shall possess the land."
(Matthew 5:4)

HE COULDN'T RESIST STEALING

A 42-year-old Manchester, England, man was being questioned by police on suspicion of shoplifting.

During the interrogation he seized the opportunity to practice his dishonest art. He saw a policewoman's handbag nearby and managed to edge close to it.

Police were so busy throwing questions at the man that they didn't see his hand dip into the purse and come out with six pounds—the equivalent of $16.80 in United States currency.

He was sentenced to six months in jail for this last bit of sleight of hand.

One of the great handicaps of allowing ourselves to fall into bad habits is that they become so dominating that we become slaves instead of masters.

Despite the best of intentions, evil tendencies that are not curbed take such deep root that they can scarcely be eradicated. Be especially kind to those who are the victims of bad habits. Show patience with them and encourage them with confidence. The help that you alone give may be the turning point in a life that would be a hopeless failure had you failed to do your part.

God's grace is always available to those who are gripped by bad habits and handicapped by more than the usual share of human weakness. God's grace is with you too when you offer a helping hand to those who have fallen.

"My grace is sufficient for thee." (II Corinthians 12:9)

⋖§ Have mercy, O Lord, on those who fall through weakness.

TROUBLE WHICH YOU CAN CORRECT

For days police in the Argentinian city of Cordoba tried to track down a counterfeiting ring. Not one clue was left unchecked. It was exhausting work.

Recently the vexing mystery was solved but under unhappy and embarrassing circumstances, almost too delicate to reveal to the public.

For the bogus money was being made by inmates in the city jail itself.

In looking for the causes of trouble over the world today we may often make the mistake of failing to observe what is wrong right under our very noses.

To be sure you should be interested, as Christ said, in bringing His love and truth to the "whole world." But at the same time it would be folly to neglect rectifying what is at fault within your own heart, soul, and mind or in the immediate surroundings.

Peace is urgently needed over the world today. Do all in your power to bring it to all nations. But while saving others make sure not to overlook the obligation to those closest to you.

The more you purify your own life and increase your own interior spiritual strength, the better equipped you will be to make the world itself better for your being in it.

"But I chastise my body, and bring it into subjection: lest perhaps, when I have preached to others, I myself should become a castaway." (1 Corinthians 9:27)

◄§ Remind me, O Lord, to recognize my defects as well as my virtues.

HE LEARNED AT LAST

A 21-year-old Buffalo, N. Y., man quit five good jobs within 18 months while his wife and infant were receiving welfare assistance.

The man was ordered to jail for six days on the recommendation of the assistant county attorney who found the wife and child were subsisting on welfare funds.

After his release from jail, the husband promised City Judge Willis G. Hickman he would get a job and be a "good husband." "Judge, I've learned my lesson," he said.

The chief reason for unhappiness in so many marriages is the lack of adequate preparation.

In the home, the church and the school a great contribution can be made in training young people with such a high esteem and reverence for marriage and the setting up of a home, that they would start preparing for it in their early teens.

Young people show a great generosity and spirit of sacrifice when the goal is a challenging one. Once they become deeply aware of the fact that they can be partners with God Almighty in the creation, sustenance and training of new life that is to go on for all eternity, they more gladly assume the responsibilities that accompany their rights. Purpose makes the difference.

"A man shall leave father and mother, and shall cleave to his wife. . . ." (Genesis 2:24)

❧ Bless and strengthen in a special way, O Lord, those who are undertaking Holy Matrimony.

ONE WAY TO DISAGREE

It was the Christmas season, and a certain grocery store in Minneapolis was open quite late. It had been a long day, and the grocer and his wife were tired.

They were ready to lock up when two young men came in. One of them pulled out a pistol and said, "This is a stick-up!"

The grocer's wife was sitting at the back of the store. "I don't think this is funny," she said pleasantly but firmly to the young thug.

The gunman looked at her carefully. His expression changed. "No, I guess you're right," he said. He put away his gun, and suddenly he and his friend began to leave. "Happy New Year," they said as they left.

No matter how difficult the situation is in which you may find yourself at times, you never completely lose when you strive to find the best that is in the worst of men. Even if you do not succeed, God knows you have tried. More often than not, He will bless your effort with a pleasant but unexpected surprise.

If you temper firmness with kindness, you can accomplish great good in your home, business or social life.

"A mild answer breaketh wrath; but a harsh word stirreth fury." (Proverbs 15:1)

⋐ O Lord, teach me how to disagree without being disagreeable.

THE GIFT THAT LASTS

Last Christmas, department stores in Pittsburgh successfully demonstrated that "where there's a will there's a way."

A crippling strike prevented them from being able to deliver their goods. At this time of year when the demand for large articles is at its peak, this could be disastrous to business. But three stores came up with an ingenious idea which enabled business to continue "as usual."

When a customer purchased a gift that was too large to carry to the intended receiver, the store provided a large photograph of the article with a message reading: "This is your Christmas gift. We regret the delay, but it will be delivered as soon as possible."

Seeing a picture of a gift is only a reminder. But if it carries with it a guarantee that the real gift is to follow shortly, it is more than just another picture.

In countless ways God gives us a preview of the sublime gift of heaven that He has prepared for each of us for all eternity. He reminds us over and over again that it is ours for the asking. All that we have to do is to think, work and act in such a way that we show that heaven is our one and only destination.

"Come ye blessed of my Father, possess you the kingdom prepared for you from the foundation of the world."
(Matthew 25:34)

A STANDING CHALLENGE

In March 1778, two years after the birth of the United States of America as a nation, Benjamin Franklin made this significant comment in a letter that he sent to the government in France:

"He who shall introduce into public affairs the principles of primitive Christianity, will change the face of the earth."

Fortunately for all of us, the truths of Jesus Christ are eternal and therefore the same today as they were 1900 years ago. But very seldom in history have a large number of individuals taken the trouble to bring into government, education and other important areas the divine solution for the problems that vex mankind.

It is a breathtaking challenge to realize that here in the twentieth century each of us can still do something worthwhile to blend these sublime truths into human affairs and do much to bring about the lasting peace for which all men yearn.

Yes, you have the opportunity to play some part, however small, in bringing into the market-place the changeless truths which are so much needed in our changing times. However small the opportunity may be, make the best of it. By prayer and work make your influence for good felt.

Think often of the forceful reminder of Benjamin Franklin that whoever plays such a role "will change the face of the earth."

"I am come to cast fire on the earth and what will I, but that it be kindled?" (Luke 12:49)

IF YOU ARE IN WASHINGTON

If you happen to go to Washington, D.C., by train, you can see the words of Christ from the Gospel of St. John (8:32) prominently inscribed above the main arch leading into Union Station. Here at the very entrance to the seat of the government of the United States are the words: "The truth shall make you free."

Nearby is another inscription cut into enduring stone, the words from the Eighth Psalm of the Old Testament: "Thou hast put all things under his feet."

A third inscription reiterates the spiritual theme: "Let all the ends thou aimest at be thy country's, thy God's, and the truth's."

It is a tribute to those who erected the many buildings and monuments in our nation's capital that they made such frequent and pointed reference to the dependence of our Republic upon the guiding hand of Almighty God. But it is even more important that this same knowledge and reverence for eternal truths be engraved in the mind, heart and soul of each and every individual.

Try to reach those who have drifted into the deceptions of atheism, agnosticism or indifference, or who may be in the grip of disloyalty or treason. A prayer, word or deed on your part may help bring them back to God.

"There shall be joy before the angels of God upon one sinner doing penance." (Luke 15:10)

⋙ Inspire me, O Lord, to carry as far as I can the Truth upon which this nation depends.

A BASIC TRUTH

George Washington, Father of our Country, closed his presidential career in the same spirit of true greatness in which he had opened it. His Farewell Address bears testimony to his abiding faith in the spiritual. We quote only a few lines here, but anyone would draw profit from an entire reading:

"Let us with caution indulge the supposition that morality can be maintained without religion. Whatever may be conceded to the influence of refined education on minds of peculiar structure, reason and experience forbid us to expect that national morality can prevail in exclusion of religious principle."

No father could give better advice to his child; no "father" could give better advice to "his country." It would be well if this warning of the "father of our country" was printed in every paper from time to time, put on every billboard, and proclaimed from every platform.

Today, more than ever before, there is need of the truth being made known in every phase of our national life, in government, education, communication, and labor relations. Nations learn too late that social morality cannot thrive without God as its foundation.

"In all thy works remember thy last end, and thou shalt never sin." (Ecclesiasticus 7:40)

⋙ Keep our people mindful of Thee and Thy law, O Lord.

REVENGE WITH A VENGEANCE

Police in Reading, Pa., were wondering what could motivate someone to wantonly twist parking meters out of shape.

From one part of the city to the other, parking meter bases looked like pretzels. Was it a delinquent juvenile? A burglar? A practical joker?

The mystery was solved with the arrest of a man who was caught bashing the face of a parking meter in the mid-city area. And why did he purposely damage city property?

He told police he received a parking ticket in an area he thought was not restricted. To get revenge, he said he did not pay the fine and resolved to damage meters each time he came to town.

Those who allow themselves to go into a fit of rage actually lose control of themselves. The ability to have complete mastery of one's self under all circumstances is one of the highest and most distinctive traits of a human being. It distinguishes him from an animal. One who "loses his temper" acts like a "lost person" whether it be momentary or for a long period.

You can reflect the glory of God in your own life by showing the self-restraint that all admire and too few practice. Encourage this same quality in others also and you may save them many a heartache.

"Whosoever is angry with his brother, shall be in danger of the judgment." (Matthew 5:22)

ᴥ§ Grant me the grace, O Lord, to show self-restraint in all that I do.

HIGH STANDARDS

The Grenadier Guardsmen who are stationed at their posts in front of the Tower of London and Buckingham Palace in London, have long been a sort of legend in British military tradition.

These men, colorful in their scarlet tunics and black bearskin headdresses are trained to stand statue-like at their posts looking neither right nor left and impervious to the weather. When in parade if one faints he is completely ignored by the others, and furthermore he is severely reprimanded later for his weakness.

Therefore, it was no surprise that recently when a 19-year-old guardsman fell asleep at the sentry box at the Tower of London he was punished by a sentence of 84 days in the guardhouse.

The example of high standards of discipline inspires most people. In a day and age when laxity and ease is the order of the day one cannot but be moved by it.

And if men can discipline themselves so well for an earthly duty or cause, how much easier should it be to do so for God and His Kingdom.

Try to display a high moral character wherever you are. Try earnestly to put it to work where it counts most and where others will benefit from it.

"And every one that striveth for the mastery, refraineth himself from all things: and they indeed that they may receive a corruptible crown; but we an incorruptible one." (1 Corinthians 9:25)

⟞ Show us Thy way of discipline so that we may follow it and show it to others.

FOUR REFERENCES TO GOD
IN THE DECLARATION

When in 1776 our Founding Fathers drew up the Declaration of Independence, they based its authority on Almighty God. They wanted to emphasize truths which they feared others might discard not realizing they were fundamental to democracy. Woven, therefore, into the texture of the Declaration of Independence are four significant references to God:

1. Note the reference to God in the very first sentence: "When in the course of human events, it becomes necessary for one people to dissolve the political bands which have connected them with another, and to assume among the powers of the earth, the separate and equal station to which the *Laws of Nature and of Nature's God* entitle them. . . ."

2. In the second sentence we read: "We hold these truths to be self-evident, that all men are created equal, that they are *endowed by their Creator* with certain unalienable Rights, that among these are Life, Liberty, and the pursuit of Happiness. . . ."

3. In the next to the last sentence, the Founding Fathers appeal, in their own words, "*to the Supreme Judge of the world,*" for the rectitude of their intentions.

4. The last sentence reads: "And for the support of this Declaration, *with a firm reliance on the protection of divine Providence,* we mutually pledge to each other our Lives, our Fortunes, and our sacred Honor."

"*Let every soul be subject to higher powers: for there is no power but from God.*" (Romans 13:1)

A CATHOLIC PRAYER BOOK

Edited by Dale Francis,

Introduction by Thomas Merton

Here are prayers that have come down through the centuries as well as prayers inspired by modern times, modern needs. As the prayers are offered, there are explanations of why Catholics pray as they do. So it becomes a book that will help Catholic and non-Catholic alike to come to a better understanding of the Catholic faith. It is a book designed to bring men a little closer to God.

The book includes prayers from
    the Mass,
    the Divine Office,
    the Sacraments, and
    Private Prayers for all occasions

DELL FIRST EDITION LC-112—50c

If this book cannot be obtained locally, send 50c plus 5c for postage and handling for each copy to Dell Publishing Co., Inc., 10 West 33rd Street, New York 1, N. Y. If order is for five or more copies, no postage or handling charge is necessary.